# The Power of Dramatic Form

# The
# Power
# of
# Dramatic Form

by

# Frederick J. Hunter

**Professor of Drama**
The University of Texas at Austin

An Exposition-University Book
EXPOSITION PRESS   HICKSVILLE, NEW YORK

Dedicated
to Elberta
for
all she has meant
all these years

*PN
1631
H 8*

*1-21-75 Eastern 7.65*

65938

F<small>IRST</small> E<small>DITION</small>

© 1974 by Frederick J. Hunter

Library of Congress Catalog Card Number: 78-80682

ISBN 0-682-48018-5

Printed in the United States of America

# Contents

# List of Charts

# Preface

In view of the changing and variegating types of theatrical experience in the contemporary world, it might be well to re-examine some of our presuppositions with regard to them. In this last third of the twentieth century, the theatre extends from the insipid anguish of soap operas through playful bedroom farces in dinner theatres and extravagant spectacles in musical productions to extreme violence in act and word among various protesters in coterie theatres.

There seems to be some uncertainty as to why so many different people like so many different kinds of theatre. Perhaps human taste is such that a great variety of aesthetic experiences are possible to enjoy without doing injury to good judgment. Perhaps the habituation of taste through the experience of rich variety has lead to the acceptance of a broader scope in the cycle of dramatic forms beyond comedy and tragedy.

The reason for the uncertainties which have arisen is the lack of clarity with which writers approach problems of definition in theatre and drama. For example, theatrical production is seldom shown as being the essential transmitter of dramatic art. Plays cannot be known or felt by reading them. As a consequence, one must notice that the theatre contains many modes of expression, and dramatic art is only one of them, albeit the most influential one.

The dynamic image of human engagement which we find enacted in drama grows directly out of the dynamic processes in the purposive behavior of human beings. A re-examination of human action must lead to a reappraisal of dramatic action and of the forms which it may take in our experience.

What one may discover is that certain kinds of human action are preferred above others by large groups of people, and that this will make up the major subject matter treated by dramatists. It will also be the case that certain theatrical qualities will be more effective with discriminating audiences than with others. When significant human interaction appears in an effective style of presentation, the audiences' preferences will be that much better satisfied. The theatre's content as well as the audience's taste can be improved by the aesthetic process of habituation.

What this book attempts to do is to point out the most often noted kinds of dramatic art that have appeared in the theatre and to determine the aesthetic qualities of those which seem to have the same essential form. The qualitative experience which they evoke has to do with the reason that we respond to them as we do. Since what is here discussed is what happens in the experiences of spectators rather than in those of readers, this text will concern what a person undergoes, or feels, or knows at a performance of a dramatic work. It is, therefore, the substance or essence of these experiences which determines what statements can be made about them, and therefore, what statements are made herein.

# I.

# The Aesthetics of Dramatic Form

"They surveyed all the types of literature . . . they brought forth the question of how to choose between Corneille and Racine . . . Then his young niece countered by asking which fruit— the orange or the peach—had the most exquisite taste and merited the most praise."

—Marmontel, 1772

Whether drama in a theatre is certainly, or even potentially, an effective and whole art depends upon what one means by "drama," "theatre," and "art." If art is that which is made by man to give some pleasure and which is most exciting when it attracts and holds his attention, then both drama and theatre may be worth some study in this regard.

On the basis of a whole history of the theatre, it is not likely that we will ever be entirely deprived of the living actor as a center of interest there. In the most primitive times and in the darkest ages, there have been individual itinerant players to bring laughter and tears and wonder to the hearts of even the most casual spectators. What has been so much less common since the dawn of history are those occasions when a company of highly trained players has projected to a large, eager, and waiting audience a dynamic action devised to be performed in word and movement as a whole emotional experience for that same audience. The question has been: How do we distinguish between the two resulting kinds of phenomena? Since we call the written composition an example of drama and since we call the performance, by either the individual or the group of players, an example of theatre art, it would seem appropriate to refer, at least tentatively, to the total experience of the drama in the theatre as a work of "dramatic art."

The term "theatre" may on occasion refer to any one of many types of empirical performance such as pantomime, puppetry, acrobatics, juggling, dog tricks, trapeze stunts, clown acts, or song and dance routines in addition to the longer performances of operas, movies, motoramas, plays, masques, pageants, ballets, modern dance, and the various hybrids of these. What they all seem to have in common are the visual and auditory elements of action, space, light, and sound organized in colorful, rhythmic, and meaningful patterns which seem to attract human attention. There has been relatively little dispute about the attractiveness of theatrical performances, but it has always been difficult to determine what effective qualities are in some of them which hold the attention, which become a matter of deep concernment to an audience, and which have the power to stir them deeply and emotionally. Some have said it is the series of incidents, or the characters, or the dialogue, or the action, or the conflict, or the crises, or the "message." Whatever is thought to be the essence of drama is thought to be the cause of the moving power which it seems to possess. Sometimes it is felt that this power is inherent in the written drama without a theatrical manifestation, and sometimes it is felt that the theatre is the only adjunct to the realization of drama's effectiveness. There can be very little doubt but what some manner of theatre will exist in the future wherever there are people, just as it has in the past. What is of real concern, therefore, is whether the theatre will continue to bring us "dramatic art" or whether it will give way entirely to spectacular and sensational substitutes.

Since drama as an art in the theatre has had a long and respected history in the development of Western civilization, it is only now, with a profusion of nondramatic dialogues, that we realize it may not last forever. Only now do we see that its dissolution is as possible as its formation. Only now do we see that *the theatre* was born with man and that it may go with him to the grave, but that *dramatic art,* having endured the fall of empires and the dark ages, may dissolve along with its presently recognized fundamental forms.

What, then, are the fundamental forms of dramatic art? This depends upon the meaning of dramatic art. Physically, the arts are probably just what they appear to be. If painting is the application of a visible substance to a visible surface and music is the making of audible sounds, then drama is the enactment of imagined human activity which is both visible and audible. To become artistic in these instances, the means or materials are carefully selected and symbolically arranged in meaningful configurations. In dramatic art, the means are words and actions, and the configurations of them are symbolic and rhythmic sequences of human incidents as acted out in a theatrical medium. But these pragmatic explanations can only serve until we inquire more about the essential nature of drama.

What seem to be symbolized in such performances are those human encounters which show the will of man expressed in the pursuit of his own future. It is this purposive behavior in the rhythm of man's confrontation with life, of his interaction with others, and of his response to consequences which holds our attention. It is the performance of man's encounters in such sequences that move audiences in basic and essential ways. Confrontation, interaction, and consequence then become the dramatic *analogue* of human engagement. In a dramatic theatre, this analogue appears in the experience of spectators as a rhythm of aesthetic responses in certain fundamental contexts.

Some of the responses recognized in this experience have been: the sense of imminence created by the anticipation in certain devices of suspense, the sense of awareness or revelation created by scenes and speeches of discovery and recognition, the sense of involvement we feel from the kinship and from the conflicts which are present among the characters, the sense of commitment created by the decisions of characters to make choices, the sense of fulfillment which comes with the final knowledge of the fortunes or destinies of the principal characters. To experience these aesthetic qualities of imminence, revelation, involvement, commitment, and fulfillment in the rhythmic continuity of a play, is to experience the aesthetic quality of dramatic action in the theatre. It should be quite evident from this and from the history of dramatic art that what is performed on a stage is never and never has been human life itself. What is performed is a symbolic representation of those aspects of human experience which show men engaged with life, *i.e.*, being willing to accept the consequences of living in a world of people. Human engagement, then, being the substance of drama, has taken on a variety of forms in the consciousness of its spectators because of its quality in their experience. Under these circumstances, it is the kind of experience in which we wish to participate as an audience that determines the kind of form we recognize in dramatic art. In such a context, form is not the structure of scenes and acts, it is not the pattern of devices, it is not the general mood, nor is it the general style of the performance. There can be no romantic form, or naturalistic form, or presentational form, or television form in dramatic art because these terms refer to the manner or style in which things are done. They belong to the customs and the fashions of the period, of the theatre, of the performers, and of the media, but not of the form.

What is needed, therefore, is a concept of artistic form which will account for the many variations in aesthetic quality which are found in the experience of plays in the theatre (*See* Chart I).

### The Growth of the Idea of Form

The idea of artistic form, of course, has had a long history of discussion in the Western world. It was probably Plato who was the discoverer of "form" as a fundamental concept in our thought.[1] In referring to "eidos," Plato, on some occasions, meant the immediately perceptible shape of the thing just as we still do in everyday speech. In his theory of ideas, however, "form" had to do with the internal structure which could be grasped only by the mind and which might or might not be reflected in the world of sense appearances. It was especially in *The Symposium* that Plato revealed the "essence" of an ideal to be its unique form:

> What would happen if one of you had the fortune to look upon essential beauty entire, pure and unalloyed; not infected with the flesh and color of humanity. . . . What if he could behold the divine beauty itself in its unique form?[2]

Likewise, in *The Republic,* he insisted that:

> Unless a person can strictly define by a process of thought the essential Form of the Good abstracted from everything else . . . he knows neither the essence of good, nor any other good thing.[3]

CHART I

THE KINDS OF PLAYS

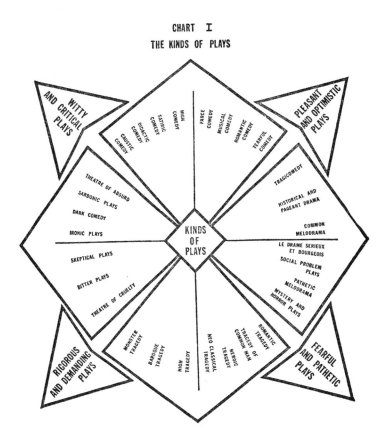

What this seems to mean in the study of dramatic art is that in discovering its proper form (or the various forms which can be abstracted from it), one will be seeking its essential nature or essence, and this essence will be unique, entire, and unalloyed. Following this line of thought, one would not seek for any mechanical structure of lines or scenes or acts or choral interludes to distinguish the "form" of drama. Nor is it conceivable that rigid structural patterns of plot and unity from neoclassical theory or textbooks in playwriting could satisfy the intention of the Platonic *eidos*. Form will need to be defined in such a way as to stand free of the structure of incidents, to be abstracted from them but appear as something more than a physical arrangement.

It was Plato's pupil, Aristotle, who actually took it upon himself to analyze the structure of drama sufficiently to observe that its essence consisted of the action or plot together with two other "objects of imitation," namely: *character* and *thought*. The end to be achieved or the objective sought in making a play would be, in Aristotle's system, the formal cause thereof; and it was in plot, character, and thought that he found the "form" of drama. Aristotle gave us a description of tragic form which would yield the "proper" effect, as depicting a hero, not unlike ourselves but perhaps somewhat better, acting through a probable series of incidents connected by cause and effect in an entanglement which would lead to discovery, reversal, and unraveling in his fortunes, all of which action would evoke such emotions as pity and fear, leading to their catharsis in the audience.

Much of Aristotle's criticism is difficult to apply to all the drama which has been written since his day, but this last phrase of his definition of tragedy which includes the effect on the audience as the final cause of drama is fundamental to any new look at the meaning of dramatic art and its forms. When due consideration is given to the stimulation of such emotions "as pity and fear," then our concern will not only be the characteristics of that which causes the stimulation but also what there is about the audience which is conducive to that kind of stimulation. We need to know what kind of dramatic action affects audiences and we need to know what kinds of feelings and experiences in the audience will allow for, or be receptive to, the effects produced. Aristotle was most concerned with how the abstract elements of plot, character, thought, diction, melody, and spectacle could be logically combined in a unified work of poetry. We must now be concerned with how *any* discernible and palpable elements might be of interest to and excite an audience in a work of dramatic art. By way of contrast it would be appropriate to say that in Aristotelian criticism a particular structure of incidents should elicit a definite response provided certain characteristics of unity, probability, causality, and universality could be achieved throughout.[4]

One thing that criticism, psychology, and aesthetics have

taught, however, is that aesthetic characteristics or qualities do not inhere in the physical work of art alone. Such quality is always partially subject to the experience and perceptual capacity of the spectator. As a consequence, even in Aristotle's terms, tragedy and comedy are forms of drama which are different partially because of their palpable structure together with their subject matter and partially because of the emotional, cultural, and perceptual contexts in which their spectators view them. It is for this reason that a brief description or synopsis of a plot will not tell us either the "soul" of the play or its "essential form." Such synopses are usually nothing more than the structural outlines or the sequential patterns of a narrative and would serve equally well for epic poems, short stories, or novels. Something more will be needed to discover the nature of "form" in dramatic art.

One approach to the problem of the disparity between the dramatist's intentions and the responses of the individual members of the audience has been the exploitation of rhetorical or stylistic devices to achieve specific effects. Beginning with Horace in 18 B.C. with his "Letter to the Pisos" and ending with the innumerable twentieth-century texts on how to write plays, we find admonitions concerning the structure and the devices which should be most effective for the audience. Horace wrote:

> Five acts a play must have, nor more nor less,
> To keep the stage and have a marked success.
> Let not a God come in, save to untie
> Some knot that will his presence justify;
> Confine your speaking parts upon the scene
> To three, a fourth should never intervene.[5]

The neoclassicists of the Italian Renaissance even suggested that "rhetorical" principles of structure be applied to the drama. In his work, *On the Composition of Comedies and Tragedies,* Giraldi Cinthio wrote:

> The Latins have held that a plot should be divided into five acts. In the first the argument should be contained. In the second the things contained in the argument begin to move toward their end. In the third come impediments, and perturbations. In the fourth begins to appear a way to remedy what

is causing trouble. In the fifth is given the expected and with a fitting solution for all the arguments.[6]

It may be that such schemes stem from Aristotle's *Rhetoric,* but, in any case, they persisted to the nineteenth century when we find them taking on a new shape in the dialectical analyses of Georg Wilhelm Friedrich Hegel (1770-1831). The latter's *Phenomenology of the Mind* and *Philosophy of History* bring to bear the dialectic sequence of thesis, antithesis, and synthesis upon all the phenomena of the world. In his aesthetic, dramatic action was not only an expression of human will but of conflict:

> Dramatic action, however, is not confined to the simple and undisturbed execution of a definite purpose, but depends throughout on conditions of collision, human passion and leads therefore to actions and reactions, which in their turn call for some further resolution of conflict and disruption.[7]

For Hegel, the conflict grows out of active volition on the part of individual characters which goes through a process of assertion, of development and collision, and finally resolution or, more specifically in tragedy, a "reconciliation."[8] The tripartite pattern of assertion, collision, and resolution did not exactly reflect the Aristotelian scheme of complication, peripety, and denouement, but it was apparently noted by William Archer that there was an artistic logic in understanding dramatic action in some rhythmic sequence: "It is the business of the dramatist to analyze the crises with which he deals, and to present them to us in their rhythm of growth, culmination, and solution."[9] The difficulty that arose from such descriptions of structure in drama was the unyielding rigidity of the total designs suggested by various critics. One influential book was Gustave Freytag's *Technik des Dramas* which contained a pyramidal diagram with the following component parts: Introduction, Exciting Force, Rising Moment, Climax, Return, Final Suspense, and Catastrophe.[10] It may now seem incredible that such a narrow stringency could be applied to the dynamic process of dramatic action, but it was not uncommon for the theorists of the next one hundred years to prescribe similar divisions in the play. William Archer proposed a scheme which required the dramatist to establish a "Point of Attack," fill in a clear and complete "Exposition," definitely show the "finger posts" in the "Preparation," always include the "Obligatory Scene," be certain there is an adequate "Climax," and bring the end to a "Full Close."[11] In much more recent times, this general approach is reflected in the rhythmic interpretation of tragic action proposed by Francis Fergusson in his book, *The Idea of a Theatre,* which suggests that the constituent "movements" of Tragedy are "purpose, passion, and perception."[12] These terms may apply to the volitional tragedies of necessary destiny such as those of Sophocles and Shakespeare, but one will recognize that most of the schemes and patterns suggested thus far do in fact describe the progress of the action only in certain limited types of drama. What they do not do is to illuminate the whole body of drama or to offer adequate differentia for defining the possible fundamental forms of dramatic art.

In what is perhaps one of the most complete discourses on the structure of drama, John Howard Lawson, in *The Theory and Technique of Playwriting and Screenwriting* maintained an objective pattern of structural divisions including Exposition, Rising Action, Obligatory Scene, and Climax.[13] It is true that Lawson treated them as dynamic parts of the "conflict" which he felt to be the essential character of all dramatic action. In looking over his whole theory, one is particularly impressed by the clear-cut relevance which it has for the "realistic," "social," "thesis," or "problem" plays written from the day of Dumas *fils* to those of Lillian Hellman. This circumstance is probably due to the fact that Lawson's theory is founded on the social conflicts and dilemmas which appear in most of his illustrations. What is, in the present context, particularly notable, however, is that this analysis of structure in the technique of dramatic writing leads to no definite "form" in the sense of Tragedy or Comedy or any other. Apparently what he hoped to reveal was the structure of something that might be called the "modern play." What he did not take into account were the experimental "styles" of playwriting put forth by Wedekind, Strindberg, Kaiser, Toller, Lenormand, Claudel, Schnitzler, Pirandello, Betti, Lorca, Andreev, Evrinov, and Brecht. Although there is no specific element in his guide to

dramatic construction which would negate the dramatic character
of the plays by these playwrights, there is a sense in which certain
of their fantastic, symbolic, expressionistic, and mystical scenes,
incidents, and actions do not correlate with the patterns of
Lawson's dramatic construction such as exposition, progression,
and climax. Only in a purely mechanical way, can these patterns
by applied to such episodic sequences of action as those in
*Spring's Awakening, Reigen, A Dream Play, Man and the Masses,
No More Peace, Anathema, Theatre of the Soul* or *The Road to
Damascus,* any one of which were available to Lawson in translation for the purposes of his book. It is not that these plays are
devoid of structural unity; it is simply that they are not amenable
to rigid structural analysis as recommended by such writers as
Cinthio, Freytag, Archer, William T. Price, Elizabeth Wood-
bridge, and others.[14]

All such schemes to describe the structural form of drama
are literal and objective modes of analysis which have often
proved helpful in understanding the sequence of incidents in a
specific plot. Unfortunately, these are all segmental analyses
which could lead to a patterned repetition in plots if they were
ever literally employed by a playwright. Some such repetition
actually did occur in the nineteenth century in connection with
the writing of "*la piece bien faite,*" the well-made play, in Europe,
England, and America. We think of the plays of Eugene Scribe
and Victorien Sardou as appearing to have been written to a
formula which influenced so many other playwrights, including
Ibsen in his "social" period, that the formula which was outlined
by William Archer (see above) eventually became anathema to
critics, playwrights, and theorists alike. Shaw was to condemn
for all time the formula play as an exercise in "Sardoodledum."[15]

The lesson to be learned from this historical experience is that
such structural formulae are simply not good guides to the
interpretation of dramatic "form" in the sense of Plato's "Essence"
or Aristotle's "Formal Cause." The natural essence of drama is
more likely to reside in the substance of what we experience at
the performance of a play, and the substance quite plainly consists of our response to human action in its various nuances and
ramifications, including not only the obvious physical aspects of

bodily movement and speech but also the thought, emotion, and interaction of characters. The latter kinds of action can, of themselves, be spectacular or sensational in a theatre, but when they arise from the depths of man's engagement with life to be symbolized in dramatic art, they become moving, disturbing, turbulent images of the world in which they were conceived. The intent of the present work is to show how these dynamic images which appear in the mind of the observer have been incipiently structured from basic biologic drives. It is then the analogues of the resulting behavior which appear in the creation of different forms of drama and which we value in different ways when we attend the theatre.

## The Aesthetic and Biologic Contexts of Form

Fundamentally what is called aesthetic is a part of that vast body of human experience of which we can truly say that we are aware. We normally say that whether we are tasting or touching, or smelling, or seeing, or hearing, we are at least *perceiving* the world around us or something that is in that world. We say that we perceive the qualities: the color, the texture, the vitality, the uniqueness or perhaps the form of the object or event which is in the field of our awareness. We also notice that there are a great many things existing outside of us which may be bright, noisy, sharp, distinct, or moving objects to which we pay little attention. There is the constant noise of traffic, the flash of neon signs, the flutter of flags, the pinch of our shoes, and the whistle of wind, which we only notice when something calls them to our attention or we decide to attend them. Potentially, the moving clouds across the sky, the roaring breakers on the beach, the swift rush of rivers, and the brilliant throbbing fluorescent lights in our offices all have properties which might be expected to attract our attention. In everyday experience sometimes they do and sometimes they do not, but at least potentially they might.

That which brings these things into the aesthetic sphere of experience is the intrinsic value we find in them. When we note that they are satisfying and complete within themselves as we attend to them, they achieve aesthetic value for us. This does not compel us to reject the plays of Ibsen and Shaw just because they have some sound moral ideas in them. Such plays will always be the more satisfying because they are aesthetically complete and morally helpful in our experience. Of course, we should not go to the theatre to acquire a moral lesson any more than we should go there just to hear pleasant sounds and see pleasant sights. Professor Archie Bahm has put it succinctly:

> That which is both aesthetic and moral may be more completely aesthetic than that which is aesthetic merely; and that which is both aesthetic and moral may be more completely moral than that which is moral merely.[16]

This explains why a play *may* be more enjoyable than a fireworks display and why it *may* be more enlightening than a sermon. Unfortunately, a play also *may* be neither one nor the other. It is, after all, a performance in a theatre; it is a display of auditory and visual stimuli; and it may not, for lack of competence, be presented in a way to interest anyone in its sensuous quality or in the meaning of its action and words. The audience may not be convinced that it is human: that it is human language in a human action in a human environment. Regardless of its style, it must seem to be human; it must symbolize the human condition. Everyone knows that it is not real life, but they must believe in it as true. The movement, the throb, the course of life must, as Susanne Langer has said, be "virtual" in our experience of them.[17] In an artistic experience, therefore, whenever we are perceptually aware of objects or events, visual or auditory, in time or space, their aesthetic qualities are potentially and virtually available to our experience. It is for this reason that we find contemplation, study, and repetition all valuable in the appreciation of a rich and extensive work like the performance of Shakespeare's *Hamlet*. One may return again and again to see such a play with the realization that the enjoyment grows with the discovery of more and more of its aesthetic quality. It is, therefore, in the consummation of adequately "funded" experience that one discovers the full *potential* of artistic form.[18]

In order to distinguish forms in our environment, we not only look for the external shapes or structures of various things, we also seek to understand in each object, the essential qualities which are salient in our experience of them. It is much safer for a human being to approach a king snake than a rattlesnake. We learn this by coming to know the markings, shape, colors, and sounds belonging to each. A rattler coiled to strike is an unforgettable experience; it demonstrates by its imminent position and its threatening rattle the very essence of its kind. The essence of its form lies in what we fear it is about to do—in its *potential* power to strike and destroy. The imminence of danger is the power of its form. One must be able to recognize its external characteristics first in order to avoid it, but the essence of the rattlesnake is not known and felt except in this dynamic moment of encounter. It might be said that, in life, man encounters the whole of nature and that, because of his social and communicative propensities, he becomes *engaged* with his fellow men. It may be possible to depict any of the encounters of man in drama, but it is his engagement with human life that seems to be of deepest concernment to him. It concerns him because it shows him exerting his will, coming to grips with the exigency of remaining alive in a society of others.

The dynamic image of human engagement which we find enacted in the theatre grows directly out of the biologic processes in the purposive behavior of human beings (*See* Chart II). Human action, for artistic purposes, is not all or everything that a person might say or do; it consists especially of those things he is impelled to do by those inner drives which serve a definite purpose, and those activities which he can honestly say he chooses to engage in or wills to do. It is the purposive behavior of man that furnishes the content of the most interesting scenes in all of drama. It should not be out of the way, therefore, to note briefly the kinds of things humans *will to do* and, thereby, reveal certain fundamental characteristics of dramatic engagement. It should be remembered, of course, that differences in ethnic origins do create different patterns of behavior, but in the monogamous society of the Western world, our drama has revealed the same kinds of human encounters for nearly twenty-five hundred years.

The reason for our interest in these encounters seems to stem

## CHART II
## FUNDAMENTAL SOURCES
## OF DRAMATIC ACTION

Some archetypal patterns of purposive
behavior which stem from biologic
needs and drives

**YOUNG YEARS**

MALE DRIVES                    FEMALE DRIVES

HUNTING                              BLOOMING

PLAYING

FINDING                          ENTICING

FIGHTING

CONQUERING          ACCEPTING

MATING IN PLAY

**USING ENERGY**

**CRUCIAL YEARS**

REJECTING PLAY                    RE-ENACTING PLAY

REVENGING YOUTH

FIGHTING FOR FREEDOM          APPEALING TO LOVE

MATING IN LOVE

POSSESSING AN HEIR          GIVING BIRTH

BUILDING A HAVEN                  NURTURING YOUNG

REJECTING CHOICES

**MAKING CHOICES**

**MATURE YEARS**

ACCEPTING RESPONSIBILITY

DESTROYING MISTAKES          CONSERVING THE PAST

TRANSFORMING THE WORLD    POSSESSING A HOME

REMEMBERING THE ACTION
AND
SEEING IT WHOLE

**SEEKING WISDOM**

from the fact that certain fundamental characteristics in human biology tend to create the basic objectives of our purposive behavior and that these objectives constitute the essence of the life force in us. Although this force is universally directed to the creation of more life on earth, there are fundamental drives in both the male and the female which tend to bring them into confrontation throughout their lives. Whereas man seems innately driven to impregnate the earth with his seed—and, by extension, to fill the earth with life—woman seems innately driven to germinate that seed and to nurture all consequent life. Man, the impregnator, hunts until he finds fecundity. He then possesses and pierces the fecund source or he attacks and destroys all that prevents his doing so. Woman as the source of fertility, is impelled to bloom and entice men until she has conceived or until she has possessed some symbol of the male archetype and is able to re-enact the enticement and the fulfillment of the biologic process. It is the animalistic principle in the male carnivore which makes him attack and destroy to get food. It is the vegetative principle in the female which makes her want to blossom again and again in a series of re-enactments which may become symbolic. She, too, by taking on certain masculine, animalistic propensities, may attack and destroy whenever she meets with frustration or opposition just as the male may take on feminine vegetative proponsities and resort to re-enactment with symbols and fetishes when he is frustrated. In both cases, the symbolic acts may be the basis of our art, drama, and religion, but the total effect of the life force will always be to populate the earth. This is as certain with our species as with others.

In this process, the male is further impelled to transform the earth by clearing it and building havens for the life which he spreads. The female, on the other hand, is impelled to continue to conserve all havens and all of that earth which will nurture more and more life. Whereas the male must dominate a certain territory of land as his own, the female must dominate a certain haven for her young. Together they need to possess and hold property, but they do so under the shadow of the possibility that such ownership will become an obsession rather than a need. Whenever any drive becomes an obsession, the human being faces the danger of opposition. The life force is directed to the end that any encroachment upon human freedom will be opposed until it is destroyed.

Because these drives cannot all be satisfied immediately in a world of other people, much of the purposive behavior of both men and women must be accomplished by sublimation. The basic drives of the male are persistently brought into conflict with those of the female, and they both must seek substitutes, symbols, and surrogates for the objects of their desire. We have devised innumerable taboos, customs, manners, fashions, and laws organized to control the total process of procreation. But because the will of the male to hunt, to impregnate, and to transform the earth, and the will of the female to entice, to give birth, and to nurture life tend to remain with them all their lives, they find themselves engaged not only with each other but with all the institutions which affect the biologic process. These human engagements become dramatic when they are symbolized to evoke aesthetic experience by their virtual representation in the theatre.

For example, in drama when the purposive behavior of both sexes becomes successful in achieving the probability of procreation, then their encounters are virtually happy and salubrious. When transmuted into an analogue of dramatic action, such human engagements become the basis for Comedy (*See* Chart VII). Comedy demonstrates that the drive to procreate, to fill the earth with life and to preserve it, is shared by both the male and the female. Comedy depends upon the fact that this drive in either sex may be thwarted by those who have other purposes. In Comedy, the monogamous marriage which is necessary to family life can be completely demolished by any of those opponents who first desire money, or fame, or sex outside of family ties. In the Western theatre since Aristophanes, such opponents of marriage have been laughed to scorn and defeated or deflated in the action we call Comedy. When the opponents are essentially vicious and powerful, and those on the side of the life force are in danger of their lives, we find the essential elements of Melodrama, provided the latter are victorious in overcoming the former. On the other hand, when the life force is set aside or thwarted by a powerful human being who has done so in the very attempt to create or conserve more of human life or the future possibility of such life, we will find an analogue for Tragedy. Likewise, when the avowed destiny and purpose of human life is brought into question by the ambiguous or ambivalent needs of self-destructive or frustrated human beings, then we may find still another analogue. Thus, it is in the vivid symbolic action representing the basic drives and encounters of human beings that we find the essential patterns which we associate with fundamental kinds of drama.

To know the essential form of a work of art is, therefore, to know more than the outer surface, the external action, and its obvious perceptible characteristics. By more careful scrutiny and closer analysis, by intuitive insight and more enduring experience of it, one may come to know its inner nature, its "essence," how it functions in experience, how it captivates attention—what its potential power may be. A painting, a sculpture, a selection of music, a dance, or a play may each be more than they appear to be on the surface. The trite, obvious, casual, and commercial examples of each may be nothing other than their sensuous exteriors would indicate, but those which have been deeply wrought will deeply move those who feel the power of their inner form.

It so happens in the living theatre that many people in an audience will laugh together because they find the same thing funny; many people may even cry together because they find the same thing sad or filled with pathos. Since we have said that our responses are just as likely to be very different, the reason for the concurrence of feeling in an audience must be due to something in the performance, either in what the playwright has created or in what the performing artists have created. In terms of the action and the meaning of the play, we do, in large numbers, feel strongly in similar ways about those who suffer; about those who succeed; about certain ideals such as freedom, justice, truth, and beauty; about all basic biologic drives; and often about certain prudent norms such as thrift, generosity, diligence, and punctuality. Because we do have, as human beings, a large number of convictions in common regarding human conduct, we can recognize these same levels of conduct whether ideal in one kind of play or practical in another.

To the extent that different people do recognize similar characteristics in various human acts and judge them in quite similar ways, an audience can probably be convinced of the "universality" of a specific human action by the manner in which it is performed, and will look for familiar consequences of that action at the final curtain.

It is this very similarity in the deep-set ideas and beliefs of human beings which characterizes the descriptions by Carl Jung in his theory of archetypal forms in the "collective unconscious." He wrote:

> The original structural conditions of the psyche are of the same astonishing uniformity as those of the visible body. The archetypes are something like the organs of the pre-rational psyche. They are eternally inherited identical forms and ideas, at first without specific content. The specific content appears during the individual life span when personal experience is absorbed in just these forms.[19]

That Jung thought of these archetypal ideas as based upon primordial images with which the creative mind of the artist is able to build universally effective structures is shown in the following:

> The man who speaks with primordial images speaks with a thousand tongues; he entrances and overpowers, while at the same time he raises the idea he is trying to express above the occasional and the transitory into the sphere of the ever-existing. He transmutes personal destiny into the destiny of mankind, thus evoking all those beneficent forces that have enabled mankind to find a rescue from every hazard and to outlive the longest night. That is the secret of effective art.[20]

It is our inherent feeling for the tragic experience found in its symbolic image or analogue in drama which makes of Tragedy an archetypal Form. When we see and hear the chief figure in a play confronted with the necessity of performing a crucial act of will, we become aware of the seriousness of the drama.

When we know how imprudent it is for him to act, we realize that he has made a tragic judgment just as Antigone and Oedipus did. When we see him prepared to die, we know the consequences of his choice and we are satisfied that this is a great person among all others. It is then that we have experienced the artistic fulfillment of what is known as Tragedy.

A similar case may be made for the archetypal permanence of the form of Comedy in dramatic art. Not only in the Western world but in the Eastern as well, do we find the aesthetic experiences of comedy from ancient times to the present. Whenever, at the performance of a play, we come to sense the confrontation of men with women, we find the willful effort of the male to reconstruct environment—to destroy and to build again—opposed to the will of the female to entice, to nurture, and to bear fruit. In either camp, the male or the female, there may be deviationists, those characters who with exaggerated bent, make it impossible for the others to live prudently; their interaction elicits the very essence of comic danger and the sense of imminence.

When the opposition is craftily organized by a Plautus or a Molière, it is the discovery of the mistakes of identity in the intrigue, and the mistakes of poor practical judgment which provide the greatest sense of comic revelation.

Up to a point, all may be frustration for those who relish a love for freedom and the joy of living. When the latter are the victors and they are to celebrate in some symbolic way a wedding, or as in Aristophanes, a festival of procreation, then we are satisfied and will have achieved a rich fulfillment in our experience of Comedy as a Form of dramatic art.

The forms of Tragedy and Comedy, then, are not found in their structure of scenes and acts but deeply in our consciousness of their biologic meaning and their flow of feeling. We must combine, therefore, our appreciation of innate humanity with our appreciation of artistic structure. But no specific drive or goal defines any particular kind of art or drama. It is man's emotional response to archetypal patterns that ultimately motivates and characterizes the making of dramatic forms. How and why we are impelled to represent these patterns of purposive behavior grows out of our need to explain and justify human existence itself.

To solve the mysteries of the biologic process, we are led by curiosity to learn as much as possible about ourselves, our world, and each other. We listen to the sound of wind, ocean, and birdsong, and we try to imitate those sounds with reeds and strings. We watch the rising and setting of the sun, and we try to imitate the colors of these displays and the vistas of the distance in front of us, and the changes from darkness to light and light to darkness. We wait for the seasons to change and for life to grow and bear fruit, and in the waiting we imitate the passage of time. But time is also action, and it is the action of life which attracts more and more of our attention because it holds the secret of all we seek in biologic fulfillment. Movement and growth among animals and vegetables give us the knowledge of our own food supply. The actions of other human beings give us the knowledge of our own biologic purposes and ultimately of our own destiny (*See* Chart II).

We are impelled, therefore, to imitate human action in all of its surroundings because we want to know more about what faces us in life. By imitating and observing motivations, we learn the drives, the needs, the frustrations and the satisfactions which accompany the whole course of our action. We come to understand these things best in their actual surroundings, and we tend to imitate or represent these surroundings in all of our representational arts both in the theatre and out.

Fortunately, almost all of the light, sound, space, time, and action of the world can be represented by symbolic structures which may be more complex and richer in their significance than that which they symbolize. By metaphor, by ambiguity, by implication, and by symbol, the artist links potentially more experience in the minds of spectators than any computer could ever handle. It is for this reason that we depend upon virtual images of physical elements to create the magic world of the theatre. We hope the symbols will mean more and more to more people. But the danger in symbolic representation is that the symbols may be valid only within a limited cultural context. The customs and ceremonies of one country are not the same as those of another. Only the basic patterns of human behavior are similar and can be symbolically represented. Hunting and blooming, enticing and possessing, accepting and rejecting, building and destroying can all be represented in dramatic terms in the theatre. On the other hand, it has only been in very extreme circumstances that either killing or copulating have been actually performed on stage; they are almost always symbolized in the dramatic action. What the performer has discovered is that all basic human action can be effectively heightened, elaborated, and made more emotional by the virtual images of life which he can transmit in the theatre by meaningful gesture.

And our responses to dramatic action are demonstrated by

## CHART III

## AESTHETIC PROPERTIES OF STRUCTURE

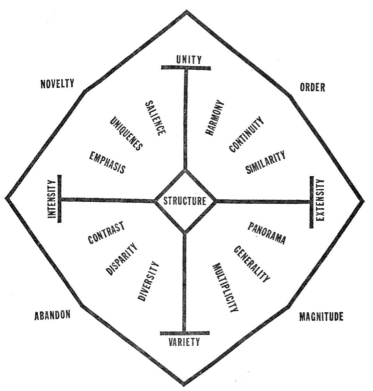

the manner in which we accept the imitations. We accept them in ways which are colored by the taste which we have developed for them. Many people can both understand and believe in the elevation, the will, and the destiny represented by Tragedy as well as the desire, the frustration, and the celebration in Comedy. But for those who do not enjoy both, it is not entirely a matter of recognizing or not recognizing the basic behavior which is represented in the action. It is much more a matter of their training and education which has determined what it is they have grown to like in dramatic art. Some have developed a taste for Comedy of one kind or another and may or may not have gained a taste for Tragedy. Dramatists, being a part of the body politic, also acquire or reject a taste for the various kinds of art and drama. Not that their taste will reflect in any way what is liked by the rest of society, but their preferences may lead to the creation of works which are within the realm of public taste. The dramatist is aware of taste only to the extent that he hopes society will attend to what he has to offer. As a consequence, how taste is acquired and how it governs the kinds of drama which are most prevalent in the world is essential to this study.

## Aesthetic Preferences

Part of what makes the forms of Dramatic Art cohere and coalesce in a fairly recognizable cycle from Comedy to Melomantic Drama to Tragedy to Ironic Drama and again to Comedy is the scope and progression of aesthetic tastes. The qualities of dramatic experience: imminence, involvement, revelation, commitment, and fulfillment are such that in the theatre it is possible to feel nearly the whole gamut of affective states from pleasure to pain. Our anticipation can be for the most exquisite delight in vision or sound. Our involvement with characters can extend from the most ardent love to the most jealous hate. Our discoveries can be of the most desirable sensuous images or of the most gruesome ones. Our willingness to be curious can apply to the destiny of the most selfless hero or to the greediest (but most captivating) monster. This is possible because human beings apparently have the ability to enjoy a wide range of things from the most saccharine sweet to the most lemon sour and from the greasiest richness to the most acrimonious bitterness. Some people can take great delight in the gay and frivolous and also find occasion to dwell upon the most lugubrious and excruciating misery in human affairs. Not only in painting and music but also in the theatre do we find that some of the most fatuous and silly products are exceeded in popularity only by the most morbid and clinical exposées of mental and physical pathology.

As a consequence, it is said, "One cannot account for differences in taste." What is needed is not so much an accounting as an understanding of how it is that tastes are developed. It may be that in different times and in different places, the artist may appeal to a wide variety of aesthetic responses without doing any injury to his artistic values.

One can readily find precedent for this wide variety in our interests in the aesthetic properties of structure, texture, movement and sound. Our attention to structure is drawn by those tensions which exist in our sensitivity to Contrast and Similarity, Harmony and Diversity, Emphasis and Panorama, Continuity and Disparity, Salience and Multiplicity (*See* Chart III). Whatever perceptible differences can be discriminated can be noticed by a sensitive artist or by a sensitive spectator. The use of emphasis and contrast by Van Gogh was different in an essential way from the panoramic effects and continuous spectrum achieved by Cezanne. In terms of texture, the coarse effects achieved by the iron-welded art of Lipschitz are different in essence from the smooth sculptured stone of Henry Moore. The deep pile of a traditional Chinese rug presents a very different effect to both sight and touch from the murals of Diego Rivera. In terms of movement, a sensitive spectator can distinguish between the random, coarse gestures of one actor like John Wayne as distinct from the economical and refined movement of another like David Niven. Not only gestures in the performing arts but lines and plains in plastic arts seem to possess the qualities of movement. Any one of these may be described as either sharp or broad, curved or angular, expansive or confined, simple or complex, and with experience we are able to accept and appreciate a long range of variations in all categories (*See* Chart IV). The crystalline tones of the upper register of the piano are very different from the coarse rumbles made by the low G string of the bass viol. We can learn to appreciate either one, but what is difficult to assimilate is an unfamiliar sound or movement which is sustained or repeated for too long a period. Saturation comes readily with unfamiliar materials. But nearly all the properties of sight and sound can be accepted and then appreciated after a period of time.

One also can find precedent for aesthetic variety in the likings of the human palate. It is apparent that all the steps between sweet and sour, between fat and acid, between dull and brilliant, between insipid and caustic, between bland and pungent are possible areas of appreciation. We find that not only do people differ from each other but also differ within themselves from time to time. Some may begin by liking the blandest foods such as cream cheese and mashed potatoes but later acquire a taste for stronger cheese and brussels sprouts. What happens in the interim may be termed the process of "habituation" which simply refers to the fact that we "grow" to like other things by trying first one thing and then another with enough frequency to become accustomed to the taste and to acquire a liking for some of the new items.[21] It is possible, for example, to work our way along by trial and rejection from a bland variety of cheese such as cream cheese through habituation to Edams and Cheddars, through smoked cheeses to blue cheeses such as Gorgonzola and Roquefort, and from there to more potent experiences in Limburger and Camembert (*See* Chart V). There is no guarantee, of course, that all people will proceed from the most bland to the most pungent in their tastes for food or anything else. Many will stop short of extremes simply out of the need for self-preservation. Others will make very few if any trials and develop no additional tastes at all beyond their childhood habits. Experience will show, however, that tastes can be developed from those things that are simple and bland to those that are much more complex and pungent.

Strangely enough, it is possible to find a correlation between the taste for the products of art, drama, and music and the range of taste for other sensuous experiences such as food, drink, or

## CHART IV
## AESTHETIC PROPERTIES OF MOVEMENT

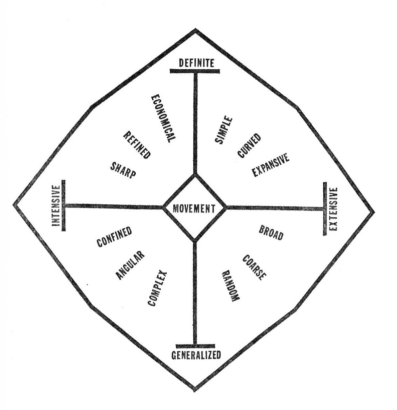

textures. It may jar someone's sensibilities to discover that his preferences in works of art are similar to choices of liquor or cheese, but even those who deny the similarity realize that within each category the process of habituation does occur. They can see in their taste for art that, after persistent trials with ever-different products, they can notice a subtle change in their choices from that which is more difficult in its aesthetic acceptance. That which is easiest is bland, soft, simple, and innocuous. That which is most difficult is astringent, pungent, rigorous, and possibly mordant. It does not seem to matter whether it is a product of the brewer's art, of culinary art, or of dramatic art. We grow to like the more pungent and the more difficult examples *provided* we make trials of these more complex experiences. Those who try the new and different experiences seem to do so when the old ones have worn thin or have become "old hat." Although there may be many who *do not* seek new experiences, there are at least as many who do.

In our present culture, it seems easy for a large majority to accept musical comedy, popular tunes, and magazine illustrations to the same degree that large numbers like to eat mild cheese, ice cream, and mashed potatoes. Apparently, the most palatable foods are the soft, sweet, mild products that abound in every supermarket of the Western world; and, in a similar way, but perhaps not for the same people, the majority are pleased with soft and sweetly fragrant flowers and also, soft, sweet, mild works of art and theatre which abound in the "Cultural Centers" of that same world. It is not that people should be condemned for liking cottage cheese, fields of larkspur, calendar painting, musical comedy, and television serials; these easy products have been pressed upon them since childhood and they may have acquired no other tastes. They have been led to believe that their simple tastes are less dangerous to their morals; that simple emotions, whether true or false, are less embarrassing. What they have not attempted to understand is that easy, mild works simply are not the same as the rich, spice-laden examples of more potent and incisive art which are available to them in all areas of experience. (*See* Chart VI).

### Forms of Drama

The number of different kinds of drama which have been distinguished historically, one from another, are not, strictly speaking, innumerable; but there are quite a few as shown in the first chart (*See* Chart I). What was not shown was the way they may be grouped in terms of the kinds of human experience which they tend to create (*See* Chart VII).

Aesthetically speaking, there are some plays which seem happier and more pleasant than others; they seem to be more

## CHART V

## THE HABITUATION OF PALATAL TASTE

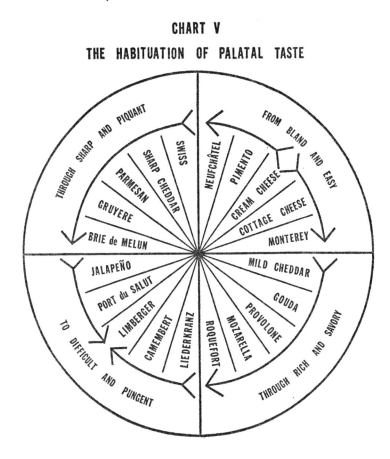

optimistic, more inspiring in their philosophy and are thereby, for a large number of people, easier to accept, easier to digest mentally, and more quickly amusing. In such a group it is not difficult to recognize immediately such types as light farces, romantic comedies, musical comedies, sentimental comedies and tearful comedies. By adding to the sentiment of the latter variety a more serious and obvious struggle between incredibly good and beautiful people whom we love and the incredibly ugly ones whom we hate, the playwright may suggest a whole syndrome of dramatic writing characterized by such terms as "melo-

## CHART VI

## A SPECTRUM OF
## AESTHETIC EXPERIENCE

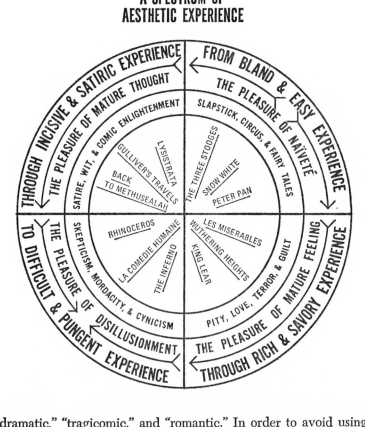

dramatic," "tragicomic," and "romantic." In order to avoid using just one of these terms, it would be convenient to coin the term "Melomantic Drama" to include them all. Within this archetype are some tragicomedies such as *A Woman Killed With Kindness* by Heywood and *Who's Afraid of Virginia Woolf?* by Albee; others include historical plays such as *Henry V* by Shakespeare and *Queen Elizabeth* by Maxwell Anderson, which contain a few facts of history but which depend upon the victory of good heroic figures for most of their appeal. In the vast majority of examples of this type, goodness is entirely a matter of moral

## CHART VII

## A SPECTRUM OF DRAMATIC FORMS

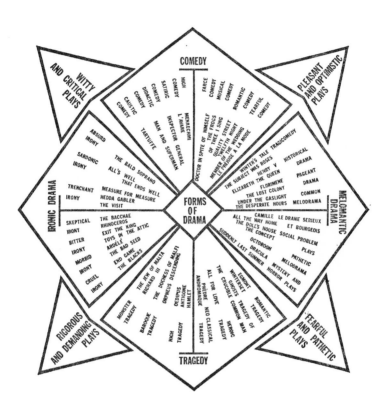

virtue, and we find many moralistic melodramas, such as *The Drunkard,* which teach an obvious lesson in virtue, or which, in some way, show that lovable people will always win either happiness or a moral victory against any opposition from strong, but finally inept, villainy. These plays have become known as "melodramas," and perhaps they should keep that title in whatever period or medium of theatre they may be found. The latest secret agent or detective movie is no less a melodrama for all its modern jargon and automatic equipment.

That which links both light comedies, tragicomedies and

simple melodramas in a spectrum of various types is the fact of their happy endings, their moral certainty, and their optimistic philosophy. These factors also cause them to be the most frequently played, the highest attended, and the most universally appealing of all types of drama. Since these three groups do not include all of the commonly named types of such plays, one needs to pursue the spectrum further. Seeking in the direction of deeper sentiment and emotionalism, one finds much sadder and more frightening effects in the more sombre melodrama and "horror" plays. But prior to the deepest pathos, one comes upon a serious order of moralizing known in the eighteenth century as *le drame*. The plays of Diderot, of La Chausée, and Destouches, together with *Nanine* by Voltaire and *Eugénie* by Beaumarchais began this type of mixed seriousness. Later works of the nineteenth century, which became known as thesis plays—written by such dramatists as Ibsen, Hauptmann, Becque, and Brieux—also fall in this category because they were structured to demonstrate the moral defeat of inhumane beliefs and decadent practices. In chapter five more examples will be shown, but for the present it can be said that in presenting a social thesis, the forces in opposition are kept as clear as in melodrama, and a double ending for good and evil is often to be expected. The devices of murder, tears, misfortune, and horror become more prominent in mystery melodramas with their fearsome imminence, in pathetic melodramas like *The Octoroon* with its sad end, and in the even more romantic *Superstition* and *Francesca da Rimini*, which were spoken of as tragedies in their day. It is usually the Gothic or horror melodramas such as *Dracula* by Deane Balderston and *Goat Song* by Franz Werfel which attempt to lead us to the limits of love, fear, and hate in the theatre without the tragic implications of these feelings. One senses the extremity of melodrama in the horror versions of science-fiction on the screen.

Tragedy as a type, and without defining it further at this point, draws us into a world of much more demanding commitments and much more unrelenting finalities from which there can be no rescue or escape. Among such serious plays, we again find pathetic types such as romantic tragedies like *Hernani* and *Winterset* with their grand ideals and plaintive sacrifices together with the bourgeois and common-man tragedies like *Maria Magdalena* and *Death of a Salesman*. In the realm of fatalistic tragedy stand the Heroic and Neoclassic plays, like *Andromaque, All for Love,* and *Phèdre* which contain some fortuitous incidents but which may evoke the same degrees of imminence, involvement, revelation, commitment, and fulfillment as do older examples.

Once we leave the more pathetic tragedies, which usually contain a hero who is a victim of circumstance, we come upon the more demanding and harsher kinds of tragic form by Sophocles and Shakespeare. For one thing, these great tragic dramatists have given us more dedicated and more self-sacrificing heroes who are willing to face insurmountable obstacles in order to preserve the ideals of the body politic. Note especially Lear demanding filial piety; Othello demanding purity in marriage; Brutus, freedom from tyranny; Hamlet, integrity of the royal court; Oedipus, the sustenance of the people and the integrity of the king; Antigone, the freedom of the individual. These plays do not contain the excesses of sentimentality found in pathetic tragedies or in heavy melodramas; instead, they have heroes who make irrevocable moral choices, who know they are responsible for their own destiny, and whose suffering is genuine.

When we approach Baroque examples of tragedy, we find that the insurmountable obstacles in the path of the hero appear more often to be ambitious and sinister agents like Bosola in *The Duchess of Malfi,* who makes impossible demands of the heroine and seems to be bent upon her destruction. Actually, it is the invincibility of such a villain, like the inevitability of fate, which keeps such plays within the realm of tragedy. The victim-hero, like Val in *Orpheus Descending,* in his pursuit of right and truth, still makes his fatal choice in the face of inexorable death, but his destiny is now in the hands of a misguided human being, Lady Torrance, instead of in the hands of the gods.

Moving further into the realm of tragedy, we find that the hero becomes more like the villain because he accrues to himself more and more power for molding destiny. Both Richard III in Shakespeare's play and Barabas in *The Jew of Malta* become indomitable villains before our very eyes, and although they may at times pay lip service to moral awareness they are truly monsters and their plays are "monster tragedies." To carry this vein further, the modern theatre has contained some plays with "anti-heroes" like the young Rhoda in *The Bad Seed,* who is a perfect villain without moral scruple and with no concern for her fate. Such a play evokes a sense of morbidity but fails to achieve a more serious tragic form because there is no awareness of self or purpose, no commitment by moral choice, and no fulfillment in either fortune or destiny.

In certain plays of similar bent, the audience is forced to anticipate the failure of those who try to succeed, and it seems ironic when the unscrupulous achieves a final victory as in *The Physicists* by Dürrenmatt. In such plays, the twist of fate leaves doubtful characters ironically in an uncertain and ambiguous world. Ironic Drama, which is here proposed as a generic title for this broad spectrum of plays, is rich in the revelation of paradox. It bids for little commitment because of the ambiguity of its action, but its resolution in failure and decay is the essence of despair as a type of fulfillment. The despairing and cynical resolutions to such plays as *Endgame* by Saumel Beckett and *Sticks and Bones* by David Rabe are the logical conclusions to themes of cynicism and cruelty. Ironic Drama, in its harsher forms, would include many plays from the Theatre of Cruelty and especially those which develop bitter or morbid ideas by means of dramatic irony.

To the extent that the Ironic Drama becomes more rational, more paradoxical, and more sophisticated it takes on the generic characteristics of its form. An exemplary play in the form would be *The Visit* by Friedrich Dürrenmatt, but as we proceed through the dark comedies of Chekhov and O'Casey, we come to the sardonic works of Jean Anouilh and finally to "the theatre of the absurd" with plays such as Albee's *The American Dream,* Ionesco's *The Bald Soprano* and Henry Livings' *Eh?* Many of these piquant plays are extremely effective in the theatre, and their ironic form is obvious. Their engagement of sad success and happy failure is always skeptical if not cynical in its import. The resulting sardonic humor, like sentimentality in the opposite kind of play, may wear thin on occasion and reach a limit of palatability. It is not just any sardonic or skeptical attitude which creates this form; it is more likely to be the disjunction of ideals, the disaffection with the status quo, and the dilemma in the end which are essential to ironic rhythm. Whatever types of ironic drama may be in existence can be clarified only through an analysis of plays and the relevant analysis of aesthetic preference. Let it suffice for the present that Ironic Drama is distinct from its neighbor in a list of types, namely: Caustic Comedy.

At the intellectual extreme of the spectrum of Comedy stand those caustic and critical plays by Molière and Shaw which bite into the decadent mores of society at the same time that they laugh stupidity to shame. Perhaps a few moments of irony appear, but the technique is one of satire and wit. One of the most caustic is *Tartuffe* because one finds in the performance that the clergyman comes close to being a monster in a comic plot. Probably the most didactic of rational comedies is *Man and Superman* by Shaw, whereas *The Doctor's Dilemma* and *Mrs. Warren's Profession* are ironic in form, and certainly the most essentially satiric comedy is *The Inspector* by Gogol. Those comedies that have been noted for two centuries as having the most refined wit are *The Way of the World* and *Le Misanthrope*, but they are essentially caustic whereas those plays of Congreve and Molière that achieve the truly generic requisite of evoking laughter in the theatre are the classic structures of *Love for Love*, and *L'Avare*.

### Preferences Among Total Experiences

As one can see from a survey of theatre criticism, those who are doing the criticizing at any one time are not always in sympathy with those who are writing the plays. Preferences among the special coteries for whom the playwright may be trying to create new types and styles of theatre will be different, if not actually advanced, from those of the critics. What is more common than the cry that the critics do not understand the theatre? For example, tragedy in the classical sense may not be appropriate in the modern theatre, may not be appreciated in it, and may not be created for it very often.[22] It may be that a certain type of romantic drama from another period is no longer the charming and heart-warming experience it was in 1910 and someone will miss it as does Joseph Golden writing in *The Death of Tinker-bell*.[23] There is nothing to guarantee that any particular kind of drama or theatre will be popular or even appreciated in any two successive periods of theatrical activity. It is the dramatist who creates the incipient artifact, the play script; and if the preferences among the audience are going to follow his vision, the theatre will have to create the physical work of art—the stage play—with that taste in mind. How ever many coterie types of audiences there may be, there will be that many different kinds of taste to please. It is apparent that more mature people prefer more mature aesthetic experiences. They may like the kind of rich and savory experiences that they associate with emotional works of art. Others may like that which is more intellectually stimulating. Most adults will continue to extend their experience to include more and more sophisticated kinds of art. Some will go so far as to prefer the pleasures of disillusionment and to insist upon the more difficult works of art, *i.e.*, those which are more pungent, more skeptical, or perhaps even cynical in their quality. Along the way, many will stop and find that, for their own fullest satisfaction, certain kinds of easy art will be the ones which they prefer. Even in the richest and fullest life, one would not expect a taste for *every* kind of aesthetic object. Nor would it be reasonable to consider one kind of taste better than another provided all examples show a comparable artistic polish and skill.

In the world of artists, some individuals and some groups will be trying to help in the development of new preferences, but others will pander to the old. In order to defend the continual production of "easy" works (the Pablum of art), a theatrical producer may claim to "give an audience what it wants"; but since an audience can have a taste only for what it already knows, the "hack" writer or "camp" merchant is simply admitting that he is unable to create anything new or fresh in quality.

The preferences of the audience, of course, will depend not only upon essential forms and their qualities but upon their physical appearance and other palpable effects as well. What is more, the fundamental forms may be limited in number, while the types and styles of plays in which their basic essences appear will show an infinite variety in the theatrical treatment of individual works.

For example, our preferences apply not only to essential forms but also to language. Some members of an audience will have acquired, by habituation, a taste for the rigors of melodic verse in their experience of theatrical sound. Actually, it has been only in modern times that both Tragedy and Comedy have been acceptable in both verse and prose. In the theatre, we may sense when an actor has revealed his character most aptly and most fully, but we may have neither occasion nor opportunity to analyze the versification or melodic patterns he has used. What we experience will be effective sound, and we may pay no attention to the means by which it becomes relevant to the dramatic quality present.

In a similar way, it is also evident that our aesthetic judgment is influenced by the production techniques employed. On some occasions we may enjoy realistic scenery with real properties and hot and cold running water, but there will be those who feel that their intelligence has been insulted if every blade of grass and scrap of paper has been realistically portrayed on the stage. Others will feel that a bare platform tends to rob the environment in a play of its essential "living" qualities. Some will notice that modern dress changes their attitude toward a Shakespearean play. Others are disappointed when Antigone is dressed in traditional Grecian robes. In case of lighting, some will find it too dark and some will find it too bright. Some will find proscenium stage lighting entirely distasteful on the open stage, or the arena stage, or on television and cinema screens. In many cases someone will notice whether there has been a proficient performance, whether the acting, settings, and costumes are relevant to the thought and reliable to the feeling of the dramatic engagement and whether the actual performance has projected the essence of the play's meaning. In any of the ways in which it seems deficient, our expectations may be disappointed and our tastes irritated. What many will realize, however, is that the conceptual image behind the production may be just as provocative to our responses. In fact, many in the audience will want the meaning of the play to be as satisfying as the visual image.

The experience of drama will show us what the receptive spectator finds to be effective is a congeries of emotions within himself, evoked, in part, by artistic devices within the structure of a play. In every kind of drama, its "virtual" qualities seem continually to color our responses in terms of moving experience. The virtual qualities of drama, as indicated earlier, consist of such experiences as that of feeling a sense of expectation or imminence, becoming involved with appealing characters, discovering by dramatic revelation both character and motivation, sharing the commitments of the chief agents of the action, and feeling a sense of completion or fulfillment at the end. We do not come to know these things abstractly; nor are they the actual sights and sounds produced on the stage. We know comic imminence from waiting to see if Harpagon will lose a single sou of his fortune. We know melodramatic involvement from the sympathy we have for the beautiful heroine. We know tragic commitment from the inevitable doom which Hamlet is determined to pursue. We know ironic revelation when the peasant, Lopahin, tells Lyubov he has bought the cherry orchard. Human taste is such that many will prefer the easy discovery of good and evil in melomantic drama to the revelation of moral choice in tragedy. Many will prefer the easy thrills of outer-space monsters in motion-picture melodramas to the difficult dilemmas presented by the ironic characters of Jean Genet's *The Balcony*. What we discover, then, is that the dramatic qualities of romantic comedy and melomantic dramas are so pleasant and so easily accepted by an audience as to make these kinds the most popular of all, and that the qualities of ironic drama and of serious tragedy are so rigorous and demanding in nature that they are least frequented by the general public. The latter types are highly prized by those who have grown to like them through persistent attendance; this would mean that they become appreciated through growth and learning and habituation.

It seems apparent, therefore, that different kinds of value accrue from different kinds of dramatic art, and that much of the value is due to the qualitative experience of the spectator. It is quite evident that the audience's knowledge, sympathy, prejudice, and emotional capacity, may all contribute to the pleasure felt by them individually and as a group. This does not mean that the audience does in fact participate in the making of the physical work of art, but it does reinforce the belief that within the limits of their perceptual attention, they do inadvertently contribute to the creation of the different forms of their experience to which they attribute certain aesthetic qualities. This is most clearly demonstrated by the transformation of the conceptual image of the playwright into a virtual image of human engagement for a responsive audience by what may be called a creative or artistic process. What we will learn from this transformation is that plays are written with definite structures and that forms are essentially in the experience of the spectators.

# II.

## The Artistic Process

"In genius of the highest order, that sudden, incalculable, and puissant energy which pours up from the hidden depths is controlled by a will which serves a vision—the vision which sees in chaos the potentiality of Form."

—J. L. Lowes, 1960

### The Making of Drama

If there may be something about imagining and making which is the same for dramatic art as it is for other arts, then it may very well be that the physical performance of a dramatic script can be considered as are other works of art: an architectonic structure molded of the materials of earth and impregnated with a living "eidos," or form, from the brain of man. The written script is made by a playwright, and the performance is made from that script by a group of artists who mold the physical structure that is seen and heard. Artists of the theatre include actors, directors, designers, and craftsmen; and they are all "creative artists" in the sense that they collaborate to make or create the actual performance which is seen, heard, and felt by the spectator. The playwright should also be considered one of the artists in the theatre because he makes the plans, the outline, the drafts and the script from which all the other artists build to the ultimate realization— the physical work of art—the performance on the stage. Both theatre artists and dramatists are also "interpretive artists" because in order to create they must interpret the incipient products of those who have gone before. The dramatist interprets the story or stories upon which his play is based; the theatre artists, whether as lone actor or as a team of various artists, interpret the script of the play as set down by the dramatist. Both art and nature seem to precede all of the tentative plans; these in turn precede the more proximate artifacts or early drafts of a work, but all art and nature seem to serve as sources for ideas in the creation of dramatic performances (*See* Chart VIII).

If these artists were not all compelled by some genuine need, they could not endure the struggles and disappointments which accompany the process of making—in this case, the writing and producing of plays. But there seems to be a most impelling need in man to make a *something*. This *something* might be the actualization of any conceptual image or idea which can appear to the human mind, but to make it *actual* is to have the skill to give it form; and to have some conceptual vision of an incipient form is to begin the creative process from the beginning.

The creative process is not easily explained or described. Although it seems to be possible to produce a formless "happening" without structure or organization or plan, it is not usually thought that man's insight and imagination can create works of effective or "moving" art without rational guidance. It is even less conceivable that an effective play could be written by a robot simply on the basis of being fed certain exalted rules, techniques, or structural patterns. From the point of view of Arthur Koestler, an artist bound by such rules would be little more than an automaton:

> Habits are the indispensable core of stability and ordered behavior; they also have a tendency to become mechanized and to reduce man to the status of a conditioned automaton. The creative act, by connecting previously unrelated dimensions of experience, enables him to attain to a higher level of mental evolution. It is an act of liberation—the defeat of habit by originality.[1]

Such creative arts can be illustrated by numerous examples in the history of dramatic art as well as in the history of any other art. The miraculous insights of all great dramatists are cases in

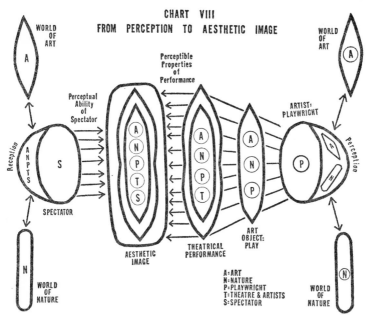

CHART VIII

FROM PERCEPTION TO AESTHETIC IMAGE

A: ART
N: NATURE
P: PLAYWRIGHT
T: THEATRE & ARTISTS
S: SPECTATOR

point. They can be observed in the plays of Aeschylus, Sophocles, Euripides, Aristophanes, Plautus, Terence, Shakespeare, Jonson, Molière, Racine, Corneille, Lessing, Goethe, Schiller, Ibsen, and Shaw. What is remarkable in these dramatists is the intuitive flashes which helped them in the creative production of their plays. Their intuitions were not merely unusual but were possessed of a recognizable essence—an inner structure of articulated feeling—which was familiar and satisfying as well as excitingly new in many respects. They gained recognition in Western culture not only for the invention of new stories but for their treatment of old ones. They adapted old tales and old plays to their own times. They borrowed stories and human engagements and made them dramatic by putting into action the purposive behavior of the agents, their basic drives and responses, and essential modes of their will and choice. Whether they were first to find the story is of less importance than how they excited the interest of their audiences by way of fundamental human needs and desires. They each picked up a story and made it dramatic, gave it dramatic form, regardless of the previous treatment or interpretation. None of them repeated the same story in the same way. This may account to some extent for the wide and enduring appeal sustained by the simplest dramatic forms and the oldest stories in the theatre.

The basic forms of any art, therefore, seem to spring from the fusion of familiar feelings, obtainable materials, and insistent present needs. This can be seen among the thousands of utensils which have been made at all levels of craftsmanship from primitive native wares to those of the finest silversmiths. For example, there are as many shapes for the spoon as there are societies of man. There are different needs to be served; there are different shapes to be achieved; and there are different degrees of feeling, imagination, intuition, and craft which can be employed in their making. But each spoon possesses the essence of "spoonness" which is fundamental to all of the particular characteristics of material or structure that we find in any given example. That which gives a spoon specific properties of line, weight, color, mass, and embellishment is its individual quality as a unique object (whether repeated by manufacturing or not). That which gives it the universal characteristic of "spoonness" or the ability to "spoon up" the materials of the earth, is its essential form or "essence." By analogy it may be said that "comicality" and "tragicality" are also essences, in certain instances, of whole and fundamental forms of dramatic art. Here, the relevant objects are no longer as simple and practical as the spoon, and the synthesis leading from the vision, to the structure, to the aesthetic experience of either Comedy or Tragedy comprises a subtle and complex process which may be called the realization of dramatic form. Observing some of the obvious steps in this process will be necessary to understanding the nature of essential "forms" as being inclusive of various dramatic "types" such as those discussed earlier.

Some plays, however, do not seem to be either tragedies or comedies; some do not achieve in the audience the effects which were anticipated by the dramatist; and some do not even seem to be plays at all. What might be important to discover, then, is simply whether the dramatist, or any original artist, gains a sufficiently clear conception—in terms of feeling, symbol, and import—of the essence of his work at a sufficiently early date so that he can know what kind of product it will be or whether he can guide it to its most effective form. Can a dramatist know what kind of play he wants to make and what steps must be taken in the process of its realization?

In the case of painting, sculpture, and the plastic arts, there would seem to be a ready answer in the fact that the artist's imagination creates the final physical object itself. It must be granted, of course, that many paintings and statues have been completed without ever having been planned on paper. A similar circumstance is found in the poetic arts. The poet does control the final physical work of art when he intones the lyrical, rhythmic pattern of his created sounds with all of their audible connotation. Putting lyrics into print simply omits these audible values. The writer like the sculptor, may have some advantage in putting down notes, sketches, fragments, and ideas which would help to shape or to interpret his works. And, like the visual artist, he seems to be impelled to set down more than the final lyric, epic, story, or novel. The difference that occurs in the performing arts is that no matter what score, or script, or scenario, or dance notation is created by the original artist, there is always a performing artist to modify it and make his own creative sketches for it. A dance is choreographed for a group of dancers to complete in performance, music is composed for musicians to complete, dialogue is written for players to complete. In such instances, the conceptual image may be set down in a fairly permanent artifact, but it is almost always incipient, provisional, and potential to what the performers will create in actuality. In some cases the original artist can be the final artist when he composes his own works; but the conceptual image, the incipient artifact, and the work of art are one and the same in the theatre only on those occasions when the dancer designs his own dance as he performs it, the musician improvises his own music as he goes along, and the actor, as in the case of the pantomimist, creates an entire dramatization for himself as he appears on stage.

What is more generally the case in all the arts is that some of the parts, contours, words, images, and sounds of potential works do appear in the conceptual vision of artists who often actualize these visions in preliminary sketches when they begin making the final product in the physical world. The original vision may be incomplete or only vaguely suggestive of a work of art, but whenever tentative notes are sung, or composing is begun on paper, or preliminary sketches are made, or dance steps are tried, they make up what may be called "incipient artifacts" or "the artifacts of vision." These preliminary sketches seem to serve as a guide for the conceptions of the artist and to the various matrices of his thought and imagination which will be brought together in more and more concrete ways as the early versions are gradually molded into their complete structural configuration. Every man-made object has the potentiality of some experience, some possible use, some possible action, perception, quality, idea, or value. The value, however, of a creative image or vision is not whether Leonardo da Vinci's ornithopter would work or pay a profit, but whether he could conceive of the possibility of man's flying in an earthbound atmosphere. We need not claim that he invented the airplane; we say that Leonardo, the artist-scientist, had the vision of a plausible, probable device to permit men to rise above the earth and that he left a concrete drawing to demonstrate his conception. He left behind him a visible, incipient artifact having the virtual quality of manned flight as a stepping-stone to a concrete work of art—which we now know as the airplane.[2]

The dramatist also creates incipient artifacts when he puts in a notebook or on any scrap of paper the observations and conceptions which have been motivated by his imagination in preparing to write a play. What one finds in such artifacts for a play, in the notes jotted down, in the sketches drawn, in the names listed, or in the stories and myths cited, are the implications of a conceptual image, an image of a human engagement. What seems to urge the dramatist to the creation of drama is his image of man confronting an environment, a society, a culture with which he feels impelled to interact, to respond, and before which he will take the consequences of his action. It is an image of man confronting the beginnings of his own choices, of his own acts, his own pursuits, his own structures, and his own failures. It is Antigone facing Creon, who makes the laws; it is Hamlet facing the usurper of his father's throne; it is Willy Loman facing a world which must destroy him because of its widely held belief in economic obsolescence.

When a man confronts life, when he is face to face with it, dramatic art, of all the arts, is able to depict his engagement with it, not chiefly his philosophical reflection upon it, nor primarily his lyrical exuberance over it, not especially his confessions of guilt about it, but particularly his will to interact with it. In the long history of drama, it would seem that nearly any type of confrontation in life has been able to inspire some dramatist to portray it in terms of will and interaction, of response and consequence. Drama is a symbol of an act of will which elicits another act of will which elicits another act of will and so on until a character makes his commitment or until he responds to the situation and the consequences are known. It is the enactment of such an engagement which gives palpable structure to our experience of imminence, involvement, revelation, commitment, and fulfillment. These aesthetic qualities are felt throughout dramatic art to the extent that the rhythmic and symbolic patterns of confrontation, interaction, and consequence impress the image of each form upon our consciousness. It is the rhythmic symbol of human engagement which moves us to know that the triumph of good is imminent in one kind of drama, or that the joy of living has been victorious in another, or that the irony of life has been proved in one kind, or that an ultimate destiny has been discovered in another. With clear images of these different rhythms, we in the audience are able to realize the power of the experience we have shared with the dramatist and with the artists in the theatre.

The incipient visions of a play, of course, are in the mind and experience of the playwright. We expect, therefore, to find among his tentative notes, sketches, and early versions only incipient clues to the realization of dramatic form. Moreover, we will probably find some other work which has inspired it and which he must "interpret" before he can "create" his play. We are really not looking for a play, then; we are looking for the germ of an idea. In some form or another we should seek the outline of a human engagement. In jotted notes may appear the confrontation which inspired the whole play. In sketches on scraps of paper may appear the images of the setting just as they would for a painter or sculptor. On the other hand, it will be found that the lack of fragments does not indicate the lack of a conceptual vision in the mind of a dramatist. The preparatory notes of the earlier dramatists were very rarely saved, but one need only observe the sources and the early quartos of Shakespeare's plays and compare them with the first folio versions to note how his imagination developed, changed, and expanded the earlier conceptions.

We may even wonder at the poor artistry of the early quartos. Could it not be that the shorter, neater, quarto versions of *Hamlet* and of *Romeo and Juliet* may be preliminary and less fully developed "scripts" for these plays than those in the first folio edition of 1623? Insofar as they are the lingual structures of potentially dynamic enacted dialogues, they stand as the conceptual and incipient artifacts in the total design which we call a play. They stand in much the same relation to the completed works of art as do the sketches of Leonardo da Vinci and Michelangelo for their sculptures and paintings. We might be prone to say that any printed version of a play by Shakespeare would be closer to a work of art than the pencil sketches of a painter, but the moment one examines the earliest versions of dramatic works, one can see the incipient nature of the structure that is being born. Almost all of the great plays including *Romeo and Juliet* have been expanded, changed, cut, and it was so from then on throughout history.[3] Those that are of initial concern, however, are those that precede the first performance of the play. It is among them that we find the conceptual vision in the original story, the earliest ideas and the earliest images of the play itself, together with whatever incipient artifacts may have been set down by the dramatist himself.

What seems to be evident from a comparative study of the conceptual artifact such as an epic tale and the final play script is that the dramatist has interpreted the prior work in such a way as to make it new and viable in dramatic action for a theatre. It is true that he creates the play in new language and in new structure, but in the first place he must be an interpreter of what has gone before. In the earliest versions of plays one does not expect a complete work, but in all preparatory and incipient play materials there seem to be potential elements of drama. There is an indication of the scenic background, there is tentative character-ization in the dialogue, there is a potential structure of dramatic action. It remains potentially and imminently dramatic, however, throughout the creative process until the artists of the theatre transform it into a concrete aesthetic structure within the sight and hearing of those who can respond. It soon becomes evident that each point of creative input is as important as another. Each artist is capable of transforming the previous artifact into a dramatic engagement based upon archetypal patterns or ana-logues of purposive behavior. It is possible at any point in the creative process to actualize fundamental human needs and de-sires in a sentient form. It may be that some of the earliest poets or bards in Western history illuminated the story of Antigone as a tragic heroine before Sophocles did. Or it may be that a modern dramatist, Jean Anouilh, has given her story the clearest import of universal tragedy. In either case, the resulting products have fulfilled their function as works of art in the society for which they were made.

If it can be said that our innate propensities when worked out in analogues of human engagement give us the virtual symbols of articulated feeling which we call forms of drama, then it is not necessary that any one artist be held responsible for the whole creative process. Something essentially dramatic may be added at each and every step. It is possible that each new artist may create a new structure for an often-treated story of the past. This is significant in the art of the theatre because such artists as actors, directors and designers are forced to conceive of dramatic engagement in terms of action, space, light, and sound. These are their only means of projecting the analogues of human behavior. The dramatist makes the human encounter out of words, the per-former makes it all new out of audible and visible action. One can say that the playwrights are the first to interpret and create, and the actors are the last; but the distinction between the drama-tist as creator and the performer as interpreter probably should be abandoned.

## Theatrical Effectiveness

Why people pay as much attention to works of art as they do

has been a matter of argument for centuries. In a theatrical medium, the answer is perhaps a little more obvious than in any other artistic medium. It is difficult to see how one can avoid attending to color, brilliance, contrasts, and movement which are so prominent in the organization of action, space, light, and sound in a theatre or on a cinematic screen. We only avoid the elements and properties of spectacle when they become monotonous, or meaningless, or painful, or incompetent. At the opposite extreme, we can observe with rapt attention when the perceptual experience seems to draw our senses to a point of concentration so that we literally respond kinesthetically or react physically to the real and "imaginal" action in a theatrical performance. The vivid experience which accompanies the contemplation of a performance such as that of an actor, a clown, or an athlete has been described as "empathy."[4] The empathy created in the viewer when he enters into movements of the juggler or cyclist or bareback rider, or when he watches the sparring between lions and tigers and their trainer, or when he watches any kind of contest such as a boxing match or wrestling match, is easily recognized so long as the example remains on the physical level. The assumption by Karl Groos that we enjoy conflict in drama because we all enjoy a street fight would imply that the conflict in a play is always a physical one.[5] Later, Herbert Langfeld claimed that:

> In the drama, the empathy is always very strong, and for the correct aesthetic attitude, we should empathize in all the characters as they in turn take up the action. This usually happens when one is entirely absorbed in the play. At times, however, the character is portrayed in a manner foreign to our experience or understanding. In that case it is impossible for us to respond empathically, that is, to live in the character.[6]

The confusion seems to arise when one substitutes the physiological aspects of anticipation, surprise, awe, and relief for the corresponding psychological responses to events which are more inwardly engrossing. It would seem a mistake to suppose that the suspense we feel from watching a trapeze artist is the same emotional experience as the imminence with which we await Othello's discovery of his error in judgment.

What seems to happen in the theatre is that the empathic response we make to the physical action stirs and reinforces our emotional response to the drama. What we will look for then are carefully executed theatrical effects in action, space, light, sound, and time which are *relevant* to our feeling during the action of the play.

There seems to be some truth in the claim that we feel a kind of identification with certain characters in plays and that this may be at least a partial explanation for drama's claim to our attention, and possibly for some of the intensity of our absorption in its course of action. There may be, however, considerable difference between our fear for the life of a heroine who is tied to the railroad tracks just when the train can be heard to approach and our fear for the life of Oedipus when he hears the full story of birth and of his guilt in the death of his father. In the latter case, we are morally afraid for the destiny of a man who represents all men and who, as a king of Thebes, has acted only for the good of Thebes in every instance. In the former case, we are empathically afraid because the big black wheels of an engine may crush the beautiful neck of a charming girl. We are naturally anxious for the physical safety of the young girl just as we would be if she were the trapeze artist in the circus, but unless we become involved in her relationships, or morally committed to her choices, or in some way spiritually identified with her destiny, our concern will remain on a physical plane as at the circus. At the wrestling match, we do want to see who will win and we may have reason to anticipate physical harm to one of the contestants; but in *Othello,* we not only anticipate real harm to Iago and Desdemona when Othello attacks them, we are also concerned about the destiny of Othello when he has been so wrongheaded. Even more important, perhaps, is that a clear, strong performance of the play, *Othello,* reveals the tragic destiny of a man whose ideals of truth and justice are forgotten or taken for granted in the face of malicious lies and circumstantial evidence. There are obviously several levels of our involvement in the dramatic events represented. When vividly performed, the usual kinesthetic responses will come with the physical action on stage. As the spectators become more and more involved in the interactions of Othello,

Iago, and Desdemona, they may respond even more strongly until they actually make covert muscular movements in response to what these characters do. In adapting the theory of empathy to the art of the theatre, Sam Selden wrote of the spectator:

> He may feel himself up there (on the stage). In imagination, he enters the body of the actor and becomes united with him in everything he does. . . . It is a sensuous response which involves the whole organism of the beholder, physical as well as mental.[7]

"Empathy" has been used, perhaps wrongly, to refer to various levels of conscious and subconscious response to works of art and nature including the pathetic fallacy of attributing human feelings to natural phenomena and also including the highest level of personal identification that one feels with regard to the heroes of literature. It is for this reason that it has been so difficult in the case of dramatic art to distinguish empathy from sympathy or from hero worship. On some occasions one might say that it is the nobility of Hamlet which makes us attend to his every movement. On other occasions, after seeing Hamlet performed innumerable times, one may be caught up in the action of the play only if the performer moves with sufficient grace, economy and saliency, and speaks with sufficient clarity, modulation, and brilliance. We then are charmed by the audible and visible qualities in addition to their meaning. For most people, these qualities must be present before they will project themselves into the dramatic encounters of Hamlet. If this is the case, then, not only must theatrical effects be relevant to the feeling of drama, but they must be performed with the greatest skill and proficiency before they create an empathic response in the audience. To give up the force of empathy (as demanded by Bertolt Brecht) might very well mean the loss of the power of involvement which we feel at a dramatic performance.[8]

As examples of physical effect, high-wire performers at the circus excite considerable suspense by adding first one cyclist, then another, then another, then a balancing artist on top of that. Boxers and wrestlers may, in fact, provoke considerable tension and a sense of conflict whenever the audience begins to wonder who will win the match. The magician easily arranges for birds and rabbits to hop out of hats and boxes which genuinely *surprise* his audience. The trapeze artists, hanging on with their teeth and twirling in space for hundreds of turns, get no less than audible gasps from an audience which is struck with *awe* and *admiration* at the daring feat of skill. Few spectators will deny a definite sense of *relief* when a man has sped down a two-hundred-foot wire on his head and is still able to stand up at the end and take a bow. There is *satisfaction* in such relief.

Since drama is performed in a theatre for an audience, one should not ignore the aesthetic effects of such physical events, which do in fact, during the course of plays, or operas, or musicals, or burlesques, or extravaganzas move the audience. While attending these performances we are often subject to feelings of suspense, of tension from physical conflict, of surprise for the unexpected, of awe for great physical prowess and skill, and of relief when the performer is safe at last. It is not strange that a physical or spectacular theatre in some form or other excites such visceral responses as these. It is to be expected, and these effects may be relied upon by the dramatist in creating the visual symbols which will reinforce what is thought and said in the dialogue of a play. Dramatic art seems to depend upon the psychological extension of the physical experience in the theatre. In a performance which is *reliable* to the thought of the dramatist, is *relevant* to our society, and is skillfully executed, we seem to subconsciously associate our visceral experience with our attitudes toward the action. We link our suspense for what may happen next with our sense of *imminence* in the dramatic engagement; we link the tension of conflict with our sense of *involvement*, our surprise and awe with *revelation*, our relief and satisfaction with *fulfillment*. Those playwrights who elicit such responses do obtain willing and receptive audiences. The aesthetic problem arises because not all spectators are prepared to be receptive in watching a play. Some find a dramatic performance too obvious or too spectacular; some find it too subtle, too abstruse, or too intellectual. What has been discovered in the theatre, therefore, is that definite, economical, and salient action and sound are as necessary as plot, character, and thought in any dramatic performance.

As a specific instance, one might examine the aesthetic context of a single dramatic incident: When Hamlet comes upon King Claudius at prayer, his speech reveals both his wish to kill the King and the religious but vengeful reasons for not doing so. His hand must partially draw his sword to anticipate the kill; but he must return the weapon to its scabbard to show that the time is not yet ripe. The "empathic" or clear, precise, and graceful movement of the actor at this moment reinforces the spectator's sense of imminent danger to the King and at the same time the imminent possibilities of Hamlet's revenge. As has been shown for many years in the study of theatre, this sense of imminence is one of the most prominent and pervasive qualities in dramatic art, but it does not seem to reach its full effect except at a play in performance.

Although several philosophers and critics, including Aristotle and Charles Lamb, have claimed that there is as much pleasure in a play read as in one seen, the play as constructed is only potentially effective until it is perceived in *some* way. If one admits that there are differences between reading a play and seeing a play, then the play as read can be no more than "incipient" to what it will be when performed. It is unfortunate that there are so many defective performances of exciting and powerful plays, but there can be no certainty that a silent reading will prove to be any more effective for any individual percipient. There is no evidence that all who read are experts at imagining the actual sequence of the *dramatic* engagement with its appropriate action. A play will, for most *readers*, be a literary experience and not a dramatic one. Only the expert theatre artist could be expected to truly visualize dramatic experience in a play he is reading, but no harm is done by analyzing the literary text and imagining the dramatic performance. What this means is that whenever a dramatic sequence of incidents, scenes, and actions presents a potentially effective image for an audience, then the artistry of the theatrical performance *as well as* the psycho-biophysical context of the spectators are both determining factors in the eventual aesthetic experience which is thus created. It may be said then that the rhythmic sequence of a play when reliably and skillfully produced in a theatre for a receptive audience creates an *incipiently* effective *form*.

It is not within the scope of the present work to include all of the necessary requisites for making a skillful and relevant production of a significant play in terms of acting, stage setting, lighting, and costuming. It is essential, however, to bear in mind that any dramatic performance in a theatrical medium employs in some way the elementary physical means of action, space, light, sound, and time (*See* Chart IX). To think of plays or to write plays which do not take into account the constant symbolic effects of these physical elements in each moment of performance is to ignore the audible and visible properties of dramatic art. The meaning of the dramatist, therefore, in every play, in every scene, and in every line of direction that he writes must be projected in what we see and hear. To make any judgments, then, about the reliability of a production, we would need to know to what extent that which is heard and seen is implied or connoted by what the dramatist has written. The dramatist not only writes stories having characters and ideas by means of dialogue, he also, by the exploitation of the means of the theatre, adds to man's appreciation of spectacle—of the experience of dynamic sensuous qualities which are relevant to human engagement. Whenever he fails to do so, the theatre artist will take it upon himself to supply these sensuous qualities based upon his own interpretation. The actor, for example, is forced to make the character audible and visible; short of rewriting, he has no other means than those of movement and speech.

Theatrical spectacle in any moment of time may consist of the reverberation of sound, or the stretch of light, or the movement of man's body, or an enveloping space, or all four at once. Wherever theatre art exists, we are immediately aware that it is capable of exciting us with a whole world of visual and auditory images provided we have cause to give it our attention, our interest, our thought, and our feelings, i.e., provided we apprehend it fully. We probably will apprehend it so long as the means of the theatre are human means and the forms it takes are human forms, *i.e.*, when the action is of man alive, when the space is his environment, when the light is of man abstracted from the void of darkness, and when the sound is of man as heard above all others on earth. The theatre is the voice and the vision of man's reality and of his dreams. As an artistic medium it is seldom merely the physical activity of man; it is more often the virtual image of his drive, his voice, his world, and his image, projecting his very soul (*See* Chart IX).

## The Response to Virtual Qualities

To think of a dramatic performance only in terms of lighting, setting, costumes, and movements on a stage is to confuse physical objects with works of art. When we treat the latter like so many pots and pans and lumps of stone, they are not functioning in our experience like those more exciting works which capture our attention and absorb our interest. The *Pietà* by Michelangelo is no piece of rock at the side of the road; Leonardo da Vinci's *The Last Supper* is not a cigarette advertisement; Beethoven's Ninth Symphony is not a hog-calling contest; and *King Lear* is not a telephone conversation. These works of art are expressive of human feeling not because of the physical characteristics which they possess in the concrete world but because of certain "virtual" qualities emanating from them which capture our attention and make us feel as we do. In dramatic art, the physical facts of action, space, light, and sound in the theatre *become* the dynamic qualities of human engagement in our experience there. Susanne K. Langer has described this relationship most vividly in terms of dance:

> What dancers create is a dance; and a dance is an apparition of active powers, *a dynamic image*. Everything a dancer actually does serves to create what we really see; but what we really see is a virtual entity. The physical realities are given: place, gravity, body, muscular strength, muscular control, and secondary assets such as light, sound, or things (usable objects, so-called "properties"). All these are actual. But in the dance, they disappear; the more perfect the dance, the less we see its actualities. What we see, hear and feel are the virtual realities, the moving forces of the dance, the apparent centers of power and their emanation, their conflicts and resolutions, lift and decline, their rhythmic life. These are themselves not physically given, but artistically created.[9]

# CHART IX
## THEATRICAL MEANS

ACTION, SPACE, LIGHT, and SOUND organized in TIME

When actual, they characterize the objects and events in the architectural structure of a theatre building or place of performance.

When virtual, they symbolize in a theatrical medium the movement of life, the environment of life, the color and intensity of life, the sounds of life, and the duration of life, but often simply of imagination.

### VIRTUAL ACTION

Symbolizes all that movement relevant to human engagement.
>In fantastic theatre, it symbolizes the supernatural.
>In drama, it symbolizes the result of human drives, choices, decisions, and therefore, character.

### VIRTUAL SPACE

Symbolically creates the image of environment through:
>Configuration or the linear and massive properties of objects, costumes, and decor.
>Deployment or the arrangement and organization of objects and agents which are relevant to the action.
>Vista or the dimension and distance symbolized by the setting.

### VIRTUAL LIGHT

Symbolically disengages all objects and agents from actuality and from the oblivion of darkness.
>Gives relevant color and intensity to all objects and agents according to their affective qualities.

### VIRTUAL SOUND

Symbolizes all the natural, mechanical, and imaginary audibility of life and its environment.
>Gives affective quality to the language of human engagement.

### VIRTUAL TIME

Symbolizes, through foreshortening, the duration and durability of human engagement.
>Creates rhythmically the dramatic analogue of what man undergoes in the confrontation, interaction, and consequence of each encounter with life.

Because the dance is theatre art in a most expressive manner, its physical entities create the kind of "dynamic image" which we find in all dramatic performance. What we see in the dramatic theatre are the "virtual realities, the moving forces . . . , the apparent centers of power . . . their conflicts and resolutions . . . ," or in other language, we feel the aesthetic qualities and their meanings inherent in the palpable action, space, light, and sound. Nor does this mean that drama and all other performing arts contain the same virtual realities. We find that not only the physical materials of the various arts differ one from another, but that their objectives also differ. The "moving forces" in the dynamic image of the dance as described by Miss Langer are not exactly the same as the involving, imminent, and committed images in dramatic art.

Theatrical action is all that movement of our natural and artificial experience fused in the image of a transformation. We find in the theatre the miracle of reality created by the impersonation of life; we find there the miracle of the supernatural created by the simulation of the impossible.

Theatrical space is the symbolic image of configuration, deployment, and vista fused in a virtual physical environment. We find in its configuration the shapes of objects, the silhouettes of personality, the structure of decoration. In its deployment, we find the arrangement and organization of the paths of motion, the ways to go, and therefore, by analogy, the virtual directions of our goals. In its vista, we find the limits of our view, the shape of our environment, the scope of our world, and by analogy, the virtual distance of our ideals.

Theatrical light holds in its power the revelation of that of which we are to be visually aware. Whether the space is realistic or imaginary, whether for *Merry Wives* or for *The Tempest,* it is light that disengages it from darkness and gives it the color and intensity appropriate to its effective force and meaning. Because light has the power to render the most distant horizon salient to our vision, it does by analogy disengage all that is unknown in our hearts from the void of oblivion.

Theatrical sound is the audible means to the creation of all the verbal, musical, and environmental imagery that can be heard by an auditor. Artistic sound is the symbolic image of heard relations and proportions. It is the connotative value of all our languages. As theatrical music, it is the essence of emotion; as theatrical language, it is the archetype of verbal abstraction. As the virtual sound of environment, it is the affective symbol of waterfall, train whistle, foghorn, or coyote's howl. As the sound of language it is the rhythm and melody of our song and speech.

Theatrical time is the duration of the symbolic image of life presented on the stage. In the theatre, time is *usually* foreshortened in order to create a virtual image of each human encounter necessary to the whole dramatic story in an endurable sequence. Virtual time creates rhythmically the dramatic analogue of what man undergoes in the confrontation, interaction, and consequence of each engagement with life.

In an objective and literal analysis of drama as it is performed, one is able to observe the qualities and effects resulting from the artistic devices and techniques used by the dramatist as well as those actualized by the director, the designer, and the actor. In recent experiments with theatrical means, it has been discovered that anti-realism and anti-theatre movements since Artaud have projected the use of actual space, light, and sound on the stage and actual human motion in a variety of contexts such as "happenings." What has proved less exciting in some instances is the continuous confusion of actual means with virtual means as in those cases when the stage is just a stage but the performers are entirely imaginary.

Theatre for theatre's sake, or theatrical positivism, posits other premises than those set forth here. Dramatic form is dependent upon the creation of the analogues of human engagement—on the dramatization of life. What the dramatist has to offer to the theatre artist is a structure of dialogue and stage directions which imply the virtual qualities of human encounters as he sees them. He is only concerned with actual means when he can transform them with his words, as in *Our Town*, into the world of his play. The dramatist must know when the means are actual, or borrowed, or become virtual by his use of them. He must have an understanding of dramatic art in its complete forms as they are experienced by audiences; he must attempt to distinguish whole congeries of aesthetic quality which he finds symbolized by all the means in the theatre; and he must discover the relationship of the visual and auditory symbols to the rhythmic sequence of the audience's emotional experience.

"Imitation" as a property of dramatic art has received many long and serious discussions which cannot be repeated here;[10] but from an aesthetic point of view, Aristotle's "imitation of an action" would seem best to be described in the present context as the symbolic representation of human engagement. As intimated earlier, an artistic representation will, in every authentic case, be a symbolic structure of feeling, representing in an artist's experience something which has touched his mind and heart. In the world at large, it is archetypal, purposive behavior in human engagements which apparently interests the dramatic artist. It is the rhythm of the confrontation, the interaction, and the consequence of that engagement which he hopes to capture; and it is with the dramatic analogue of this rhythm that he is able to move a body of spectators to feelings of imminence, involvement, revelation, commitment, and fulfillment. There does not seem to be any law which any longer wields the authority to prescribe the boundaries of "imitation." The one hundred years between Hebbel's *Maria Magdalena* and O'Neill's *Long Day's Journey Into Night*, indicates the period in which drama had been thought of chiefly as a representation of everyday living. Yet, neither "imitation of an action" nor "imitation of life" would seem to necessitate such a naturalistic interpretation as these plays would indicate. Even the limitations of "human action" and "human life" could conceivably incorporate all that is possible in human experience, both external and internal. For example, the expressionistic play is often rich with the dramatic rhythm of lifelike engagement. The modern dramatist is widening the scope of the representation to include all that is imaginable in experience whether it be inner or outer—psychological or social—experience. Whether or not the theatre is a mirror of life is no longer a question simply because, as an effective art, it will continue to be the symbol of *whatever* experience, real or imaginary, may be represented in a theatre.

In dramatic art traditionally, all the means of theatre may be employed in a given production. Whether actual, virtual, or borrowed, they may create for the audience the semblance of human life either of the external and concrete world or of the inner world of the imagination. In dramatic art, both worlds are "real" worlds, and the function of the theatre is to make both worlds "virtual" in the experience of an audience whether it be Prospero's island or Jean Genet's balcony. In the modern theatre the question is not whether a play should be produced realistically or stylistically; it is whether the dramatic engagement seems to call for actual, or virtual, or borrowed means to create its relevant environment. Whatever the means used, they may become virtual in the creative process of making images which are symbolic of the inner form of the drama. Stage scenery can be made to represent anything from the heath in *King Lear* to a river dock in *A Man for All Seasons*. Sometimes light with a minimum of other visual clues can abstract such a place from out of the dark void of the theatre. Often it is the language of a play which makes "virtual" the reality of such a place by means of melodic and figurative words—the most famous being:

> But look, the Morn, in russet mantle clad
> Walks o'er the dew of yon high eastern hill.[11]

These words have transformed many a bare stage for as many audiences into a springtime view of the parapet of the castle at Elsinore. The reality of any stage space is, therefore, experiential fusion and acceptance of all those means of the theatre which may be used to delineate it. There is nothing about action, space, light, or sound which would necessitate or even call for the "representation" of an external "reality" on the stage. The artistic process is not to imitate life in a photographic way but to transform the actual theatre space into a "virtual" environment for an exciting dramatic engagement.

Unlike theatre for theatre's sake, dramatic art as a whole is not at one time "representational" and at another "presentational" because it *always* symbolizes something quite beyond itself. Like other arts, it always means more than it says. It need not be considered an illusion of life because it may be a symbol of anything on earth or in the mind of man which evokes emotion. It is evident, however, that certain plays are more didactic and more discursive than others. It would appear that some which pretend to be lifelike—such as *The London Merchant, The Drunkard, Uncle Tom's Cabin* and *A Doll's House*—may be intended to teach a moral lesson while at the same time "holding a mirror up to nature." There are others which have been called "expressionistic" such as *Woyzeck, Erdgeist, Massemench,* and *The Cradle Will Rock,* which apparently hope to teach their lesson by means of allegorical figures and overtly didactic speeches.

One of the most popular examples recently of this type of theatre was *The Motel* in *America Hurrah* called by its authors "a masque for three dolls." Its performers were encased in huge doll-like costumes which were grotesque reminders of their sex and their attitudes. One figure only did all the speaking while the other two acted out a travesty of a couple moving into a motel room. Obviously, there was very little visual correspondence with what one would find in the actual world. The figures were allegorical symbols, their action was surrogate and noncohesive, and the pattern of the performance was a rhetorical structure of communication rather than a dramatic structure of human engagement. Such have been the distinguishing characteristics of the masque since the Renaissance, and these properties are now appearing in increasing number in theatrical presentations.

Many performances since mid-century have gone much further in the abandonment of dramatic structure. In some cases they have failed to show the engagement in any way; they simply substitute theatrical devices which may or may not be related to the vague dialogue being spoken. For example, in the play entitled *Balls* by Paul Foster, the action is the movement of ping-pong balls swinging, floating, moving in space, sometimes fast, sometimes slow, sometimes touching but always with the voices of human agents in the background. The use of theatrical means in this production are vivid and startling, but it is discursive and imagistic in its effect. It lacks the kinship, the warmth, and empathy which can be created by live actors in their embodiment of human encounters. Listening to the dialogue is to note the noncohesive nature of the visual and audible elements which create a purely theatrical experience in contrast to one that is also a dramatic one.

This also occurs in more serious and in more complex productions before audiences. When the symbolic representation does not contain a human engagement in terms of confrontation, interaction, and consequence, then purely conceptual symbols or abstractions are likely to dominate the image of what is performed. It is then that a serious masque rather than a drama may result. Masques and pageants have colored much of theatrical life in the world for centuries. There have been didactic and historical masques like the *Paternoster* and *Everyman* in the middle ages and *The Miracle* and *The Eternal Road* of this century. There have been masques of cruelty like the Dance of Death in thirteenth century Europe and like the *Marat/Sade* and *The Investigation* by Peter Weiss in the theatre of the 1960's. There are moral implications in these masques, as in all allegories, which are widely applicable to man, but their main effect is that of remonstrance rather than of dramatic experience because they tend to substitute statements for confrontations, arguments for interactions, pronouncements for consequences, and allegorical agents for human ones. One senses no involvement or commitment in the play *Marat/Sade* because no attempt was made by the dramatist to draw the audience into a recognizable human action. One is alienated not to the point of intellectual objectivity (as suggested by Brecht) but to the point of confusion and disgust at the futility of man in his deficiency. Many masques from the middle ages to the present day have been titillating in the theatre, but they have shared in the power of dramatic art only occasionally and in a fractional degree.

Dramatic art, to be effective and relevant, therefore, must be a symbolic representation of human engagement, but it is neither an allegorical disquisition nor is it necessarily an imitation of life as it is lived; it may simply be an act which we can accept or believe in as human. Brander Matthews once described the spectator's point of view in the following way:

> The Playgoer . . . is willing enough to accept any frank departure from the actual; he is not insistent on the mere facts of life. If he can get the deeper truth, he has no objections to

make believe if he is invited to do so; he is willing enough to accept the supernatural, for example, and to follow with unflagging interest the actions and the words of ghosts, of witches, and of fairies. . . . All he demands is that these nonexistent creatures shall be represented as obeying the law of their own being.[12]

The supernatural agents who have appeared in all forms of drama from Darius' ghost in *The Persians* to the expanding corpse in Ionesco's *Amédée* also attest to this fact. One must acknowledge that many of these beings have had essentially human characteristics, but the abundance of extranatural creatures from other planets, the robots, computer systems, and the walking-talking abstractions in contemporary films and plays would indicate that it is man's engagement with all experience, natural and unnatural, which we find represented in drama and not merely a "mirror of nature" *per se*. We might conclude, then, that instead of being an imitation of life, dramatic art is the symbol of human engagement extended in action to the limits of our imagination before our very eyes.

The "receptive audience" is one that earnestly desires to know what the dramatist means. If, as has been suggested, the receptive audience is a requisite in the creation of dramatic form, it is simply in the sense that they have the psychological and intellectual background to understand and appreciate this form of art. Such an audience is not entirely an unlikely phenomenon since there is so much that is "dramatic" in all of human life. We speak of the dramatic and tragic character of automobile accidents, of sinking ocean liners, and of plane crashes. We speak of the "drama" in the presentations of our rituals, christenings, initiations, weddings, and other ceremonies. We find an even greater abundance of dramatic incidents in the events reported in daily news releases. At times it would seem that there are more moments of tension and excitement in the contemporary scene of national and world affairs than could possibly accrue from an organized stage performance. On the one hand, this may limit the need or desire for dramatic experience in a theatre, thus reducing the development of new works; or on the other hand, it may work two ways in the theatre itself: one, to increase the exaggeration and sensationalism found in plays old and new, or for more knowledgeable spectators, to increase the dramatic values instead of the more spectacular ones in each performance.

A receptive audience will be most pleased with that for which it has developed a taste. Almost anything in life can be portrayed on the stage, but an audience usually prefers a fresh and different image provided the theatre presents relevant material. Life can be very exciting, but we attend to drama especially when it is greater than life—greater not only in loudness and brightness—but greater in meaning as well. The fullest dramatic experience, therefore, is available to an audience when the text has been made from a story or experience within the knowledge and the taste of the audience, when the production has been an effective recreation of that text, and when the audience has been sufficiently prepared for the kind of performance which is presented. Their preparation will depend upon their habituation to dramatic experience. Those who work so assiduously toward "theatre for theatre's sake" eventually realize that, in a free society, audiences are not forced to attend theatres; they discover what they like by going again and again by choice. They will return most often to that theatre where the images have been created for their sake.

# III.

# Dramatic Experience and Its Values

"This organization of energies to move cumulatively to a terminal whole in which the values of all means and media are incorporated is the essence of fine art."

—John Dewey, 1934

Speaking metaphorically, one might say that one's faith in God, or in Truth, or in Justice could die in the abyss of a cruel and relentless world. Our ideals are compromised by the exigencies of biologic drives, but they have been persistently maintained as values in order to adjudicate the conflicts that arise between one human being and another. In spite of the difficulty of man living with his animal nature, the ideas of Justice, Truth, Beauty, and Faith persist in their essential nature, or *eidos,* and may never disappear from the mind of man. Their significance, the essence of their "forms," is being recreated eternally in the thought, the work, and the desire of many living people.[1] In all probability, their essential forms will remain in our collective subconscious as long as man exists. Beyond man, they may or may not have any existence, but so long as there is man, his fundamental ideas will be the measure of his life. His ideas of God, of Goodness, or Justice, of Truth, and of Beauty will stand over and above all that he does or says so long as he acts or speaks upon the earth. By analogy, it may be said that the essence of Comedy and of Tragedy will also endure in spite of what some may say to the contrary.[2] This does not mean that either Greek Tragedy or Greek Comedy will appear again just as they were once created within their own eternal or surface textures. Surface textures, like fashions, belong to their own time. Artists do us no service in attempting to recreate the surface textures of the past because we will see again and again that fundamental and significant forms are usually clothed anew in each artistic epoch in new and different shapes. Such change is imminent in every art and every culture, but it is not the essential form—the *eidos*—that changes.

For example, the ways of dealing with Justice may change from time to time, depending upon man's social and political organization or system. The numbers of judges and jurymen, the procedures of trials and of penalties, even certain ideas about justice have varied from age to age and from country to country, but what does not change is the essence of Justice. It is not inappropriate to speak of Justice here since all great tragedies and many other kinds of drama have touched upon man's engagement with the just and the unjust. Our understanding of the idea of Justice is both a requirement and a result of our experience with such plays as those of Sophocles, Aristophanes, Shakespeare, Molière, Ibsen, and Shaw. By comparison with its example in these great dramas, we may not find even a semblance of Justice in our courts on any given day; nor, would we find a comparable semblance of Tragedy in our theatres. But that is not to say that either one is dead. The physical conditions, the properties and devices, for both Tragedy and for Justice may vary from time to time, but certain attributes of each seem to remain essential in our world.

In the case of Tragedy, the problem is to discover these attributes as they appear in the actual confrontation, interaction, and consequence of a dramatic structure. It is, then, conceivable that these attributes may also be discovered in other symbolic archetypes which have equally distinct rhythmic structures but which are always dramatic in their essences. To find these distinct essences is to distinguish between structure and form.

The rhythmic structure of Tragedy will appear to have different qualities from that of Comedy; the rhythm of Melomantic Drama will be different from that of Ironic Drama. Our experience of their aesthetic qualities in the dramatic action should be reliable clues to our apprehension of each essential form. What should claim our attention, therefore, is how the structure of action gives us the experience of these qualities.

## Symbolic Rhythms and Dramatic Qualities

The reason for difference in our pleasure, then, seems to be associated with the kinds of drama that can be distinguished one from another. In the first chapter, the distinctions in kind were made according to different qualitative arrangements and the different names applied to them. What has been suggested by the writings of various critics, however, is that particular rhythmic patterns of feeling may apply to the distinctive forms in which we experience dramatic art. If drama is not a copy of life but is a symbol of life, if dramatic action is not simply human movement but an analogue of human beings engaged with living, then it may be said to symbolize the *confrontations,* the *interactions,* and the *consequences* in the vital and dynamic situations of that engagement.

In Tragedy, the symbol of the confrontation appears in the entanglement of man's will with his moral choice; the interaction of man's will with his destiny results in a reversal of his fortune; the consequence leads to his moral vindication in spite of death.

In Comedy, the confrontation is established with the desire of certain lovable characters like Olivia and Viola for love and life. The interaction develops when other characters, by their deviations, seem to frustrate those with the desire for happiness. The consequence is made clear when those who frustrate are overcome by those who have a desire for love, which is then celebrated in any of several ways. In Melomantic Drama, the confrontation arises from those like Uncle Tom and Little Eva or James Bond who have been subjugated or frustrated by the forces of evil; this leads to a crisis of terror or expected failure in the interaction and it is resolved by a heroic response in which the hero, or heroine, is brought to safety or inviolability. In Ironic Drama, the confrontation grows out of the disjunction which appears between two disparate ideals such as those of Hedda and George Tesman. The ironic interaction consists of the rebellion which either or both contestants foment against each other or against society in spite of any law or rule of conduct; and the consequence may be the destruction of one or both of them as in *The Visit* by Dürrenmatt, but always with the ambiguous possibility that both may be right. It is thus that we may proceed from easy confrontations, optimistic interactions, and happy consequences to those more rigorous, more pessimistic, and despairing. Depending upon the rhythmic symbol with which we are confronted, we experience the qualities of drama in a different light and in a different form. (*See* Chart VII.)

When a play means something to us, whether it be serious or funny, sardonic or silly, sentimental or cruel, exciting or dull, we can ordinarily find within it the devices of art and the virtual qualities which elicit these responses. It has long been noticed that incidents happening early in either a narrative or dramatic structure have a tendency to excite us with expectation or suspense provided they contain anticipatory signals, foreshadowings, unanswered questions or merely a general sense of imminence. Actually, these devices do not occur only in the beginnings of plays. The audience is probably even more expectant at the play *Hamlet* when Gertrude drinks the wine in the last scene than they ever are when she sits upon her throne with Claudius in Act II. As soon as we know something about the characters and the situations, we begin to be more interested in their destiny. We do not become deeply concerned about them, however, until more has transpired; until additional forces work upon our sensibilities. In dramatic experience, the nature of our expectations seems to be a correlation of our feeling of imminence with the immediacy of the consequence. Again, in *Hamlet*, one does not need special instruction to sense the imminent danger expressed by Marcellus in the earliest moments of the action when he says: "Peace, break thee off; look, where it comes again!" It should be noted that it is a *virtual* imminence because it is what the spectator feels and not what the actor feels that renders this quality being *present* in a factual sense. His whole position, gesture, tonal quality, and expression will tell us to be afraid even though he is not. If this example is too obvious, one may attend a performance of a somewhat more subtle and sophisticated play, *The Sea Gull*, and notice one's feelings of anticipation when Treplef is asked why his mother is in such low spirits. He answers: "She is bored. She's jealous." We, the audience, before ten minutes of the play have passed, are curious about the mother of this boy and how she may influence his destiny. We need not be mortally afraid in an audience in order to feel a sense of imminence.

After a number of different plays, it becomes apparent that those which interest us in the theatre, whether they are realistic, naturalistic, cubistic, expressionistic, or futuristic, all seem to evoke in us a sense of expectation or imminence. This quality carries us along with the action and never needs to be explained; nor does it seem to call for description or analysis. We anticipate the lovers and their embraces, the clowns with their pratt falls, the gunslingers and their wounds, the swordsmen and their points, Harpagon and his lost chest, Oedipus and his own expulsion from Thebes, and the freedom-loving Algernon Moncrieff caught in a domestic web by his supposed friend, Mr. Earnest Worthing. We say the serious endings are "inevitable" and the comic endings are *"faits accomplis"* when it is simply the case that we have been held in suspense for them. Even in that masque of cruelty, referred to as *Marat/Sade*, although it may lack every other dramatic quality, the author has insisted that we wait for the death of Monsieur Marat. All kinds of theatrical performances, thus far, have persistently evoked a sense of expectation. In dramatic art, we feel strongly the imminent possibilities of human confrontation.

During all representations of life, love, and war in the theatre, we are not really more excited by their suspense than we are by the entanglement of our affinities, our biases, our prejudices, our loves and hates. As soon as any interesting play has progressed more than half an hour—even so vaguely elusive a play as *Waiting for Godot*—we are interested, whether we are aware of it or not, in the fortunes of all those characters for whom we feel some *kinship*. We not only anticipate the appearance of Godot, we also may want Vladimir and Estragon to somehow achieve a measure of happiness after their long-enduring wait. And surely we would rather that Romeo win Juliet than that Paris did; they have shown their love in a rich and touching way; we cannot help but love them. We would rather that Orlando, who loves Rosalind, win the wrestling match than Charles; rather that Orestes, who has revenged his father, be acquitted than indicted; rather that Claudius, the usurper, should die before Hamlet does; rather see John Proctor in *The Crucible* die than forswear his name and his honest convictions. We feel our kinship to those persons and those ideas of which we approve; we want those to win a conflict who fight for beauty, love, truth, and justice; in a word, we are "involved" in such dramatic action. We sympathize with the characters and settings and ideas which we would like most to have in our own experience; we laugh at those who deviate from our ideals of thought and action; or if they seem to be a danger to us, we try to scorn them into oblivion and sometimes even hate them unto death. It does not matter whether the play was written in the fifth century B.C. or yesterday; the spectator responds to the emotional stimulation of "virtual involvement" in dramatic art whenever there is either a positive or negative "cathexis" aroused, whenever the audience feels it must take sides in the struggle between the desirable and the undesirable. It is for this reason that some of the more painful or irritating plays, such as *The Connection* or *The Toilet*, are more popular than those that elicit merely vague or unidentifiable responses as in the case of *The Enchanted* by Giraudoux, *Jim Dandy* by Saroyan, *Balloon* by Padraic Colum, or *Hotel Universe* by Philip Barry. Only a few critics have gone so far as to say that these plays by well-accepted playwrights are poor ones, but some have pointed out that they did not involve their audiences in any aesthetic relationship.[3]

Some audiences probably would prefer to be thoroughly disgusted if they cannot be delighted, and most would prefer to show pleasure at the shockingly new plays in any age than to be bored by innocuous nonentities written by traditional craftsmen. It is not uncommon for fashionable audiences to go along with the "nouveau" elite whether it is the *Sturm und Drang* with Goethe, the *romantiques* with Hugo, the *esthetes* with Oscar Wilde, or the prestigious *avant-garde* of the present. As a result, critics and audiences find themselves applauding and sometimes even demanding plays for which they have neither mind, nor heart, nor stomach. But there are two things at least that a large audience will have difficulty in resisting: one is the anticipation of all those things for which they feel a sense of *imminence* within a play, and the other is their *involvement* in the lives, the problems, the conflicts, the sufferings, and the loves of those characters for which they feel an inescapable kinship.

Fortunately for art, there are more than the easy virtues of involvement and imminence which keep a play alive and vital, which make it memorable and long remembered, which make us glad to have attended it, and desirous of having it played again and again. There may be some truth in the claim that we go to a sentimental play to enjoy the experience of suffering with a hero, or watching him suffer and crying our eyes out simply for the satisfaction of crying. Perhaps we do these things out of sympathy; perhaps we do them sometimes because the performers have created in us an empathic response which we cannot resist. It seems that we also do these things at a great many performances because we want to learn something. We want to learn how, through the suffering of the chief figure, it has been possible for him to attain his moral victory; or how, in the case of tragedy, his destiny shows a reconciliation of opposing ethical demands.[4] We learn that such a victory would not be possible except for the inevitable discovery of finding himself faced with an insoluble problem. In other words, we discover the truth about Justice, and Freedom, and Love, and Beauty, and Peace, for which heroic characters struggle with all their might, but for which most of us fight only when it is expedient to do so. In the comic drama, we also learn the truth about such matters as fame and fortune, generosity and selfishness, economy and waste, marriage and sex, larceny and "big business." We learn these things after our interest has been excited and after we have become involved in the fortunes and destinies of the characters who please us. The way in which we make these discoveries as members of an audience is through our observation of those within the play who make their own discoveries of the people in their family, their neighborhood, their community and their society; who discover their own capacities, their own failings, their own selves. One of the greatest pleasures in watching the sombre play of *Ghosts* by Ibsen is to observe Oswald and Mrs. Alving discovering the motives and natures of Pastor Manders, Regina, and Engstrand, and how these discoveries do, in fact, reveal the essence of the long-buried beliefs, acts, and words which make up the "ghosts" of the past. Our sense of *revelation* concerning the environment and society of this small group of characters can hardly be denied. In the course of a more recent play, *The Chairs,* it is difficult to make any discoveries of character at all, but we do learn that the Orator is a deaf mute and that the Old Man and Old Woman will never be "memorialized" because they decide to commit suicide.

One need only recall the famous line, "Something is rotten in the state of Denmark," to realize that *Hamlet,* as a play, is not only the tragedy of an embittered young man; it is also the story of the discovery by the Prince of Denmark of the corruption into which his father's court has fallen. We learn as he learns, scene by scene, that he can begin to correct its faults only by the boldest means possible, including the sacrifice of his own life. Some of the memorable discoveries in modern dramatic art include: the discovery by Lyubov in *The Cherry Orchard* that her estate has been sold at an auction; in *The Madwoman of Chaillot,* the Countess Aurelia's discovery of the greediness of modern entrepreneurs; in *Death of a Salesman,* Biff's discovery of the hose on the gas jet in the basement signaling his father's possible suicide attempt; the discovery by Jean in *Rhinoceros* that the world of men, including all his companions, is turning into a herd of rhinoceroses.

In both classical and modern drama, some of the most striking and moving discoveries have been those which reveal to the audience the destiny of the principal character in the drama. In the *Oedipus* by Sophocles, we are told in the very beginning by Tiresias what is in store for Oedipus, but we are no more ready to accept such statements about the King of Thebes than he is himself. The play is one continuous revelation, therefore, of the truth of what Tiresias, the old blind priest, has predicted to the elders of Thebes. Each scrap of information from a messenger, or shepherd, or from Jocasta tell us more—just as it tells Oedipus more—about the facts of his early life and of his origins. Simultaneously with these discoveries comes the step-by-step realization for the audience that Oepidus is no ordinary man, that he is not willing to accept half truths, that he is not willing to stop his search after finding one unpleasant thing, that he means what he said in the beginning about seeking out the guilty man in Thebes even if it be himself. We come to know the meaning of moral courage. We discover, in other words, how great a man can be under the most difficult and harrowing circumstances in all the world. This we find good to know, but it is no *easy* lesson. It is hard to swallow and we need some practice to enjoy a tragic discovery.

It should not be difficult to see how it is that revelation is one of the chief aesthetic pleasures in those works which have the pattern of a search as in a detective story, or murder mystery, or a sheriff's hunt for a killer, or in any similar structure of human events.

Quite obviously, however, finding out who killed King Laius is neither the end nor the point to Sophocles' play. There comes the moment in the dramatic action when Oedipus knows that he is a guilty man—guilty of murder and incest—and that he is responsible. By the power of his office, he could say that nothing he has done in the past can be held against him, that the people should forgive and forget, and that if they do not, he will destroy all those who oppose him. Such is the power invested in the hands of a king. But Sophocles was a serious dramatist who saw that the important thing and serious thing which Oedipus did was to commit himself to finding the truth and then to set about meting out justice in the way he promised. Oedipus was committed to his promise. He intended to keep his commitments to justice in the same reliable way in which he kept his commitment to seek the truth. From an artistic point of view, Sophocles saw that such commitment was necessary to the acceptance of the end of the play.

For those characters with whom we become involved, there is a willingness among us to accept their commitments whether they be somewhat foolishly mistaken as was Richard in *Ah, Wilderness!* or whether they are such a victim of retribution as Ill in *The Visit*. Commitment, therefore, is the binding quality that links the spectator to the ideals, beliefs, needs, and desires of the agents in strong and powerful plays. We may not prefer the commitments of tragic and ironic agents at first, but we can grow to appreciate them. Commitment is usually associated with the most sympathetic situations in Melomantic Drama because we like what the hero likes, but there is a sense in which a spectator must be committed to the prudent way of life and the *joie de vivre* of comedy before he can be caught up in the comic spirit of that form. In the case of Ironic Drama, one is, at the very least, committed to the stoic acceptance of disjunctions, or paradox, or ambiguity when the chief agents are thus disoriented or at war with their society and with themselves. Such commitments as Madame Zachanassian's to kill her former lover may be bitter to the taste at first, but in spite of the resulting ambivalence we learn to accept them as necessary. In any case, whatever commitment is established in the play motivates the end of the drama. We may sympathize with both Claire and Ill, but the latter's death is inevitable.

The end of a play, in terms of structure, has been called its *denouement*. This term, during its century or more of use, has meant not only the "falling action" and "final catastrophe" at the end but just as often the quality of certain music which achieves a crescendo at its crisis and then diminishes to a silence at the end. Neither music nor drama, however, can be bound to rigid or repetitious structural patterns. The most climactic moment may come very close upon the final curtain as it does in the "Drama of ripe condition" whether by Ibsen, or Dürrenmatt. Such plays as *Hedda Gabler* and *The Physicists* leave us with no soft romantic feeling of *"denouement"* in the sense of a quiet resolution after the turbulence of the preceding action. A more extensional term for the feeling quality evoked by the end of a play is "fulfillment." Even at such an elusive play as *Waiting for Godot,* we are left with the sense that waiting is all that one may expect of "existential" life and that this is the conclusion one must reach. In this case, there is no resolution to a conflict; there is no denouement; but the demands of the action of waiting—of waiting through a long mystical incantation—have finally been fulfilled. The demands made by the action in both Tragedy and Irony will be rigorous and sometimes harsh, but the transcendent close of the one and the bitter end of the other may be equally fulfilling.

In the case of Oedipus, we accept his self-blinding and his self-exile because we know that his commitments must be met. We are also left with the realization of man's great capacity for suffering, his capacity for truth and justice, and of the consequent solutions to human problems, the consequent reconciliation of differences which such capacities can realize in the world; and we are thereby satisfied. Our satisfaction in tragedy is the realization that the promise of the beginning has been kept in the end, that commitments have been met, that prophecies have been fulfilled. It is true that we often are made aware that a struggle has ended, that in comedy the characters who deviate from the norm are no longer destroying the well-being of others; that, in melodrama, the fighting has stopped, that good fortune for the lovable good people is about to be achieved. If conflict were the essence of drama, such forms would be the only possible ones. It should be noted, however, that in the more powerful tragic plays, it is not only the conflict which has been resolved; it is both the issue and the destiny at hand which have been fulfilled. In the ironic play, the conflict may stop, but the dilemma remains and, if nothing else, our skepticism is enlarged. Fulfillment, then, is the aesthetic experience which one finds at the end of dramatic art. It may be similar to that found at the end of all temporal and fictional arts as well, but it is definitely the fulfillment of destiny in terms of the consequence of human purpose which defines drama as a kind of aesthetic experience.

We are ready, then, to bring the idea of drama into focus. In simple terms: *Drama is the virtual image of human engagement enacted for an audience in a theatrical medium.*

All forms of drama are symbols of articulated feeling transformed into analogues of action from man's experience of purposive behavior. These analogues may be interpreted out of Myth, out of History, out of the concrete moment, or out of the dramatist's imagination. Each play is shaped in the rhythmic sequence of confrontation, interaction, and consequence from the materials of language, vision, and sound for performance in front of an audience. Each form of drama, in their separate analogues, will give us a different quality of pleasure in the specific areas of our feelings denoted by *imminence, involvement, revelation, commitment,* and *fulfillment.*

What this means in terms of society and culture should be taken up in other studies; but in terms of a theory of form, the older criteria of unity, probability, and universality, like traditional structural analyses, must here give precedence to considerations of drama as experience.

### Unity: A Relevant and Coherent Analogue

From the very beginnings of dramatic theory, it has been felt that the most effective means of marshaling the interests and the responses of the audience is that of a unifying principle. Aristotle had suggested that a single structure of dramatic incidents—possessing the relationship of cause to effect and having a beginning, a middle, and an end—would result in a unified play. Later Renaissance writers suggested that unity could be given to plays simply by mechanically limiting the time, the place, the action, the number of agents, and the number of incidents in the structure of the whole. To realize the difficulty of achieving this type of structure, one needs merely to sit down to try to write such a play and to keep it interesting to an audience. There have been numerous plays which obeyed the rule of the three unities but which were scattered in their effects as in Dryden's *The Conquest of Granada* and Maxim Gorki's *The Lower Depths.*

There is, then, the other kind of situation in which certain historical and panoramic dramas give vast scope to time and place and action but which manage to retain a high degree of singularity in their purpose and in their images as whole works of art. This might be said of the tragedy, *King Lear,* of the ironic drama, *A Dream Play* by August Strindberg, and of the melodrama, *Uncle Tom's Cabin.* The rhythm of dramatic quality through these three plays is so insistent in our experience of their forms that we ask for no other unifying principle. In all three, the audience is caught up in a long pursuit after fortune and justice, even though in different ways and for different reasons. The structural details of such multi-scene plays may be called unified on the basis not only of relevant incidents, of coherent dialogue, of consistent characters, and of answers to the questions which have been posed in the course of the action but even more insistently, on the basis of a single rhythmic and symbolic flow of articulated feeling which is the *"form"* of the play. On the other hand, when a causal necessity between antecedents and consequences is required of these plays, it will be noticed that necessity may be interpreted merely as a requisite condition of action which is relevant to the audience, so that what is necessary in one culture may not be so in another. Scarcely any of the action in a Renaissance play motivated by a socal code of honor and duty, as in Calderon's *The Physician of His Own Honour,* would be felt to be necessary by audiences of the twentieth century. What, if anything, may still be effective is the play's dramatic feeling—the fusion of its dramatic qualities surrounding the love affair, the discovery of infidelity, the struggle for secrecy, and the rejection of love. However unified this plot seems to be, it will be unacceptable to a modern audience to the extent that they see no reason in its motivation. The social code which motivates the action is no longer binding in the world at large. Under such circumstances, social necessity as a requisite for dramatic unity cannot be maintained.

We will discover, therefore, that, while many structural details of a play may be well organized, the necessity of the action may not be universally accepted, and the emotional experience of the play may or may not be unified. What we look for, then, is the rhythm of its feeling in terms of the human engagement represented. What is unified in our experience is the rhythm of the dramatic analogue: the confrontation, the interaction, and the consequence. We feel the power of this rhythm to the extent that the sequence of events presented is infused with the qualities of imminence, involvement, revelation, commitment, and fulfillment. We feel these qualities to inhere in the rhythmic pattern, and the dramatist has created this potentiality by his organization of the relevant evocative devices in the structure. As indicated earlier, it is the conceptual image around which the dramatist evolves his whole play that makes it one complete entity *for him.*

When the conceptual image can be said to have unity for its creator, it may possibly have unity for those theatre artists who attempt to re-create it with at least a potential unity for an audience. As can be readily seen, there are an infinite number of accidents which can disturb the unity of a play before it is witnessed by a spectator. The author may have included irrelevant scenes in the beginning; the actor-director may have included irrelevant business or sound; the designer-costumer may have included irrelevant objects or clothes; a fashionable performer may cause a spectator to envision a luxury liner when Hamlet sets sail for England. Unity is, therefore, one of the most tenuous characteristics in dramatic art, whereas organization for a unified effect may very well be the chief aim of the artists concerned in its creation.

It would be unfortunate if any interpretation of unity were to deprive us of such extensive and various panoramas of drama as found in *King Lear, Hamlet, Faust,* and *Peer Gynt.* All of these plays seem to be richly organized, or planned, in terms of structure, characters, and evocative devices; but their unity is evident over and beyond the extensive spread of their many dramatic qualities. At a reliable performance, we may experience, firsthand, their rhythmic coherence and the consistency of their import and of their feeling. This is when we know them to be unified.

### Believability and Common Humanity

Likewise, the audiences's acceptance of the probability of ghosts, Martians, and robots in dramatic action will depend as much upon the experience of the auditors as upon the logic of the play. Fortunately for Aeschylus, and Shakespeare, we still believe in ghosts as figments of the imagination, and fortunately for us we still believe in the actions of the supernatural characters which some of the older dramatists created. It is not generally considered probable that Cassandra and Tiresias could have the powers of divination and prophecy which they exhibit in the Greek tragedies, but for most of the audiences which have attended *Agamemnon* and *Oedipus Tyrannus* since they were written it has been believable that such gifted persons, having the vision and knowledge which they possessed, would have spoken as they did to their kings. Something of the same rational view of life has been shared by the ancient world of Greece, the world of Elizabethan England, and the modern Western world. To the extent that this is so, the plays from each of these cultures will depend equally upon generally acceptable criteria of probability and truth for their acceptance. To the extent that the modern audience understands the culture of the past, they will find the actions and motivations in the older plays believable, or, at least, acceptable. For example, once the premises of time, place, and magic established in the early scenes of *The Tempest* have been accepted, then all that follows is a probable consequence of the beginning.

This has long been a problem in criticism. In 1671, René Rapin, in his discussion of Aristotle, wrote:

> 'Tis only by adhering to Nature that the probability can be maintained, which is the sole infallible guide that may be followed in the theatre. Without probability all is lame and faulty; with it all goes well.[5]

More recently, in his brilliant exposition of the quality of *The Cherry Orchard*, J. L. Styan has written:

> Every detail is relevant . . . to the creation of that particular balance of sympathies which can re-create for an audience the

fluid feel of life. It is not a gallows humour, he offers, nor a
mere exuberance, but it embraces each of us in its restless appeal
to truth.[6]

This is not to say that one should accept a single spectator's opinion concerning the plausibility of a play, but it does show that
plays have long been criticized for their truth and believability,
and that no form of drama is likely to be exempt from such
criteria.

Our concern, then, may not always be with the logical probability of motivation and the causal sequence of the action of a
play as it might be analyzed; it may be more especially the
credibility with which an audience can accept it on their side of
the footlights. We may be able to project ourselves back to the
primitive days of Ajax and find good reason to accept the suicidal
humiliation of this warrior hero after slaying the sheep, but in
our own time, we would find such a suicide just insane. The
punishment which Menelaus dictates in having him left unburied
is entirely contrary to any modern practice, but once the code of
ethics and customs of the ancient world are accepted as the
premise of the play, then these actions can be considered probable
in a logical sense and at least acceptable to receptive spectators.

One of the ways in which the playwright has attempted to
achieve probability in his plays has been to create widely-recog-
nized, "such-or-such" characters to carry on the action. Typical
characters have generally been easy for a large majority in the
audience to accept. Typical characters are appealing because of
their immediate recognition by the audience, but it is no longer
to be expected that every dramatic agent be a stereotype. Many
great dramas of the world have been noted for the psychological
depth of their characters, and realistic drama for more than a
hundred years has been much more concerned with true portrayals of human individuals than with immediate recognition. In
all artistic characterization whether by writer or actor, one will
find basic human motivations, traits, propensities, idiosyncrasies,
and failings, to be important clues to the believability of the
agents. They are also the clearest marks of their common humanity. Whether the play is as remote as Aeschylus' *Persians* or as
near as the local cinema, the audience tends to believe in and

become involved in what they share with the agents in the drama.

One will find the idiosyncrasies and failings of some characters exaggerated in the avant-garde styles of expressionism, epic realism, and absurdist theatre. Once the exaggerations and distillations of human personality are found to spring not from stereotypes so much as from single traits of character, the agents of these plays are more understandable. The character of Madame Zachanassian seems to epitomize man's tendency to recriminate; Baal seems to represent man's concupiscence; those of Beckett and Joan Dark—the human desire for martyrdom; the old couple in *The Chairs*—human gullibility; the man and wife in *Amédée*—the human predilection for escaping involvement. So long as the spectator recognizes the human propensity which is dominant, the dramatist and the actor are often satisfied with this characterization by typical traits because it presents an easy way to reach a large general audience. In all richer textures of dramatic engagement, of course, the characters are more complex, more fully human, and therefore, more appealing. As an example, the power of Ionesco's *Rhinoceros* is sustained in great measure by the sincerity and believability of the character of Bérenger. One then needs to accept only the typical traits represented among the other characters in order to believe in their transformation into rhinoceroses. Much the same would need to be accepted at a performance of the very quixotic and amusing ironic play called *Eh?* by Henry Livings. One needs to willingly disregard the customs of ordinary society long enough to accept the premise that human character and human problems can be symbolized by these strange agents in this irrational context. Very little that is done or said in this play ever occurred in the real world. What we come to believe from such a play is that modern life often appears to be incoherent and also whimsically ironic. Once we accept the premises of the action in the opening scene, the remainder of the play is no more difficult to believe than the melomantic fantasy in Maeterlinck's *The Blue Bird*. Both plays require this ready acceptance although they are poles apart in our dramatic sensibility; the latter being a dramatic symbol of the search for happiness in Melomantic Form; the former being the symbol of man's futile engagement with technology in Ironic Form. In spite of the fantastic unrealities in dramatic art—the ghosts in Tragedy, the coincidences in Comedy, the fairylands and mystery in Melomantic Drama, and the artificial dilemmas and ambiguities of Ironic Drama—there is still a sense in which believability is an artistic property of effective dramatic action.

Both believability and the acceptance of a common humanity present problems of society and culture which will have to be taken up elsewhere; but here, their interpretation is briefly that which is required in the realization of specific forms. Wherever believability, or the acceptance of the premises, has been achieved for a performance of a play, to that extent has the understanding of the play's essence reached its audience. To verify this axiom, one needs merely to witness reliable performances of a number of foreign plays and to observe the audience at the time. At performances of *The Sea Gull* from Russia, *The Little Clay Cart* from India, of *The Circle of Chalk* from China, of *The Trojan Women* from Greece, of *The Miser* from France, of *Mother Courage* from Germany, of *The Cradle Song* from Spain, of *Ghosts* from Norway, and of *The Country Wife* from England, American audiences have been rapt in contemplation of the action and moved at appropriate times by the drama within. They feel a sense of imminence, of involvement, of revelation, commitment, and fulfillment. There can be little doubt but what these productions have been of wide general interest and, to that extent, amenable to a broad general acceptance among their many audiences. This is what is meant by their common humanity.

This common humanity is demonstrated each time a reliable performance of an old or foreign play is effective and appreciated in a new cultural context. When such is the case, it means that the symbolic structures of these human encounters have not expressed merely the individual action of the specific agents portrayed but have meant to the spectators a human engagement touching upon all their lives; and these plays become, therefore, of wide import. Shakespeare has been effective in many countries in the twentieth century, and so, also, have Euripides and Molière. Not every play can be expected to please every single person, everywhere, but those drawing the largest and most generalized audiences have been thought to be most significant to art and culture because the theatre, is, and always has been, the seeing place of the people. It is in this sense that "universality" can be said to be a significant attribute of dramatic art.

What one discovers, therefore, from a study of various kinds of plays, is that their coherence, their symbolism, their believability, and their common humanity may add important values to their total effect. But since these properties are evident in aesthetic experience chiefly in connection with different kinds of dramatic rhythm, it will be necessary to associate these properties with each fundamental form, including: Tragedy, Comedy, Melomantic Drama, and Ironic Drama.

# IV.

# Traditional Forms

"As Comedy presents the vital rhythm of self-preservation, Tragedy exhibits that of self-consumation."
—Susanne K. Langer, 1953

## Tragedy and Its Effective Qualities

As discussed earlier, Tragedy is a form of drama which has been prominent in the development of Western culture; it was rather carefully defined at an early date in Aristotle's *Poetics*. Something of what we learn from that definition is that Tragedy has to do with the greatness of man, particularly the greatness of his moral choices in the face of irreparable wrongs. We fear for man's end because we know it will be catastrophic, and it could be so in our own experience. We pity man because we know that his catastrophe is not deserved according to any rational sense of justice. What is often lost sight of in Tragedy is the fact that however inscrutable is man's destiny, however predetermined it seems to be by fateful powers, this form of drama has, from the very beginning, shown man expressing his will and making the choices which lead to his own destruction. It is the hero who chooses, whether we are speaking of Oedipus, Antigone, Hamlet, Phèdre, Egmont, Mrs. Alving, or John Proctor (*See* Chart VII). Each of their choices, beginning with Antigone's, would seem to be avoidable by simple acts of prudence; but there is not only a supernatural force which seems to be driving these characters to their ends; there is also an unmistakable inner belief which will not permit any one of them to do otherwise and still remain true to his own convictions. What these fatal choices mean to the art of drama is that they make possible a conception of tragedy which demands the fullest possible evocation of the spectator's sense of imminence, involvement, revelation, commitment, and fulfillment (*See* Chart X).

To hear Antigone's answer to Creon's decree, to hear Hamlet's answer to his father's ghost, to hear Phèdre's admission of love for Hippolytus, to hear from Egmont that he will not escape from Brussels, to hear from Mrs. Alving the extent to which she intends to remove the thought of Captain Alving from the mind of her son, to hear John Proctor say he must find the faction against Parris and join it, is to feel the possible danger to these heroes whose choices thwart the laws and customs of the land. To know that they speak out of inner necessity and out of real conviction for what they believe, and to know that what they say will have significant consequences, is to feel the imminence of serious drama. As soon as we realize that the personal convictions of these characters could indeed have fatal consequences for them or, at the very least, could offer a life full of suffering as for Mrs. Alving or full of guilt as for Orestes, then we feel the imminence of tragedy. The consequences may be foretold early in the play as in *Oedipus* when Creon brings the statements of Apollo's Oracle at Delphi and Tiresias tells Oedipus that he himself is the guilty person. Or the consequences may be withheld until the end as in *King Lear* where Cordelia is disinherited in the first scene and it requires the whole play to show the full extent of suffering and death which result therefrom. And though the whole of Western culture has long been aware of the fate of Antigone, Oedipus, Lear, and Hamlet, it is the rhythmic continuity of the action, the confrontation, interaction, and consequence of these human engagements which foster not only the

# CHART X
## THE ANALOGUE OF TRAGEDY

The Symbolic Rhythm of Tragic Engagements

| Confrontation | Interaction | Consequence |
|---|---|---|
| Man Confronts Society by Will and by Choice. | His Choice Collides with Destiny and He Discovers Himself. | His Will Is Reconciled with Moral Law in an Ultimate Suffering. |

The Aesthetic Responses to Its Dramatic Qualities

| The Sense of Imminence | The Sense of Involvement | The Sense of Revelation | The Sense of Commitment | The Sense of Fulfillment |
|---|---|---|---|---|
| From the Anticipation of Catastrophe in the Life of a Proud and Determined Man or Woman. | From Our Kinship with Conflict and Suffering. | From the Discovery of the Strength and Greatness of Mankind. | From Our Faith in Truth, Justice, Honesty, and Love. | From the Manifestation of Man's Destiny. |

imminence but the common humanity of their tragedies. It is the experience of the play and not simply a casual reading, not the hearsay of criticism, which evokes dramatic feelings.

In romantic tragedy, it is particularly difficult for a reader in our present disturbing and disruptive world to concentrate on the opening explanatory passages which describe in detail the situation and intention of the hero. For example, it requires three of the five acts of the tragedy *Egmont* to discover with any certainty the deep affection that the title character has for his beautiful Clare. The affairs of state, the problems of a Protestant country governed by a Catholic country, the intrigues of the Princes and their Regent Margaret ruled from a great distance by King Philip of Spain, all are part of the story, but all together they make it difficult to become involved in the dramatic action of Goethe's play. In the performance of the play, when some effort is made to expedite the time when the Duke of Alba is expected to oppose the gentle rule of those in Brussels, one can sense the opposition which Egmont faces as well as the love of Clare who holds him there. To become interested in Egmont's problems is to be involved in his drama, and this is possible in a performance; but Goethe was mistaken that such involvement could be evoked by the commonplace discussions of soldiers and workers in the first scene of the play. One is aware that, in other great tragedies, the spectator's feeling of involvement is evoked from the very beginning of the action.

For us to be fully and richly involved in the problems of Oedipus, we should be made to see from the beginning the kinship and affection which he feels for the people of Thebes. We should also feel involved when he is faced by those who appear traitorous in his eyes, *i.e.*, when Creon and Tiresias seem to be opposing his rule by their insinuations of his guilt. It is in his love for Thebes and in his fight against those who would stop the search for truth that we in the audience become involved in the fortunes of Oedipus. However well we know his end, our real concernment is with the way in which he pursues his faith in knowledge. A little prudent silence on his part would have kept him happily married and king of Thebes for many years; but, in addition to the Oracle of Apollo, we have the belief ourselves that this man, having such a steadfast faith in truth and in justice, could do nothing other than he did.

We are likewise drawn into an involvement with the problems of John Proctor in *The Crucible*. He does not fight for justice under kingly rule but discovers its necessity in his own community and in his own home. In the latter he knows his guilt much better than Oedipus did; in the former he sees it only at the end. In his interaction with the trials he makes some effort to deserve no further the title of lecher, to live in peace and honesty with his wife in whose goodness he believes above all else. That he should be faced with the vengefulness of Abigail and at the same time be forced to struggle against the whole court at the Salem witch trials, moves an audience—a large and sympathetic audience—to become involved in the fate of John and Elizabeth Proctor. Their motives and basic drives become important aspects of their relationship. Tragic involvement, then, may be our entry into the guilt as well as into the passion and destiny of the hero.

The order of revelation in *The Crucible* is an artistic accomplishment in itself as it proceeds from its disclosure of the confrontations of the early scenes: the girls in their deception, the church in its dogmatism, Abigail as the seductress spurned, the victims in their denial, and the reasonable community in its incredulousness. We know these things by vivid example before the end of the first act, and we come to see them boldly elaborated in the interaction of the second. We then see the discovery by John Proctor of the danger of the trials to the well-being of his wife whom he protects with all his will. His next discovery is that Elizabeth, in a position of danger, is willing to lie to save his life. This is exceeded in intensity only by the final major discovery in which he believes in his own truth and that of the other victims to so great an extent that he is willing to go to the gallows rather than sign his name to a false confession. The essential meaning of this tragedy seems to lie in Proctor's discoveries and we in the audience are satisfied with our feeling of revelation, just as Elizabeth is, when we realize that John "has found his goodness now."

A major discovery, then, is not only the culmination of the

interaction between the chief figures of a tragedy; it is the revelation of that to which the hero is committed. There has been much said about the indecisiveness of Hamlet, but in a reliable performance of this play, all acts following his discovery of the guilt of Claudius are characterized by the commitment of Hamlet to make right what is wrong in the state of Denmark. He draws his sword on the King at prayer but realizes that his purpose could not be satisfied there. He shows in the Queen's chamber, by killing Polonius, that he will pursue his task expeditiously to the very end. Before he leaves his mother, he promises, "But I will delve one yard below their mines/And blow them at the moon:" indicating that he means not to be stopped by his traveling companions. His letters to Horatio and the King confirm that his commitment is more certain than all else.

In yet an older play, the strong-willed Antigone cannot be doubted in what she intends to do about burying her brother. The choice she makes is clear between obeying the decree of Creon and abiding by her spiritual faith that she must show reverence for the body of Polyneices. It is just as clear that Oedipus must seek out the murderer of King Laius and must find his true parentage. There is no wavering in their commitments from their opening speeches to their last. The tragic reversal is in their fortunes but not in their minds or wills. What is added in the course of the action in a Renaissance play is the change which seems to come over the hero in his confrontation with new circumstances and external powers. Macbeth is committed to his ambition *after* he meets the witches; Othello is committed to find the truth about his wife *after* Iago fills his mind with doubt; King Lear is no longer confident of his judgment *after* he visits Goneril and Reagan; Brutus is not truly dedicated to the overthrow of Caesar until he has been persuaded by Cassius.

By way of contrast, one does not sense any change in commitment for the anti-hero or monster such as Richard III, or for Barabas in *The Jew of Malta*, or for Rhoda in *The Bad Seed*. The commitment to destroy seems to be present in these characters from the very beginning. Macbeth, on the other hand, must be goaded by all the powers of hell to commit his infamous usurpations. The consequence is death in each case, but the more tragic figure has the greatest sense of guilt for the tragic mistake in judgment. There does not seem to be any such commitment for the pathetic victim of a Baroque tragedy such as the Duchess of Malfi, or for Lessing's Emilia Galotti, or for Lady Torrance in Williams' *Orpheus Descending.* The Baroque play exploits the violence, the terror, the pitiable victims, and the destruction of life and property but seldom explores the commitment of an agent with the will to make a moral choice.

In the neoclassic imitations of the Greek classic structures of Tragedy, we find more instances of single-mindedness throughout. Phèdre feels no further commitment than her duty to Theseus and her love for Hippolytus; Anthony is doomed to failure in Egypt from the moment he loves Cleopatra, which is prior to the action of *All for Love* by Dryden. Egmont has no other thought than the peace and freedom of his own people even to the neglect of saving his own life, but he is less a classic hero in not striving with all his will to preserve that freedom. In two modern tragedies of Catholic martydom, *Murder in the Cathedral* and *A Man for All Seasons,* we find a classic single-mingedness in Thomas à Becket and Thomas More who set their wills against those of their kings.

In the tragedy of the common man, *Death of a Salesman,* Willy Loman is depicted over a period of seventeen years as coming finally to a decision to take his own life as the only way in which he can justify himself to his family and to the world. When the action is considered to be in the present, Willy Loman is thinking back over the years at the same time that he is planning single-mindedly to commit suicide—which he does. In this sense, his commitment is clear, and it is merely pathetic that he has no other faith than the false dream of being "well liked." He is, then, not committed to the welfare of the state as are Oedipus and Hamlet; he is not committed to the ideas of religious faith as are Antigone and Sir Thomas More; he is not committed to the ideals of monogamy as are Othello and Phèdre; Willy Loman, as one might expect in a twentieth-century economic culture, has only his profession of salesman and he makes the fatal mistake of choosing false ideals for himself and his family, that is, choosing all the "wrong dreams." This tragic mistake is meliorated only by the strength and sincerity of his will, and the question will always remain as to whether his sincerity is great enough for him to be admired by a broad general audience.

Our sense of commitment in the theatre is engendered through all the acts and scenes of a play. We know what these great tragic figures stand for before they make their fatal error in judgment. In the course of the rhythmic structure of Tragedy, whether of ancient plays or of modern ones, the hero reveals his commitment in his interaction with the forces of destiny which present a choice for him to make. By his character, we will know what his choice will be, whether he is committed to romantic ideals of love, honor, and duty or more pragmatic ones of honesty, truthfulness, and lawfulness. In any case, the probability of the consequences will be established only if the commitment is clear when the choice is made. John Proctor does not see his place in society until he envisions his name signed to a false confession. Having an inherent honesty and discovering his own integrity both lead him to his final choice.

It is, therefore, only in the final moments of a Tragedy that we feel satisfied: Oedipus walking away without eyes, Hamlet and Lear expiring in the arms of those dearest to them, Egmont and John Proctor going to meet their executioners, Othello and Phèdre in their final self-reproaches before dying on stage. These are the acts which complete the image of consequence for the tragic hero. It is with these actions that we feel the sense of fulfillment which has been the final evocation of tragedy for centuries. It is not simply an end for which we seek, not simply a kind of total destruction of all contentious parties as in the melodrama, *The Tower of Nesle*, by Alexander Dumas *père*. Indeed, nothing can proceed after such a holocaust, but in tragedy it is the destiny of those who have been engaged in crucial interaction for which we wait with awe. Not usually do they die together as with Antigone and Haemon, Romeo and Juliet, Dona Sol and Hernani, and Rosmer and Rebecca, but more often separately as with Oedipus and Jocasta or Phèdre and Hippolytus, or Macbeth and Lady Macbeth, or Oswald and Mrs. Alving. Such tragic figures may come to their death or final suffering at different times and in different ways; yet realizing the finality of their interrelated lives gives added force to the sense of fulfillment at the end of the play. This ultimate feeling of completion, including the resolution of whatever tensions may have been present, has always been a satisfying experience in the theatre. It occurs at the end of all theatrical performances, but it is nowhere more poignant than in the tragic form. In Tragedy it is the sense of fulfillment which is evoked when we know the destiny of those about whom we have become concerned, and know their final response to the human engagement in which they were involved, *i.e.*, know the choices they made and the consequences of those choices. As Oedipus comes forward (after gouging out his eyes) to say farewell to the Council of Thebes and to speak to his daughters, we know that he has fulfilled his promise of banishing the guilty man and that his destiny of exile and suffering are certain.

To realize the complete fulfillment of the play, *Ghosts*, we must depend somewhat upon the performance. The actress playing Mrs. Alving can achieve a greater sense of finality and destiny for the audience by being more positive about giving the morphine to her son as he had requested. It is true that she is forced either to nurse him through his last moments of life after the destruction of his brain or to relieve him of his gruesome existence. To show her determination to do the latter before the curtain fell was one of the brilliant insights of Alla Nazimova, who made the character of Mrs. Alving fully emancipated and free to act outside the bounds of false Victorian restraints. This gave a greater sense of fulfillment at the actual performance of the play than could ever be felt in the mere reading of its last scene.[1]

## Comedy and Its Universal Image

Comedy is also a dramatic experience, but it is of a different kind. As Susanne Langer has so succinctly put it, "Tragedy is the image of fate, as Comedy is of Fortune. . . . As Comedy presents the vital rhythm of self-preservation, Tragedy exhibits that of self-consummation."[2] Comedy, then, being also a vital symbol of human engagement, is also bound by a single dramatic analogue (*See* Chart VIII). Its unity is inherent in its mutually exclusive form, which we recognize in man's desire for life and love as he confronts unreason, stupidity, and folly. The common sense of self-preservation is shown as interaction with the mistakes of deviation to the point of frustration. The consequence shows that *joie de vivre* can be achieved and that love can be consummated in the face of nearly any obstacle. Neither the believability nor the universality of its action can be questioned because of the truth in its premises and because of the common humanity which we all share with its typically human characters. Comedy loses its power chiefly when its sentiment becomes pathos, or its satire becomes bitterness, or its typical characters become mere caricatures.

Examples from famous comedies demonstrate the rhythmic engagement of normal human agents with the mistakes of deviation (*See* Chart VII). There are laughable confrontations of sound common sense with idiosyncrasies (which seem harmless in the end), and the persistent frustration of happiness by duty, or love by selfishness, or of youth by age. The resistance made by Harpagon in Molière's *L'Avare* to his children's desire for love and marriage is rigid, unreasonable, and ridiculous. Only by their zealous conniving and intrigue throughout the play can they gain from their father the permission to marry and have some of the money which he so greedily hoards. If Harpagon's will had been vicious, unrelenting, or cruel, this interaction might have been a matter of life and death and the moral conflicts of these agents more appropriate to Melodrama; but Comedy has to do with the prudent side of man's will, rather than with his animal aggressions.

As Samuel Coleridge wrote, "Tragedy has to do with serious consequences of maintaining or violating moral laws. Comedy has to do with prudence and imprudence, enlightening or misled self love."[3] For comic characters, then, their power of reason as well as their will power are both in conflict with the emotional satisfaction of their basic drives and appetites. In *The Birds* by Aristophanes, the desire of Eulepides and Pisthetaerus to achieve the perfect state of peace and contentment enjoyed by the birds is thwarted very often by their own insistence on worldly comforts and pleasures. Rather than the tragic rhythm of will, choice, and destiny contained in the tragic engagement of man, we find in Comedy the rhythm of desire, frustration, and satisfaction which accompanies each mundane step in the direction of the Good Life. The girls whom Algernon Moncrief and Jack Worthing cannot have as bachelors and rivals, they find to be delightful possibilities when they become brothers who are prepared to be married. In *Love for Love* by William Congreve, Valentine must suffer the dissembling of Angelica as well as his own feigned madness before he can find his happiness. Valentine's confrontation is seen in his first scene with Angelica who tantalizes him until very nearly the last minute of the play.

The response to interaction in Comedy is not commitment to a moral principle and to death as in Tragedy; it is essentially a commitment of the joy of living and the consummation of its greatest pleasures. Its unity is, therefore, the organization of events leading to that end. If historically, the consummation in a wedding feast was omitted after the old Greek comedy had disappeared, at least the wedding has been implied in thousands of instances since that time. Even in Terence's *Hecyra,* Pamphilus is not truly united to his wife in a loving marriage until both families know, at the end of the play, the truth about the ring worn by Bacchis, the courtesan. In Jonson's *Epicoene: or the Silent Woman,* there can be no happiness for Sir Dauphine until his uncle Morose has signed over his fortune and has been cheated of his "bride," which action ends in no wedding but in the satisfaction of all the normative agents concerned. In Jonson's comedy the use of good sense and prudence has banished not all the evil forces but at least the folly of old Uncle Morose. The prudence in Comedy also mitigates the stupid suspicions of Pamphilus' relatives and the miserly obstinance of Harpagon both of which are obstacles to sexual union and procreation.

By way of contrast, the satisfaction in melodramas comes from our feeling that all must be well in the world when honest, upright people have conquered or thwarted the agents of destruction. The satisfaction from comedy comes from the triumph of reason or rationality, not over evil in the Christian moral sense but over stupidity and folly in a universal sense. What is unified in Comedy, therefore, is the human engagement leading to the end of prudent self-preservation and, therefore, the preservation of life and the species.

But Comedy is not a falsification of life any more than is Tragedy. Comedy is the dramatic analogue of those human engagements which are ludicrous in their totality for being violations of good sense in the pursuit of happiness. Tragedy has its heroes who are faced with insoluble problems. Comedy has no heroes but merely has prudent agents of sound reason who are thwarted in the achievement of the good life by social deviates who may or may not discover at the end of the play how unreasonable they have been or what enemies to happiness they are. Scapin in Molière's *Les Fourberies de Scapin* seems to realize that his cudgeling and cheating of Geronte have been wrong, and he demands to be forgiven, but M. Jordan in *Le Bourgeois Gentilhomme* seems to have no idea what a fool he is nor even that he still has the same wife at the end of the play. Yet we are satisfied in both instances that the marriages of the young people will be performed in good order and the couples will be happy. Sometimes such things may happen in life, but these comedies are the representations only of things that might be and not necessarily of what has been.

One would suppose, therefore, that the demands of believability and universality would be less in the case of comedy. Upon investigation, however, one finds that the memorable figures from the works of the great comic dramatists Aristophanes, Plautus, Molière, Shakespeare, Congreve, Sheridan, and Shaw are all engaged in those actions in which such-or-such kinds of persons would *probably* engage. Even the greatest social deviates including Lysistrata, Pyrgopolynices—the original braggart warrior, Harpagon, Tartuffe, Falstaff, Dogberry, and Malvolio all seem to have some human counterparts which cause us to say these are universal creations in drama, *i.e.*, that such *kinds* of people in life might actually do such things under those circumstances. We should have to say, therefore, that comic situations may be as lifelike as those which are tragic because the interactions of ordinary characters are caused by everyday circumstances. The human engagements in serious plays are often motivated by historic or epic figures in historic or epic events. That they are, does not make their dramatization any more believable; it does provide a reference point from which their action can be judged by

# CHART XI
## THE ANALOGUE OF COMEDY

### The Symbolic Rhythm of Comic Engagements

| Confrontation | Interaction | Consequence |
|---|---|---|
| Man Desires Life and Love. | He is Frustrated by the Mistakes of Deviation. | He Celebrates Life and Love in Symbols of Procreation. |

### The Aesthetic Responses to Its Dramatic Qualities

| The Sense of Imminence | The Sense of Involvement | The Sense of Revelation | The Sense of Commitment | The Sense of Fulfillment |
|---|---|---|---|---|
| From the Anticipation of Life Juxtaposed to Mechanism. | From Our Kinship with the Battles of Sex and Politics. | From Our Surprise at the Mistakes of Intrigue and Irrationality. | From our Belief in Prudence as We Meet with Ridicule. | From the Resolution of Differences and the Celebration of Life and Love. |

those who know the life stories in history or epic. In Shaw's *Caesar and Cleopatra,* the general outline of history is only loosely maintained, and the characters and scenes were imagined or created for their comic quality and for their satire of historical traditions. The interactions of youth and age, of man and woman, of modern man with ancient history are all dramatized in the comic rhythm with comic characters and comic incongruities. One need not believe that Shaw's agents are the figures of history in order to appreciate his comedy. Having some preconception of their history simply adds to our funded enjoyment of the whole.

We may even measure our understanding of romance by our appreciation of the comic interactions of Rosalind and Orlando, Beatrice and Benedick, or Viola and Orsino, and we have every bit as much reason to remember these lovers as we do to remember Romeo and Juliet. The rich texture of the interaction of the former couples with the niceties of courtly love and Renaissance intrigue make of them delicate and sweet agents of exciting comic action.

We also look for their kind in such comedies as those of Kaufman and Hart, who made some attempt to avoid the worst pitfalls of romantic comedy in *You Can't Take It with You, Once in a Lifetime,* and *The Man Who Came to Dinner.* These plays also have had the accolade of "true to life" presented in their memory, but whether they can be said to represent the actions of universally understood characters depends upon whether the agents are recognizable to our changing audience as typical of their time and place. As suggested in connection with Tragedy, we should accept the principle that when characters and their actions, either historical or imaginary, do share a common humanity with real human beings from our mutual experience, we have a right to expect a recognition of them from receptive audiences in a wide variety of circumstances. Beyond this, universality cannot go.

## The Dramatic Qualities of Comedy

What might present the best test for the wide appeal of a comedy would be its potential power to stir the feelings of imminence, involvement, revelation, commitment, and fulfillment in an audience (*See* Chart VII). Comedy, no less than Tragedy, is provocative of the dramatic experience, and again, these feelings are uppermost in that experience. The imminence we feel in a comedy usually appears very early in the action, just as it does in Tragedy. But in this case it is from the confrontation of normal eager young people with those whose bent is antisocial or antiquarian or at least imprudent or impractical, that causes us to anticipate the misfortunes which are sure to come. Almost at the very moment that Lysistrata tells Myrrhine and the others that they must give up all sexual activity, we anticipate all kinds of possible trouble for these young women. Then there comes the time for them to tell the men what their demands are to be. Our expectations are borne out in the frustrated objections and arguments of the men. The supreme test is made when Myrrhine tantalizes her husband, Kinesias, excites him sexually in every possible way and then runs back to the safety of the Acropolis. Even at this point, the sense of imminence is high, since the maddened men could cause much more trouble than they do; but what a satisfaction it is when we see the men willing to settle their differences and sign a peace treaty in order to have their wives and girls again. It would be hard to conceive of any greater sense of comic fulfillment than that offered by the play, *Lysistrata*.

It has been suggested that we do not feel the same kinship for the characters of Comedy that we do for those of Tragedy. There is, however, a sense of involvement in the engagements represented in Comedy whenever we feel akin to those normal characters who suffer the pain of other's folly. We also feel strong sympathy for what our own sex may suffer in the play. Men tend to sympathize more often with Kinesias, with Menaechmus Epidamnum, with Benedick, with Orlando, with Valentine, with young Jack Absolute, and with John Tanner. The ladies may sympathize with Myrrhine, with Erotium, with Beatrice, with Rosalind, with Viola, with Angelica, with Lydia Languish, and with Anne Whitfield in *Man and Superman*. The battle of the sexes has always been evident in Comedy, and our involvement in the audience has centered around winning the battle or arranging a truce. This does not mean that women in the audience have any less appreciation of Falstaff, of Sir Andrew Aguecheek; of Subtle, the al-

chemist; of Tony Lumpkin, or of Felix Unger in *The Odd Couple*.
All great comic creations—the agents in pursuit of folly as well as
those in retreat from folly—are marvels of wit, energy, innuendo,
and raillery. We do not attach ourselves to them out of kinship,
but we are concerned; we are involved in the good fortune which
they may hinder in the lives of the beautiful young people with
whom we sympathize.

In *Ah, Wilderness!* we are amazed and amused by the propensities of the parents and relatives, but we are concerned chiefly
because they hinder the happiness of Richard and Muriel with
whom most in the audience come to have some involvement.
O'Neill's play is definitely a romantic comedy with all of the attendant sentimentality and tears; but the mockery of tradition,
the mistaken identities, the mishaps and the misinformation all
augment the struggle for freedom and happiness in the desires of
the young lovers. In Molière's *L'Avare,* we sympathize strongly
with Eliza and Valere simply because they act with prudence in
the pursuit of their own happiness and because they are thwarted
not by other sentimental attachments but by the avarice and
austerity of Eliza's father, Harpagon. Thus, in generic Comedy,
we are involved not from sentiment or pathos but from our faith
in the kinship of the active agents and faith in their achievement
of the Good Life, such as in a happy marriage. In both sentimental and satiric types of comedy, however, our involvement is with
those for whom we have developed an attachment and usually
from their show of affection and their struggle to maintain it. In
Shaw's *Caesar and Cleopatra* it is for an older man and a young
girl that we are most concerned; in *You Can't Take It with You*
it is not only with the love of Alice and Tony that we become
involved, though that is crucial to the ending; we are also attached
to the whole Sycamore family and even to Grandpa Vanderhof
who is the greatest nonconformist of them all. We are amused
by the latter's absurdities, but we cheer him on in his fight against
the income-tax collector because of the sincerity of his motives
and his love for his family. In *The School for Scandal,* we are
hardly able to concern ourselves with young Maria and Charles
Surface because of the intrigue, fury, and gossip set in the way
of the precarious marriage of Sir Peter and Lady Teazle with

whom we are so fully involved. It is not, therefore, just the adolescent lovers with whom we become involved in Comedy; it is our concern for the effort of all men and women to attain the prudent enjoyment of a happy sex life.[4]

Comedy is an art of surprises. It is not so much a matter of keeping secrets from the audiences as it is allowing the characters to keep secrets from each other. Lysistrata holds back the full description of her intentions from the women until all are ready to help her win peace for the city; she also withholds the full story from the men until they demand to know it. Her plan, when revealed, is a surprise to her listeners in each case and a comic revelation to the audience. It is for this reason that the discoveries of comedy are very often double in their effect. The audience learns of the twin Menaechmi before the characters do, but we are doubly pleased at the surprise it causes, since it seems like a foolish mistake to take one human being for another as if they could be so identical that a wife or a mistress would not know the difference.[5] This may explain why mistaken identity, practical errors of all kinds, and thoughtless mistakes have been the means of surprise in Comedy for such a long time. When the mistakes have been rectified, we find the natural causes for discovery to be surprisingly laughable. The discoveries of Comedy are not based upon errors in moral judgment as in Tragedy but upon the mistakes of imprudence and the ordinary failure of common sense. Our sense of revelation, therefore, comes from our discovery of such mistakes. We, in the audience, are happy to discover that all the characters are about to mistake the twin from Syracuse for the one who lives in Epidamnum. From this discovery we are not only pleased to anticipate the pleasure that the twin from Syracuse will have with Erotium; we also expect the twin from Epidamnum to be greatly disturbed by the whole thing. It cannot be too serious because they are long-lost brothers, but each time that one is taken for the other, the disconcerting surprise among the characters (when reliably represented by the actors) creates a delightful discovery for the audience.

Our sense of revelation in Comedy must also include our realization of the meaning of what has been enacted, of the feeling that has been articulated in this single structure, of what the whole thing is about. Ophelia, upon seeing the dumb show says, "Belike, this show imports the argument of the play." King Claudius after seeing a portion of the play asks, "Have you heard the argument: Is there no offence in't?" What the audience seems to want to know is what the play means, and they are usually willing to wait until it is over before they pretend to understand it fully. When they do realize what has been symbolized by the play, they feel with a sense of revelation just what it means. What it means, in discursive terms, may be the import of its feeling or in Renaissance terms, the "moral" of the play, but in either case it is what it symbolizes to the intellect or what is revealed to it. This revelation is what makes us feel that we know what it is about. We know the lesson of Aristophanes' *The Birds,* because it is quite plain from the creation of Cloud-cuckoo-town that a Utopia is extremely impractical when it deprives so many people of the good things of the world which they have learned to enjoy. The birds do gain control, but Pisthetaerus is as much a despot as any ruler anywhere. To discover this is to realize the joy of living in the present world and to enjoy the comedy.

The lessons of Congreve's *Love for Love* are many, but perhaps the chief one is that the older generation simply cannot control the younger one if it makes greedy and foolish mistakes and then attempts to purchase the loyalty of the youngsters with legacies. Sheridan's *The School for Scandal* is also concerned with young male heirs and how to test their worthiness, but essentially what is revealed by the total action of this comedy is the duplicity and dishonesty which underlie aggressive social ambition and its attendant gossip. In a sense, then, we may say that a comedy means what it teaches, and that we prize those plays which teach the age-old lessons of man. However biting and skeptical the play *Tartuffe* is to us in the audience, we cannot say we are not pleased to discover that the old impostor is to be taken off to jail. Whether his defeat is thereby related to the melodramatic defeat of the villian in melodrama may be a matter of debate, but there can be no doubt of the comic revelations concerning hypocrisy which attend the viewing of this play.

Concerning the sense of commitment, it has been pointed out that the sympathetic characters of Comedy are committed to seeking a happy life. We, therefore, in a receptive audience at a comedy become committed to the joy of living. But only after the interaction of normal characters with deviate characters is it proven that the struggle has been worth undergoing. The continual altercation between father and son in *The Wasps* by Aristophanes is so long-winded that one has difficulty in waiting to read it all or to hear it all. In most productions of *The Way of the World,* it may seem forever before Mirabell and Millamant are given permission to marry. In such instances there is little chance for the audience to feel that sense of commitment which a reliable performance of true Comedy is capable of eliciting. In a vital performance of *The Alchemist,* it is still possible to this day to marvel at the devious ways in which Subtle and Dol Common are able to dupe their "customers" into accepting their claims for making gold by alchemy. One is not so much committed to their aim of deception as to their ability to avoid being caught for such a long time. The prospects for the success of the ruse, the effort and energy spent upon it, all entice the audience to hope for a satisfactory end even when they know it is a punishable crime. A similar situation exists in *Arsenic and Old Lace* by Joseph Kesselring (who once thought he had written a melodrama). The audience is so amused and delighted with the kindhearted trio of Abby, Martha, and Elaine, that they are committed to participate in the task, not of killing lodgers, but of helping the aunts to avoid detection at all costs. Usually, killers are villains whom we hope to see dead or jailed in the course of the play, but these ladies are so witty, so affectionate, so full of the joy of life, that we cannot but laugh at their wonderful success with their elderberry wine.

Once we become involved with the characters in Comedy, it is then possible to take up the causes for which they stand and become committed to their aims—whatever they may be. Going to extremes, however, we may become too sentimentally attached to a tearful comedy such as *A Kiss for Cinderella* by J. M. Barrie or *Goodbye, My Fancy* by Fay Kanin. As more sentimental devices are added, there is less and less comedy present. The play, *Peter Pan,* may have been conceived as a sentimental comedy, but its emphasis on the mystical overthrow of Captain Hook and the return to sweet safety in the home with its lasting promise of continued retreats to "never-never land" make of it obviously a melomantic play in its essential form.

Our individual commitment at a comedy is, then, to the good fortune of those characters in whose efforts and aims we delight because we find them to be fostering a world of happiness in which we want to believe. Thus, the total and formal commitment to Comedy will probably continue to be directed to the enjoyment of the Good Life: the pleasurable, comfortable, satisfying life for which the more fortunate are able to strive in each period of human culture. Our comedies change in their stylistic and superficial traits from century to century, but the ideals of honesty, responsibility, loyalty, and fidelity which are portrayed in their deviation are the same in Garson Kanin's *Born Yesterday* as they are in Aristophanes' *Lysistrata*. Much the same can be said about the views of these two authors on War, Politics, and Love. What one discovers, therefore, is that the fullest satisfaction and sense of fulfillment comes from Comedy when it reiterates our ideals and our convictions about the practical and social world. Whatever minor differences appear in various periods, many of the same ideas are repeated. The pretentiousness and idiosyncrasies of poets and playwrights are ridiculed not only by Aristophanes in *The Frogs* (404 B.C.), but by Molière in *Les Précieuses ridicules* (1666), and by Samson Raphaelson in *Jason* (1942).

What this seems to indicate is not only the universality of comic ideas and comic human engagements but also the wealth of our deepest satisfactions in the theatre. We find fulfillment in the belief that our precious heritage will be preserved in the same clear light of criticism that it always has received. As it has been said, "There is nothing so solemn or serious that it cannot be improved with laughter." It is reassuring to find that man's foibles, his predilection to mistakes in practical judgment are ridiculed in many climes and in many ages of man. Some of the same mistakes are portrayed in tragicomedy and in melodrama, but the most incisive ridicule is found in pure comedy. The audience can feel the very greatest sense of fulfillment which is attainable in the theatre when it realizes that the world's worst hypochondriac, M. Argan in *Le Malade Imaginaire* has been tricked at last with fond words and false promises to give his consent to the marriage of his daughter and to enjoy the elaborate but fake ceremony of making him a doctor. There is satisfaction in seeing the hypochondriac bested and ridiculed; there is satisfaction in seeing the pretensions of the learned doctors ridiculed by Argan, and our sense of fulfillment is complete when we find this quality to be as prominent in Comedy as it is in Tragedy.

Moreover, it is apparent from the study of these two different kinds of play that the essential properties of drama are maintained throughout. The receptive audience apparently senses the unity of a comedy in terms of its rhythmic continuity; the audience senses its imitation of nature as a symbolic representation which is its reality rather than its illusion; the audience accepts its probability in terms of what it believes about human types; and the audience accepts its universality in terms of their kinship with the common humanity of its dramatic engagement. To the extent that a spectator finds himself a member of such a receptive audience, he will be influenced by these properties of the total structure just as he is by the specifically dramatic qualities of the form. The spectator knows it as Tragedy or Comedy by the distinct differences in his responses to its dramatic rhythm. At a comedy, he will sense the imminence of action when his common humanity is confronted with deviation; he will sense the rhythm of surprise in the interaction of common sense and irrationality; he will feel the satisfaction that comes when the devotees of pomposity are defeated by those more prudent. At a tragedy, he will sense his involvement with a serious character because of his mutual kinship with conflict and suffering; he will sense the rhythm of discovery when he sees a man's choice collide with destiny; he will sense the fulfillment of human action when he sees the hero's desire reconciled with moral law.

But Comedy and Tragedy are not the only forms of drama with which we may be faced in a theatre of the present day. Not all of the possible experiences of dramatic art are available in them. Other kinds of drama have been created throughout Western history, and some have been more widely appreciated than others. Some are easy to digest; some are difficult. Because of the variety in human personality and in human experience, it is possible for us to appreciate a large variety of works of art. Because of our sociality, it is possible for us to enjoy the same kind at the same time. Because of our similarities, dramatic art appeals to universal needs and feelings in the human spirit, but because of the variety in art, we must educate our taste if we are to know and appreciate all of the richest and most distinctive Forms.

# V.

## The Essence of Melomantic Drama

"In *Le Fils Naturel,* I tried to give the idea of a drama which should stand somewhere between comedy and tragedy."
—Diderot, 1758

Tragedy and Comedy are still possible in our world; they are still viable forms of dramatic art because they touch upon and have positive meanings concerning the universal beliefs of mankind from primitive times to the present. It has been noted again and again, however, that not all plays written are in the forms of tragedy and comedy. One needs merely to bring to mind the thousands of pleasant romantic plays including tragicomedies and melodramas, which cause laughter and sentimental smiles, which lead us through harrowing experiences, but which end happily for all the characters concerned. In the United States, today, such drama is most common in the musical theatre, on the motion-picture screen, and in television. It is seldom realized that such plays have been in the majority ever since Aeschylus wrote *The Suppliants* with its sentimental appeal to virginity and its melodramatic rescue for a pleasant ending. Such plays are never so frightening as melodramas; they are never so crucial to life as true tragedies, and they seldom affect our risibility as do true comedies. As intimated earlier, it is not merely the quality of pleasantness which characterizes the genre of Melomantic Drama; it is more particularly that kind of drama in which moral precepts adhere to the sentimental aspects of human engagements (*See* Chart VII).

## A Large Inclusive Genre

One of the most difficult distinctions that there is to make in the spectrum of happy and easy plays is that between romantic or sentimental comedy and tragicomedy. Both will satisfy a general audience in their desire for soft emotions, in their desire for sentimentality, and in their desire for a happy end. Whereas on the one hand we find pleasant comedies such as *Twelfth Night, The Rivals,* and *Arms and the Man;* on the other side of the gap in Melomantic Drama will be *The Faithful Shepherdess* by Fletcher, *Nanine* by Voltaire, *A Caprice* by Alfred de Musset, *The Admirable Crichton* by Barrie, and *The Dark at the Top of the Stairs* by William Inge. The latter plays do not contain the happy discoveries of romantic comedy and their dramatic structures give us no sense of classic or generic comedy. The experience of imminence in comedy comes from our anticipation of mistakes to be made, of awkward confrontations between characters such as those of the cross-gartered Malvolio and Olivia, of amusing exchanges such as the battle of wits between Beatrice and Benedick. In tragicomedy, the suspense is built around our actual fear for the consequences of what the stupid, or drunken, or malevolent characters may actually do to those with whom we have fallen in love.

Our involvement in Comedy is different from that in Melomantic Drama. In the former, we are delighted by the witty and pretty, the handsome and gay, the charming and brilliant characters, but we may not be engrossed so deeply in their loves and their hates as we are when it is a history, a social drama, a tragicomedy, or a melodrama. Our sense of discovery is quite distinct in all types of the comic form simply because we learn so much about human foibles, and human awkwardness, and human dullness as well as about the spirit which suffers from them, namely: the joy of living. In most melomantic types, on the other hand, we discover who the good characters are, who the bad characters are, what the relationships are, what dangers are involved, and what moral lessons may be learned but only those which concern the war between good and evil. In the case of didactic melodramas such as those of "socialist realism," we are, of course, asked to learn a great deal about the thesis of the dramatist; but this is not the same as becoming aware of the joy of living. Our sense of commitment in comedy is inclined toward the championing of prudence and sound reason in their war against folly, even when that folly is the dull mechanism of conformity as in those plays of Sean O'Casey: *Purple Dust, Oak Leaves and Lavender,* and *The Bishop's Bonfire.* In a modern tragicomedy such as *The Dark at the Top of the Stairs,* we are committed at last to the ideals of love, honor, and duty in the guise of a new morality just as surely as we were in *The Winter's Tale.* And in the scenes of fulfillment of both comedy and tragicomedy we are often pleased to welcome a marriage to be; but, whereas the marriage of comedy is celebrated for the joy, the dance, and the action of it, the marriage at the end of a melomantic play is proposed as a solution of a problem, as a test of honor or duty, or simply as the confirmation of the present social order as in the plays of Sir James Barrie and those of John Van Druten.

In all such sentimental drama as tragicomedy, our feeling of imminence regarding love intrigues and lurking enemies, our subsequent involvement with the beautiful people who are embroiled, our happy surprise at discovering the mistaken identities, our acceptance of the prudent decisions reached by the main characters, and our rejoicing in the end at the happiness which has been achieved, are all among the innumerable pleasures experienced at easy and optimistic plays. Nor does there seem to be any great difference in aesthetic experience between that associated with sentimental comedy or *comèdie larmoyante* and the latest stage and film versions of *Carousel, South Pacific,* and *The Sound of Music.* All of it seems to be a little tearful, perhaps briefly funny, but most of it is pure endearment for the beautiful characters, their easily solved problems, and their ultimate happiness. Most persons in large general audiences associate this experience with what they call entertainment and continue to return to it even as they do to something more thrilling, but just as simple, namely: melodrama.

Thus it is that romantic comedy is as easy to digest as a mild cream cheese and tragicomedy is only slightly more tasty than a good cottage cheese; one is a soft sweet wine like port and the other is a little richer like sherry. Some people obviously never change from their original preference for the sweet and the mild —in cheese or wine or plays; but in the search for variety in aesthetic experience there is always the chance that a percipient, or spectator, will come upon a change that offers a challenge to his tastes. In the case of drama, he may find his new interest in the more vigorous form of farce and then, perhaps later on, in the deeper and wider textures of classical high comedy. As in the eighteenth century after the development of sentimental comedy, a more usual change occurs in the direction of melodrama and social drama. Once the need for sentiment and the good fight of villains and heroes is satisfied by tragicomedy, it is not difficult to take up the moral cudgels of melodrama or the later serious plays of social reform. As Kenneth Rowe so cleverly shows in *Write That Play*, the structure of *A Doll's House* by Ibsen has the very structure of a well-made melodrama while at the same time pointing the way to the serious consideration of social and moral problems.[1] A drama of social reform such as *Justice* by Galsworthy, with its fight against the "establishment" and against the complacency of the public, embraces a conflict which is similar to the struggle of good and evil in melodrama. Social drama is usually Melomantic Drama because it does not possess the qualities to achieve comic joy, or sardonic irony, or tragic elevation. Social drama does not pretend to achieve that which is alien to its spirit; it seeks a moral victory for those on the side of social reform.

The pleasure we get from watching melodrama is just as great as any we get from watching tragicomedy, but it is a different variation of the Melomantic Form. We may on occasion be amused by certain incidental characters who supply comic incidents or witty remarks from time to time, but our chief concern is for the safety of the heroine and her hero. As a consequence, the greatest pleasure from melodrama is derived from the sense of imminence which thrills us as we anticipate the breathtaking danger which approaches the chief characters and seems about to destroy them, but, which we know in our hearts cannot, in the end, disfigure even one part of their beautiful faces.

It would appear, then, that there is some similar pleasure in the experience of both tragicomedy and melodrama associated with the happy outcome for characters whom we love and admire. Like the pleasant, mild, easily palatable foods of the world, melomantic plays are numerous and common to all the cultures of the world. Even the best-known classics of the Hindu, Chinese, and Japanese theatres are of this kind, as can readily be seen in *Shakuntala* from India, *The Chalk Circle* from China, and *The Famous Tree at Sendai* from the Kubuki stage. It is not merely the happy ending which makes these plays easily palatable, nor is it merely the beauty and the moral rightness of the principal characters, nor merely the sweetness and softness of the emotions expressed within the framework of fearful imminence. It is all of these things taken together which captures the sympathy of the audience and brings such plays back to the theatre century after century in almost every culture which has any drama at all. They are easy to experience; they may or may not be easy to believe; but they are always such that a large majority of the audience would like to believe them all the way. They are sympathetic plays. They are plays of "sensibility," as they were called in the eighteenth century, and it is for this reason that the whole spectrum of types from tragicomedy to Gothic melodrama has been given the one generic name of Melomantic Drama. Such drama contains within its form both the most endearing and the most thrilling experience which it is possible to exploit within the realm of soft feelings and happy endings. Here it might be well to examine the various kinds which do this.

## Tragicomedy

Beginning with the earliest tragicomedies, such as the pastorals of the Renaissance—the *Aminta* by Tasso, *Pastor Fido* by Guarini, and also, therefore, *The Faithful Shepherdess* by Fletcher—it is evident that our sense of imminence and involvement are with the lovelorn and those who prefer a simple pastoral life. In the greatest examples, including perhaps both *Cymbeline* and *The Winter's Tale*, the sympathy and affection that is aroused for the dispossessed people with all of their sweet sentiments are part and parcel of the dramatic type known as tragicomedy.

Traditionally, there is often more than one plot in such plays, with at least one of them involving a beautiful heroine and a handsome hero whom we love immediately just as in melodrama. It may be that the plots of melodrama tend to concern these endearing characters to the exclusion of all else, but in tragicomedy we discover the dismay of mistaken identities, the sad misplacement of affection for "poor relations," and the fond welcome for long-lost kindred; we sympathize with the sentiments of strong moral characters, but we are not usually terrified by an indomitable villain. Also traditionally, the plots are sufficiently interrelated so that they can be resolved with one ending. Those plays with two distinct plots, as in *The Woman Killed with Kindness*, will always find it difficult to evoke any single sense of either the quality of commitment or of fulfillment. In the case of tragicomedy, these two essential qualities consist of sentimental attachments on the one hand and pleasant solutions to difficult intrigues on the other. The sense of fulfillment at a performance of *The Sound of Music*, for example, seems to derive from the escape of the Trapp family from persecution and not from the celebration of marriage which occurs in the middle of the second act. Our dread is for the safety of these charming people and is more appropriate to tragicomedy than to any type of true comedy. Such plays do not celebrate the joy of procreation as do the comedies, but they do show the inviolability of human life in the shelter of a kindly Providence. We know that we are no longer in the realm of sentimental comedy but have crossed into a new form of drama when our sympathies, our affections and hence our involvement are all caught up in the struggles of certain main characters to maintain the moral principles of which we approve. In Melomantic Drama there appears a struggle between traditional Western morality and the seven deadly sins, which is quite different from the battle of the sexes in such comedies as *Lysistrata*, *Love for Love*, and *The Importance of Being Earnest;* or the battle of political factions in *The Birds*, in *The Non-Juror*, and in *The State of the Union;* or the battle for economic status in *Aulularia*, *The Miser*, and *You Can't Take It with You*. In the classics of comedy, we are involved in the struggle between those of prudent mind and those bent on folly, but in more sentimental comedies we are involved in our affections more than in the struggle; witness the plays: *As You Like It*, or *Le Glorieux* by La Chausée, or *A Kiss for Cinderella* by Barrie, or *Mary Mary* by Jean Kerr, all of which may be described as *comédies larmoyantes*, that is, tearful comedies. By and large, the actions in the latter plays are still primarily concerned with the comic engagements of prudence and folly; the rational agents are still seeking a certain joy in living in spite of the social deviations they find in their fellow creatures; but, in most part, we are captivated by the charming sad characters and not by any ludicrous behavior. Sometimes we leave the world of comedy entirely when there are those situations which are sufficiently pathetic to warrant our tearful sympathies and our heartfelt concern as in *Liliom* by Ferenc Molnár. The latter is tearful without being comic and is entirely lacking in any tragic implication for the destiny of man, but it does insist on the inevitable victory of good over evil. Thus, *Liliom* tends to approach the generic essence of Melomantic Drama in a way similar to serious bourgeois drama as in *Eugénie* by Beaumarchais, or *La Dame aux camélias* by Dumas, or more recently *All the Way Home* by Tad Mosel. In such plays the qualities of imminence and involvement are more emotive than in Comedy. There is no restriction on our sympathy or our affections. As a receptive audience for such plays we do not hesitate to commiserate with the destitute, the foundlings, the homeless, the lonely, the sick, the troubled legions of the world. We love them all.

### Historical and Pageant Drama

Such is the essence of Melomantic Drama, and it is observable in no works more clearly than in historical plays. Their outcome reassures us that our ancestors were strong, successful, enduring, and God-fearing. We see human engagement enacted over a broad segment of time, and it gives us a sense of longevity and stability in our institutions. When we become aware of the broad sweeps of dramatic action over long periods of time, in a wide variety of places, we realize not only the values of an enduring society but the aesthetic values of the panoramic story and its translation into dramatic terms in the pastorals, histories, and romantic melodramas which often acquire panoramic structures in order to achieve historic relevance. Our sense of involvement will often come with our admiration for the chief figure, who may be a historical one, and with our antagonism toward his opposition in whatever shape that may take. In such "history" plays we are almost always involved in a struggle between right and wrong as they are viewed by Henry V in Shakespeare's play; by Edward II in Marlowe's play; by Queen Elizabeth in Anderson's play; by Pedro Menendez in Paul Green's "symphonic drama," *Cross and Sword;* by Marco Polo in O'Neill's play, or by Pizarro in *Die Spanier in Peru* by Kotzebue. But this does not mean that every conflict in such drama is of the same sort or that our response to it will be of the same sort. There may be several examples of bitter plays such as *The Royal Hunt of the Sun* and *Beckett* which, for all their historical interest, would probably not evoke any of the essential responses of the Melomantic experience.

The struggle for power between the two queens in Schiller's *Maria Stuart* is not of the same order as the struggle for existence among Elizabeth's colonists to the New World in *The Lost Colony* by Paul Green. Even in sentimental comedy, we are still interested in the struggle between prudence and folly, but in historical drama we become involved in the conflict for political power as in Anderson's *Mary of Scotland* or in Christopher Fry's *Curtmantle.* In the histories, as in all Melomantic Drama, we are also involved with our affections for those characters who represent general goodness in human character. It is not uncommon in this form of dramatic art for the audience to espouse a cause in a political struggle, an ideal of moral behavior, or even a concept of social justice while at the same time admiring those characters who also espouse these principles. In *Richard II,* the audience may feel as much attachment to the English countryside described by John of Gaunt as they do for the old gentleman himself. It is difficult to feel any real sense of commitment for the cause of Richard II because his case is simply too pathetic. His history is irreversible; he was the victim of the greed for power. We may pity him and have great affection for him, but he possessed no tragic will or choice which could go undeserved in his death. His play is weak as tragedy but strong in its melomantic appeal to the involvement of our affections.

## Melodrama

At this point, it would be helpful to preserve certain distinctions by comparing the lighter dramas of sensibility—such as tragicomedy, pageant drama, and historical drama—with the common type of moral melodrama which is heavier but which also insists on rewards for the virtuous and punishments for the evil with the promise that goodness must be victorious. For one thing, melodrama, as a type of dramatic art, probably does not have as long a history as the others. When late-eighteenth-century French and German playwrights interspersed their light dramatic sequences with short songs to compose what became known as *mélo-drames,* they may have had no inkling of what we in a later time call Melodrama. In traditional examples of this type, including *The Castle Spectre* by Monk Lewis, *Ten Nights in a Bar-Room* by William Pratt, *Under the Gaslight* by Augustin Daly, as well as in such twentieth-century plays as *The Desperate Hours* by Joseph Hayes, or even in *The Homecoming* by Harold Pinter, there is a rather consistent use of the conflict between lovable tyrannized people and the cruel, hardhearted villains who dominate them. The human engagements depicted seem incredible in the older plays and are often improbable even in more recent ones. Like the fantasy in all romantic creations, however, we are often able to accept the premises of a melodrama and assume a real pity for the beautiful and lovable people who are unnecessarily subjugated by ruthless and greedy men. As a consequence, one of the chief differences between Melodrama and the lighter types is the more fearful nature of the opposing force whether it is known in the beginning or is some mysterious secret as in *R.U.R.* by Karel Capek. This force can be a supernatural one as easily as it can be the ugly demand of a landlord who may oppress either a hero, or a heroine, or both. The struggle to escape the oppressor's tyranny comprises the main body of the interaction in melodrama. The characters struggle until they come upon the terrible revelation that their lives are at stake if they do not solve the problem immediately. Once the point of terror is reached, there is the coincidental discovery of a solution which will save them. Whether it is money to pay off the mortgage or a clue to the treachery of the unknown villain as in a mystery melodrama, the solution of the problem brings about the consequences which are usually a kind of reward for the hero and a kind of punishment for the villain. In some instances, of course, the heroine, like the pitiable victim, Nelly Armroyd, in *Lost in London* by Watts Phillips or like the aimless hero, Alan Squier, in *Petrified Forest* by Sherwood may gain their freedom from suffering and their victory over tyranny only in their apotheosis after death. Instead of being tragic figures with positive wills, they are victims of circumstance whose fate is to die trying to endure cruelty. In their pathos we feel the power of this form.

In a receptive audience, when at last we see the destiny which comes to a tragic hero and are made to feel that it is the destiny of all men—be it the transfiguration of Orestes or the great suffering of Oedipus—then we are satisfied that the tragic action has been completed and we sense the tragic fulfillment in our experience. We do pity the heroes of tragedy, but only because they are greater in stature than anything that has happened to them. We feel their undeserved misfortune and we feel in our pity the moral triumph of a great human being who has suffered to the utmost. Our pity for them is a part of our commitment to them. This experience is quite distinct from the pathos which is engendered by the pitiable victims of circumstance in Melomantic plays, written either in the verse of historical drama or in the realistic dialogue of common melodrama. It is evident therefore, that the seriousness of tragicomedy, historical drama, and common melodrama is not the same seriousness as that of tragedy simply because the imminence, the involvement, the revelation, the commitment, and the fulfillment within them do not achieve tragic power. (*See* Chart XII).

In the case of melodrama, our expectations are aroused by the imminent danger which seems to pursue the hero and the heroine with whom we become involved at an early moment in the play. We become involved with the young people in motion pictures and in television "soap operas" because they are fighting the battles which we would want them to fight. What we discover about them is how beautiful they are, how much they are in love, how much danger they are in, and how monstrous is the opposition against them. We are truly horrified at the possibilities; and, in the end, we discover how much we want them to live and to be happy. The audience's sympathy does not reach to tragic pity, but its fear goes far toward horror in many instances; our involvement in melodrama is very great because few of our aesthetic responses are as strong as the love we have for the good characters and the hate we have for the monstrous villain. There is, however, in no "melomantic" type of drama, a tragic fulfillment which combines a feeling of great waste for the loss of life with a sense of moral victory. There is, instead, merely relief and happiness coming with the success of good people with good ideas. The victory of good over evil which is the conclusion of Melomantic Drama is a much easier thing for the general audience to accept than is the moral greatness found in the transfiguration or death of a deeply suffering tragic hero.

As it turns out, then, there is a whole body of drama which, because of its form, affects us somewhat differently from what we expect of comedy, or of tragedy, but which possesses a structure of human engagement that demonstrates, like the latter, the superiority of moral virtue and, like comedy, gives certain major rewards in the end to those characters who show the most common sense or best prudent judgment. Some of it has been called the "drama of sensibility" by Ernest Bernbaum, and it has been delineated and described in detail as "tragicomedy" by others.[2] The need is obvious, therefore, to discover a common configuration in aesthetic experience in which such pleasant and optimistic plays will be grouped according to their recognizable types but will always be recognized for having but one essence—that of a distinct form of dramatic art.

The chief reason for grouping the "drama of sensibility," tragicomedy, historical drama, and pageant or symphonic drama, with common melodrama is the essential unity of their symbolic rhythm, of their emotional appeal, of their image of human engagement (*See* Chart XII).

As was intimated in earlier chapters, these plays have qualities

# CHART XII

## THE ANALOGUE OF MELOMANTIC DRAMA

### The Symbolic Rhythm of Melomantic Engagements

| | Confrontation | Interaction | Consequence |
|---|---|---|---|
| | The Subjugation of Good Men by the Bad or by Misfortune. | The Pursuit of Virtue or Social Improvement to the Point of Terror or Dismay. | The Achievement of Inviolability in Victory or Apotheosis. |

### The Source of Its Dramatic Qualities

| | Confrontation | Interaction | Consequence |
|---|---|---|---|
| | The Sense of Imminence — From the Expectation of Dominance by Destructive Forces. | The Sense of Revelation — From the Discovery of Goodness and the Wonder of Coincidence. | The Sense of Fulfillment — From the Satisfaction of Achieving Safety or Love in the Face of Death or Defeat. |
| | The Sense of Involvement — Taking Sides in the Struggle between Those We Love and Those We Hate. | The Sense of Commitment — From the Devotion to the Ideal and the Reformation of Evil. | |

which are easily understood, easily accepted, and pleasantly reassuring in their philosophical import. They are just pathetic enough to elicit sentimental feelings; they are just frightening enough to give the audience a vicarious thrill that involves them in no real danger but increases their sense of imminence as far as possible in the structure at hand. One does not need any special information or wisdom to understand the musicals: *Carousel, The King and I, The Sound of Music* or *Fiddler on the Roof*. Nor, is it difficult to get wrapped up in their pathos, their lovers' scenes, their laughter, and their symbols of death. In the Judeo-Christian tradition, it is not difficult to accept the conclusion that in spite of the death, the danger, the tears, and the lovelorn hearts, there is a Providence that guards the faithful and the good of heart and which makes one feel that, in the end, all will somehow come right with the world. Tragicomedies, fantasies, historical plays, symphonic dramas, children's plays, and simple melodramas all tend to evoke these pleasant feelings. It is the fulfillment in such plays as *Henry V, The Lost Colony* by Paul Green, *Alice in Wonderland, Peter Pan, The Stranger* by Kotzebue, and *Richelieu* by Bulwer-Lytton that gives the audience the satisfaction of feeling that right will win out over wrong and that all will be well.

## Social Problem Plays

Beyond the common or moral melodrama, however, there is another range of types including social problem plays, pathetic melodramas, and mystery or horror plays, which are all heavier, more sombre, and more filled with pathos than any of the lighter types of Melomantic Drama. Instead of the easy confidence demonstrated by the latter, the more sombre Melomantic plays are much more serious in tone and show many more pathetic and frightening aspects of human engagement. On the pleasant side is the promise of solutions to human problems through simple love and tolerance; on the heavier side, is the feeling of urgency that the immediate frustrating problems of men and their institutions must be solved or the consequence will be destruction for all concerned. Such is the thinking behind "*le drame serieux et bourgeois*" discovered by Diderot in the works of Lillo, La

Chausée, and Destouches, and incorporated in his own play, *Le Fils Naturel* in 1757. The serious bourgeois drama, through its early expression in *Eugénie* by Beaumarchais, *Money* by Bulwer-Lytton, and *Le Demi-Monde* by Dumas *fils* fostered the development of social problem plays in the nineteenth century and is here referred to as one of the principal types of Melomantic Drama. To assist in our current identification of the type, Denis Diderot wrote the following passage in 1758.

> Do we judge a play by its subject? In the reasonable and serious drama, the subject is no less important than in gay farce, and it is treated in a more truthful manner. Do we judge by its character? They can be similarly varied and original, and the poet is forced to sketch them even more strongly. By its emotions? They will show themselves all the more vigorous as the interest will be greater. By its Style? It will be terser, more solemn, elevated, violent, more susceptible to what we call sentiment, a quality without which no style appeals to the heart.[3]

The truth and realism, the originality and emotional vigor, the violence and the sentiment which characterize Melomantic plays are all suggested here, and the effects to be achieved by them were also suggested by him:

> O dramatist! The true applause you seek is not this handclapping which is heard suddenly after a brilliant speech, but the deep sigh which escaped from the soul after the constraint of a long silence, a sigh which relieves the soul.[4]

It is the sigh of relief which we experience after certain plays in this genre which link them to the other dramas of sensibility. The sense of fulfillment in the social drama is a sense of completion, a sense that nothing further can be done as in *Pillars of Society* by Ibsen, *La Robe Rouge* by Brieux, *The Second Mrs. Tanqueray* by Pinero, *Candida* by Shaw, *The Cassilis Engagement* by St. John Hankin, and *A Raisin in the Sun* by Lorraine Hansberry. The only hope felt by the audience in many cases is for social reconstruction, but essentially, the interaction of the characters is finished, the consequences have been made salient, and the didactic or pedagogic purposes of the playwright have been satisfied.

In the early scenes of these plays, one discovers the confrontation of rational and prudent agents with circumstances and opposing forces which are difficult to overcome. The principal agent, in his interaction with society, pursues solutions which are as rational as circumstances will permit, but which, like Nora's forgeries, cannot be morally corrected until changes are made in certain social institutions such as that of marriage. The consequences of social interaction in the serious bourgeois drama were not particularly happy, considering all of the sorrow, suffering, and even death found in such works as *Maria Magdalena* and *Agnes Bernauer* by Hebbel, *The Weavers* and *The Rats* by Hauptmann, *An Enemy of the People* by Ibsen, *The Vultures* by Becque, and *Strife* by John Galsworthy; but their philosophy was inspiriting because the evils they depicted seemed to be amenable to correction. What one discovers is that, although their prevailing tone is pathetic, they possess a didactic point of view which proclaims to the world that if these problems are somehow solved, good will win out—that all will be well if man's better nature sets out to solve the problem. There is very often more skepticism and even hopelessness expressed in these plays than in certain tragedies, but most contain a lesson of moral behavior which reassures us that, for the individual, the moral way is the best way, and for larger bodies of society, it is the only way. There are not only faults to be found in individuals but in larger areas of interest such as that of slave labor in Hauptmann's *The Weavers*, the corrupt courts in Brieux' *The Red Robe*, the degrading social system in Robertson's *Caste*, and the labor unions in Galsworthy's *Strife*. There is also the feeling that humanity stands in judgment of these faults and must be led to see how to correct them. At the time of their first performance, these plays were thought by many to be lugubrious or pessimistic at the very least; but looking back through the smog of contemporary cynicism in drama, the mordant social drama of the romantic era now seems not at all distasteful but rather full of faith in the possibility of the goodness of human beings. In addition, the dramatic and aesthetic properties of some problem plays have taken on the tone of moral melodramas as in the case of *Dead*

*End* by Sidney Kingsley and *Watch on the Rhine* by Lillian Hellman.

The sense of imminence in social problem plays is similar to that in melodramas to the extent that the danger which threatens the individual in either case is external and beyond his control. We find both Nora in *A Doll's House* (1879) and Susan in *Black-Eyed Susan* by Douglas Jerrold (1829) "put upon" by inconsiderate, dangerous, and mercenary men. We fear for those beautiful young women and what may happen to them without the protection of brave men. In Ibsen's play, Nora finds no hero, but she leads Krogstad into the arms of Christina while she achieves the courage to face her adamant husband, Torvald, and if necessary, the whole world—alone. Susan, like the true melodramatic heroine she is, does not have the power to oppose her uncle, Doggrass. Fifty years later, Nora realizes that she can oppose Torvald and go out to make a life of her own after she has shown him to be unyielding and unwilling to support her actions on her behalf. In spite of the facile and unconvincing motivations of Jerrold's character, the unrelated events, and the slipshod coincidences throughout his play, there were some compensations in the theatre of his day. The sense of anticipation centered in the happiness of William and Susan, and the imminence of their separation by Will's court-martial was the clear-cut dramatic quality which sustained this play in the popular theatre of the nineteenth century for hundreds of performances.[5]

To compare, in this way, one of the best-written plays of the nineteenth century with one of the most popular is simply to show that certain plays may achieve the distinctive characteristics of subordinate types, such as melodrama and social drama, without in any way denying that they possess the essential qualities of Melomantic Form. It may be that melodrama will always be more extravagant and less believable than social drama, but our believability is strained even in *A Doll's House* when we hear Nora's tale of secrecy and forgery and hear her slam the door at the end. We are properly shocked by her last exit because Ibsen apparently hopes that we will begin to question the absolute value of indissoluble marriages. We are left at the end of each of Ibsen's social dramas with the feeling that such marriages may not be entirely defensible. In most melodramas, on the other hand, such as those of Jerrold, Buckstone, and Daly, marriage is the one stable and reliable solution to the problems undergone. It is the most common response made by a hero and a heroine to their interactions with the villain or villains. Instead of the rhythm of comedy, however, which often includes a desire for marriage, we have in Melomantic Drama, characters resigned to subjugation under evil powers, then the terrifying feeling that evil forces will completely destroy the good, and in the end the happiness that can come with freedom, or with marriage, or with any other safe solution to the problems posed. It has never seemed wholly plausible that a happy solution could be reached in Melomantic Drama whether we are speaking of Euripides' *Iphigenia in Aulis* or *Come Back, Little Sheba* by William Inge. In the former we are reassured by the gods that Iphegenia will be saved, and in the latter we are led to believe that life will go on in much the same way always. This is not particularly a happy thought, but there is a sense of equilibrium established by Inge which reflects the only contentment his characters will ever know or evince. There is less of the elevated moral vision and victory found in Tragedy; there is less of the joy of living in a prudent world as found in Comedy; but there is, in Melomantic Drama, the salvation of pure love, and the emotional stability of traditional, homespun ways. Yet, there seems to be no essential reason for a happy ending in every case.

## Unhappy Endings

At melomantic plays in the theatre, we are left with the feeling of resignation that a final destiny must be put off until another day, but we are seldom "happy" simply because there is no death scene. In both melodrama and social drama, we are probably best satisfied when the cruel or immoral characters do die from some cause. We come to expect the death of the drunkard, the prostitute, and the long-repentant murderer when they are central figures.

In *The Red Robe* by Eugene Brieux, which so brilliantly

shows the corruption of French legal circles, we are relieved to see Judge Mouzon killed after the suffering he has caused. After seeing the cruel indifference of the court and the love that Yanetta bears her children, we are glad to see her stab the judge. Our sense of justice is vindicated before the final curtain.

Another kind of solution, which is equally pathetic and equally simple in its structure and moderate in its effect, is in that body of plays which depict the death of a character who has been outside the pale of law and order, who has tried to make an effort at respectable living but must die in the end because he or she cannot endure the censure of society. Such have been the stories of "fallen women" from that of Marguerite du Gautier in *La Dame aux camélias* (1852), to Paula in *The Second Mrs. Tanqueray* (1893), to Laura Murdock in *The Easiest Way* (1909), and finally to Blanche Dubois in *A Streetcar Named Desire* (1947). The pity which is engendered for the fallen woman in these plays is no less remarkable than the criticism in them which is leveled at the "double standard" in the sex lives of men. It would seem from the majority of these plays, that promiscuity in sex as well as prostitution had created a social problem in the Victorian period which could be corrected by a shower of sympathy bestowed upon the women who went astray and by a subtle hint to the men that they learn to control themselves. Oddly enough, the only change observable at sophisticated levels in the Western world since "Camille" has been one of greater permissiveness for all parties concerned.

In other words, it is probable that the audiences within the period 1850 to 1950 held the same principles of sexual morality as those exhibited within the plays themselves. A faith in chastity and in the permanent monogamous marriage underlies the inherent criticism of society which these plays attempt to project, and a receptive audience for them will still need to understand this faith. It is evident that the tragedy, *Ghosts,* by Ibsen is also surrounded by the same moral attitudes which are appropriate to these other melomantic plays. The moral difference lies in the active character of Mrs. Alving in contrast to the passive nature of the other heroines. Mrs. Alving works out her own destiny by her will and choice throughout her entire life.

She follows the Victorian moral code and it brings her nothing but suffering. Had she sought the divorce which she deserved, she would have been branded as immoral. That which will preserve this play from age and decay is the truth and universality of the heroine's motives. Although reforms in customs and mores will change the milieu in which this play is seen, nothing will change our attitude toward her desire for personal integrity and her maternal desire to care for her son, which desire in this case commits her to a life of despair. Tragedy depends upon this stability in moral law, whereas the ideas behind social drama, or socialist realism, or melodrama, are often dependent upon the changing customs and sentiments of the society for which they are written. In the melomantic struggle between good and evil, it is the concept of social (or personal) reform which delineates the "good" and which holds the only hope for improvement in the lives of the chief characters.

In the rhythmic pattern of confrontation, there is a subjugation in Melomantic Drama which is shown as a state of discontent and unrest in the motivation of such characters as Camille, Paula, Laura, and Blanche to rebel against their lot in life. We are led almost immediately to anticipate their fate in these circumstances; we are led to sympathize with their desires and their present condition until we become emotionally involved in their encounters with society. In their interactions with others, they demonstrate vividly their desire to escape from their past lives, and we are shown the demands of the others who hold them back.

Each of these female characters is like the others in that she has lived as a "kept woman" or prostitute but has learned to despise her life and has sought to free herself from such an existence. In each case, the solution is different: Camille dies of tuberculosis, Paula commits suicide, Laura resigns herself in despair to her former way of life, and Blanche is taken to a mental hospital. Some of the social conditions and attitudes were different for the audiences of these plays when they were first produced. By and large, however, the customs and manners of each are based upon the principle of marital fidelity, which is one of the social lessons taught by the consequences of these particular dramatic engagements and becomes a part of the satisfaction which these particular audiences may have experienced. The sense of fulfillment is achieved in these cases as in all Melomantic Drama because virtue, by existing standards, reigns supreme at the end; God seems to be in his heaven, and all is well with the world. Nor do we need to despise this easy approach to life. The salubrious thought behind such drama is provocative of a sense of well-being; it gives a sense of moral satisfaction which has been desired by the vast majority of our Post-Renaissance audience and which has sustained them in their work and in their lives to the present time. Our sense of involvement in Melomantic Drama is also nurtured by a similar moral imagery from much the same variety of causes. In tragicomedy, melodrama, and social drama, we enter immediately into the sympathy that befits those who are unfortunate or who are put upon by unscrupulous men. Misfortune at first fills the lives of beautiful characters whom we love in their state of early subjugation and with whom we are eager to stand and fight in their confrontation and interaction with the opposition. Our sympathy links us to them, our pity involves us in their problems; our kinship with them keeps us out of breath until the chase is done and the villains have been subdued. And the villain still exists, although he is sometimes incorporeal as in social problem plays and particularly in the melomantic plays of the new social reform such as the anti-segregation plays of America.

In *A Raisin in the Sun* by Lorraine Hansberry, the spectre of racial discrimination and prejudice hovers over the mild little family of Lena Younger and makes us feel the force of what it is they are up against. The characters in this play all have their share of deficiencies in love, and dignity, and generosity, but they possess enough goodness of heart and enough spirited desire to improve their environment to the extent that one cannot help but become involved in what they are doing and in what they hope to do. In each scene, however, the villain's racial prejudice tends to appear in their speech and in their consciousness—long before Mr. Lindner comes to bribe them to stay away from the white residential section. Mr. Lindner is not a villain from a melodrama; he represents a very real segment of society which opposes the presence of this little Negro family. As in most of the social drama from the days of Diderot to the present, it is the defect in society which is the danger to the sincere and lovable people in the play, and we fear for this danger and for the harm that this danger can do to them. It is this fear of danger, from whatever source, that furnishes us with the greatest sense of imminence in Melomantic Drama.

In previous times there may not have been as much general consciousness of racial difference as in the United States in the nineteen sixties, and it may be that the future will greatly modify these racial problems so that the general understanding of these plays of social unrest will be somewhat limited in their acceptance. The principal weakness of social drama or *le drame serieux et bourgeois* or any other didactic drama is its lack of universal import outside of its own milieu. One clue to this circumstance is the dependence upon realistic setting and casting which characterizes this type of play. In most cases, the theatre would not be able to furnish the proper scenery or actors for such a play out of its period. The peasantry and poverty of Hebbel's plays may no longer exist in Germany as they once did. *"Le demi monde"* in Dumas fils' drama and in other nineteenth-century French plays would not be considered in the same light today. Yet, even when it is possible to recreate scenes and characters out of the past, it certainly would not have been possible for the theatre or stage to present the anti-segregation plays of today in any former time or place. What such plays must do, therefore, is to tell us as much about the world outside the theatre as they can. One of the most significant scenes of revelation occurs at the end of *A Doll's House* in which Nora tells Torvald the faults of the Victorian male's patronizing attitude toward women. Although such a scene has some relevance today, it would hardly have been conceivable in any non-comedy before Ibsen's time.

The social bourgeois dramas and the moral melodramas were, from the very beginning, revelations of the society and the physical environment which gave birth to them. We discover from them a great deal of what the culture and environment of certain types of characters may have been at the time of the play. It is for this reason that we think most didactic drama, including social problem plays and moralistic melodramas, to be "dated" or bound to their own time and place. The example of an early play of this type will best illustrate the case. George Lillo, in 1731, wrote *The London Merchant; or, The History of George Barnwell* with a dedication to Sir John Eyles, Bar. beginning as follows:

> Sir,
>
> If Tragick Poetry be, as *Mr. Dryden* has somewhere said, the most excellent and most useful Kind of Writing, the more extensively useful the Moral of any Tragedy is, the more excellent that Piece must be of its Kind.
>
> I hope I shall not be thought to insinuate that this, to which I have presumed to prefix your name, is such; that depends on its Fitness to answer the End of Tragedy, the exciting of the Passions, in order to the correcting such of them as are criminal, either in their Nature, or through their Excess.[6]

It is thus from an eighteenth-century attempt at tragedy that we learn of the basis of all homiletic drama down to the present century. Dryden accepted the dicta of Horace that the functions of dramatic poetry were *utile et dulce,* and he assumed that tragedy was especially useful if it could teach a moral lesson and deter the criminal tendencies in man. Dryden himself would not have written such a play for his own highly sophisticated and aristocratic audiences in the Restoration period, but by 1731, Lillo was able to see how the moral bent of tragedy could apply to the problems arising in the new bourgeoisie of bankers and merchants.

Lillo set his play in an imaginary world of Queen Elizabeth's London, generally speaking, about the time of the Armada; it was not nearly so definite in setting as similar plays would become in the next century. What was of interest to Lillo was not the physical environment but the moral climate of the characters. As a consequence, nearly every speech in the play is a part of a debate with another character on the morality of a given point of view: whether it be that of the Merchant Thorowgood, or his daughter, Maria, or the sophisticated woman of the world, Millwood, or the apprentices themselves. The play, therefore, turns out to be a long series of homilies not reflective of Elizabethan London but directed to the immediate edification of the eight-

eenth-century working class. A short passage from the first scene
of the play between Maria and her father shows how little attention was paid to creating a sense of imminence or involvement
but how great was the desire to teach morality:

> *Thor.* From your perfect Obedience in every other Instance, I
> fear'd as much; and therefore wou'd leave you without a Byass
> in an Affair wherein your Happiness is so immediately concern'd.
> *Ma.* Whether from a Want of that just Ambition that wou'd
> become your Daughter, or from some other Cause I know not;
> but I find high Birth and Titles don't recommend the Man, who
> owns them, to my Affections.
> *Thor.* I would not that they shou'd unless his Merit recommends
> him more. A noble Birth and Fortune, tho' they make not a bad
> Man good, yet they are a real Advantage to a worthy one, and
> place his Virtues in the fairest Light.
> *Ma.* I cannot answer for my Inclinations; but they shall ever be
> submitted to your Wisdom and Authority; and as you will not
> control me to marry where I cannot, so Love shall never make
> me act contrary to my Duty.[7]

Thus it is that we are taught the moral basis for right action with
regard to choosing a husband in English society in the early
eighteenth century. We realize how important is the moral teach-
ing, but not why we should be involved in the action that is to
come.

Not until the end of Act II of *The London Merchant* is a
major action sufficiently pronounced to give rise to a real sense
of imminence, namely, Barnwell's first embezzlement. Giving the
money to Millwood is not his initial confrontation with the opposition, but it is the first act which will assist in defining Barnwell's destiny in the end. One characteristic of this play which
makes it more melodramatic than other self-styled "Tragedies"
is the insistence of the central figure that he is doing evil, that he
cannot help doing it, and that he deserves whatever punishment
he will receive. What may have been acceptable emotionalism in
1731 seems to us today to be exaggerated, maudlin, and beyond
belief:

> Do I still live to press the suffering Bosom of the Earth? Do
> I still breathe, and taint with my infectious breath the whole-

some air?—Let heaven, from its high throne, in Justice or in Mercy, now look down on that dear murdered Saint: and me the murderer; if His Vengeance spares,—let Pity strike and end my wretched Being.[8]

Regardless of any changes that have occurred in the public attitude toward murder, a twentieth-century audience will not find sincerity in the murderer, Barnwell, who protests at length about the extent of his guilt and the degree of his wretchedness. The dramatist demonstrated for his audience how the apprentice— low on the economic scale, seduced by an older woman, caught in the mesh of his own lust, stealing from his employer to please her, and murdering his uncle—would go to the gallows for his crimes. If ever a play showed that "the wages of sin is death," this play did so. Because it did so effectively, it was performed on the apprentice's holiday or during the week of December twenty-sixth at one or the other of the theatres of London for years after its first season.[9]

*The London Merchant,* however, does not possess the form of Tragedy because it does not evoke the aesthetic quality of Tragedy. It does not show the greatness of Barnwell in the engagement, nor the will, nor the choice of a tragic hero. No other sense of imminence is present than that this foolish apprentice seems about to make some very bad mistakes, and he does so to his own sorrow. The audience cannot become involved in his destiny unless they too are apprentices who have committed errors in some such way as he has . We do not feel akin to those whom we do not admire or at least respect for their point of view. In the whole range of Melomantic Drama, the hero is "more to be pitied than condemned," but our sense of *tragic* revelation is evoked only when we realize that the hero must make a choice that he is bound to make out of his own sense of truth, or justice, or love. One feels no commitment to take on the burden of Barnwell, because he is an ineffectual, weak person for whom we can feel nothing but contempt. He is not an anti-hero out of a monster tragedy because he knows too well that he deserves the punishment which he is to receive at the end. Finally, we feel no sense of tragic fulfillment because the play has shown in the end what is wrong for man to do but not how great man can be in the face of irrevocable choices and insurmountable obstacles. For the audience to learn what is antisocial, as they might in any comedy or tragicomedy, is not to learn the measure of man's greatness as they do in Tragedy. The basic assumption of Lillo in his preface that "the more extensively useful the Moral of any Tragedy is, the more excellent that Piece must be of its kind," is proved by his play to be a misguided conclusion from his interpretation of Dryden's criticism. He may have failed at Tragedy while achieving the epitome of Melomantic form.

And so it appears in all moralistic melodrama, and in all social problem plays from that day to this, that seeing and realizing man's ethical mistakes either punished or condemned gives us the satisfaction of knowing what is the good and proper way for man to behave and sometimes how best to reform his institutions, his customs, and his modes of life. The audience appreciates, in many instances, the moral certainty which the melodramas give them when they repeat or reinforce the moral doctrines which have been held traditionally. It has been demonstrated that they may also come to accept many of the social changes which are shown to be necessary by the more polemic playwrights in such plays as *The Weavers, A Doll's House, The Red Robe, The Vultures, Strife* and even later in America by such works as *Street Scene* by Elmer Rice, *Stevedore* by Paul Peters and George Sklar, *Waiting for Lefty* by Clifford Odets, *They Shall Not Die* by John Wexley, *Roger Bloomer* by John Howard Lawson, *Dead End* by Sidney Kingsley, and *Tobacco Road* by Jack Kirkland. The reason that these plays have since been neglected was suggested by Jordan Miller:

> The failure of most problem plays to survive after many years lies in the removal of their problems from public concern. Plays created in the heat of great political or social unrest seldom endure except as historical curiosities. Such is the case with the majority of the "social" dramas which developed in America during the Great Depression.[10]

This also may be the reason for fewer polemic or hortatory plays to be written about depression problems after 1940. Except for the anti-segregation plays mentioned above, there is a continued lack of interest in such drama.

## The Problem of War

One kind of play seems to have persisted in melomantic form from Euripides to the present day, and that is the so-called "war play." A traditional tragedy, *The Trojan Women*, by Euripides seems in the present context to be a conflict between the conquerors and the conquered at Troy and is almost entirely a play of suffering. Neither Hecuba nor Andromache have been able to make any choices; they are captured and subjugated and about to be taken far from their home. Hecuba can express nothing but anguish; Andromache feels nothing but hate for her captors; Cassandra becomes hysterical thinking of how she will tell Agamemnon about his frightful death on his return home. The boy Astyanax goes unknowing to his doom. The war is painted as a stupid mistake undertaken by the Greeks for a worthless Helen of Troy. The helpless figures elicit some of the pity of tragedy, but for the audience there is no tragic involvement in the lives or actions of the women beyond that pity.

Our sense of imminence is excited by our desire to know which Greeks will take these women as prizes from the war and what will become of the boy Astyanax. The major discoveries concern what disposal will be made of each one. The audience's major commitment is to share with these victims their remorse over the fact of the Trojan War. A sense of fulfillment is established by the fact that we know the fate of each character, and nothing more terrible than the war itself can possibly happen to them. Such a direct and overpowering appeal to our sympathy for the victims of war, to our sense of the immorality of war, gives this play its position as one of the greatest dramas written in the Western world. It may be that classicists will continue to classify this play as a tragedy of suffering, but in the present analysis it is something quite different. There is an overpowering pathos when the characters whom we pity are merely innocent victims. When the agents with the power of will and choice are agents of destruction and are given no destiny, and when the whole engagement consists in the struggle between some weak but good women and some strong but ruthless warriors, we in the audience can experience no other form of drama than that which is Melomantic.

Hecuba can be no tragic heroine because she is helpless to act for her own or anyone else's good; she did not choose the war or any of its results; she cannot change her own destiny or that of Troy. The rhythm of this dramatic engagement shows Hecuba's confrontation with the powers of destruction, but there is no possibility of her interaction with them nor of her knowing the consequences. Instead, Hecuba confronts Talthybius and Menelaus in complete subjugation; she can offer no help to Andromache who must listen to the sentence of death for her boy, Astyanax; nor does Hecuba give any further succor than a final requiem of tears. As a serious and highly emotional play, *The Trojan Women* becomes so overwrought that our feelings of pity can bear no more involvement and our feelings of fear can bear no more imminence. We find ourselves unable to commit our hopes to sorrow or to be satisfied in the end with a sense of failure and destitution so long as the dramatist, whether he be Euripides or Tennessee Williams, gives no indication that man ultimately has the power to choose a destiny based upon moral law. A pathetic war play must inevitably face this emotional dilemma.

On at least one occasion, a play about war was given a much more pleasant outlook. There is an eloquent appeal in the speeches of Henry V in Shakespeare's play, showing an admiration for the soldier, showing the need for courage, perseverance, and skill in each combatant and also showing the exhilaration of victory. In depicting the victory of the English at Agincourt, Shakespeare created a moving play by including all the effective qualities of the Melomantic form. Henry is easily moved to declare war on the French who have sent the insult of the Dauphin in the form of tennis balls. We are made to anticipate almost immediately the anxious preparations for war. We may be somewhat involved with the amusing friends of a deceased Falstaff, but our most concernment is for Henry himself in his confrontation with the French, in the battle scenes thereafter, and in his ultimate response in asking Katherine to marry him so that the two countries can be joined in peace. The happy ending to this play is anticipated from the beginning scene of comic bishops, and there is nothing unpleasant about the scenes of war themselves; they reveal the very model of chivalry, valor, and comradeship as contrasted in the two camps. The less competent, the more pompous, and more hypocritical officers on the French side form the ideal opponent for the dedicated and patriotic English forces. In the interaction, Shakespeare has made us happy and pleased with Fluellen, Williams, and Pistol, and with every single blow that is dealt the enemy. The good are pitted against the bad, and our sense of fulfillment is rich with good will for the lovable Henry and his charming French bride and Queen at the end. In so feeling, we experience the essential qualities of historical drama, of melodrama, of tragicomedy, and, therefore, of Melomantic form itself.

Not all historical drama is necessarily in this form nor is it about war. The famous tragedies of King Lear, Macbeth, Hamlet, and the monster play of Richard III are all based upon historical fact, although battles and warfare are not the most prominent thing about them. Something similar may be said of later romantic histories as well. *Goetz von Berlichingen* by Goethe is filled with imperial warfare and the battle of the peasantry against the emperor. Here the friends of Goetz are pictured as entirely good and the opposition entirely bad as in any melodrama, but Goetz holds enough of his own destiny in his own hands that, if any type is to be assigned in this case, it would be simply that of "heroic history." As it stands, it appears as a panoramic sequence of scenes depicting broad segments of medieval peasant life, warfare, and political strife. There are both hero and villain to hold the story together, but it lacks the necessary qualities to give it anything other than Melomantic form.

In spite of the great panoply of war depicted in the romantic tragedies of Friedrich Schiller such as *Die Räuber, Fiesco,* and *Wallenstein,* the heroes of his plays are not sacrificed on the altar of victory alone; they stand for the very highest ideals of freedom and justice found in any drama. It is in the later development of the Civil War play that the heroes and heroines are daring spies who risk their duty, honor, and love for the sake of the war and for each other without regard to plausibility or adequate motivation. Some obvious examples would be *Belle Lamar* by Dion Boucicault (1874), *Shenandoah* by Bronson Howard (1888), and *Secret Service* by William Gillette (1895). As time went on, these plays became more and more realistic as far as the physical details went, but the heroic speeches concerning self-sacrifice in the war effort continued from first to last. In the first two, the safety of all the good people is achieved with only defeat for the enemy, but in the last, Miss Edith Varney clings to her love for Captain Thorne while he is marched off to imprisonment as her mortal enemy and spy. The subjection of their love affair to military necessity in the early scenes, the complicated interaction which it undergoes with the official discovery of Thorne as a spy, and the pathetic consequence of Thorne's failure to send the destructive message and his being reprieved from a spy's execution all give to this play the melomantic image of a sentimental romance.

Nor is the sentimental attachment to war and its pathetic heroics entirely gone in the plays following the First World War such as *Journey's End* by R. C. Sherriff (1929) and *What Price Glory* by Anderson and Stallings (1924). Even after the Second World War, the audience is treated to much more sentiment in *The Eve of St. Mark* by Anderson (1942) and in *Home of the Brave* by Arthur Laurents. In the examples of *Command Decision* by Haines (1947) and *The Caine Mutiny Court-Martial* by Wouk (1954) there are serious attempts to create more realistic dialogue and more realistic situations, but the rhythmic symbol still evokes the melomantic experience of fear of the enemy, of taking sides with certain characters against others, and of relief when the safety of the USA has been preserved by valiant effort.

Some modern drama has attempted by means of witty and satiric comedy to show the stupidity of war. War as a social disease perhaps could be attacked as any other ill in the world, either by satire or polemics. In *Heartbreak House* by Shaw and in *La Guerre de Troie n'aura pas lieu* by Giraudoux we find both. With war as a kind of villain, however, an audience would expect a vision of freedom from war which these dramatists have not been able to create. It is true that in these plays the easy victory of moral goodness does not appear as the opponent of war. The moral force of Melomantic Drama is missing, and the humorous inclusion of love and laughter seem irrelevant to the subject. Giraudoux's play permits the same women of Troy, about whom Euripides wrote, to plead for peace just before the war in the earlier play takes place. Giraudoux's play came before the Second World War, but it showed the men and woman of the war-bound world to be so weak and ineffectual as to offer no hope whatever for peace. The argument ends between Hector and Ulysses, not with a solution to the problem of war but with man's perennial resignation and apology for what we call the inevitability of war. The expectation is great that such intelligent creatures could find a way to prevent such a disaster, but unlike Giraudoux's other plays, this one ends without much satisfaction. For the dramatist, as for the politician, there seems to be no end to the necessity of war.

## Mystery Melodrama and Gothic Horror

To find more consistent examples of Melomantic Form in the great romantic period of Western literature, one might best turn to the end of the eighteenth century when Gothic melodramas and horror plays became the forerunners of all our mystery melodramas down to the present time. Gothic drama saw its true beginnings in the *Sturm und Drang* period of eighteenth-century German letters. Dramas of death, murder, and revenge included: *Die Zwillinge* by Friedrich von Klinger in 1776, which showed a case of fratricide and the revenge taken by the father right on stage; *Die Kindermorderin* by H. L. Wagner, also in 1776, in which Evchen Humbrecht is driven to kill her own child by the officer who is the father; and *Ugolino* by J. W. von Gerstenberg in 1768 in which two brothers die of starvation in front of their father during the five-act discussion of love, honor, and duty in a gloomy room. These plays had no history as successful theatre, but as literary expressions of emotionalism and terror, they were unique in the eighteenth century and seemed to have given some impetus to the Gothic thrillers in prose and drama which followed. Fearsome tales began to appear more frequently on the stage as the romantic period came to flower. Gothic drama included such mysterious and frightening plays as Monk Lewis's *The Castle Spectre* (1797), Thomas Holcroft's *A Tale of Mystery* (1790), Coleridge's *Remorse* (1813), Henry Milman's *Fazio* (1816), and Charles Maturin's *Bertram* (1816). This mode extended down through a century of melodramas to the mystery and spy thrillers of more recent times. In the twentieth century, one may call to mind Cohan's *The Seven Keys to Baldpate,* Rinehart and Hopwood's *The Bat* (1920), Willard's *The Cat and the Canary* (1921), Stoker's *Dracula* (1927), Werfel's *Bocksgesang* (1921), Emlyn Williams' *Night Must Fall* (1935), Percy and Denham's *Ladies in Retirement* (1939), Hayes's *The Desperate Hours,* and, more recently, Tennessee Williams' *Suddenly Last Summer.* Concurrently with these plays, of course, are the many motion pictures, both fantastic and mysterious, which seem to have even more frightening intentions.

What has happened, apparently, is that Gothic melodrama has acquired two different aspects, one being more spectacular and fantastic as in Richard Peake's *Frankenstein* and the other more realistically mysterious as in the case of Emlyn Williams' *Night Must Fall.* This type of mystery follows the same melomantic rhythm of engagement, but the interactions are usually more subtle, less violent, and less spectacular than in either the fantastic play, *Dracula,* or the horror movie, *The Exorcist.*

The drama of spectacular horror, one finds, is characterized by an engulfing sense of imminence which omits the pleasure of nearly all the other dramatic qualities. We do not get involved with Henry and Elizabeth while waiting with baited breath for the monster Frankenstein to find another victim. Very little of Mary Shelley's philosophy is evident in the dramatization, and we make very few real discoveries other than the startling images of terror which follow one another rapidly through scenes about the monster. We are probably not committed in any way to the revenge, to the murder, to to the destruction upon which the monster is bent. We are committed only to seeing how it will end. There is some satisfaction in seeing it end because we long for the moment when we will see some horrible punishment wrought on the terrifying creature. The aesthetic satisfactions of horror drama, therefore, are limited, with only a few exceptions, to the sense of imminence which pervades the whole action together with the sense of relief at the end.

For illustration, one might compare the mystery, *Night Must Fall* by Emlyn Williams with the horror play *Suddenly Last Summer* by Tennessee Williams. Both are melomantic plays with the same symbolic rhythm of subjugation, pursuit, and equilibrium worked out in strikingly different ways. In the first play, our understanding of the boy, Danny, and of the secretary, Olivia, depend upon the development of the early scenes so that we realize that they both have been in some way constrained in their social outlook, resulting for the girl in deference and withdrawal and for the boy in deceptive affability to hide his desire for violent revenge. The hints are subtle but definite that he sees a financial opportunity in the presence of old Mrs. Bramson. From the moment of our realization of his desire, our sense of imminence increases until we see him do what our morbid curiosity has been expecting. We can then only be happy when Mrs. Terence causes him to be apprehended. We are, of course, involved in the interaction as soon as we realize Olivia's interest in Dan. We know then that his discovery means the sacrifice of her affection for him and of her own social development through his presence. That this circumstance may have existed and that these characters could have been engaged in it no longer seems credible, but the veil of time now appears over it and its incongruities may be excused. It would appear that few melomantic plays can be held to an eternal probability because they stem chiefly from mystical or topical generalizations about human engagement. One of these generalizations is that murder is always committed by persons of great intelligence and great skill, and that all it takes to catch the villain is great craftiness as in a game of chess. Another generalization is that criminals all make some revealing mistake which is bound to trip them in the end. Working out a dramatic engagement in which the investigator is inevitably craftier and the criminal is ultimately mistaken is to fabricate a plot which may or may not be believable. At the time of the opening of *Night Must Fall* in 1935, when the dramatization of criminal psychology was still popular, the audiences of the English-speaking theatre were receptive and believing; in the latter half of the century, such a "psychological thriller" is less often seen, although there are may plays which contain frightening and grotesque elements.

Romantic grotesquerie is a common element in the plays of Tennessee Williams from the clubfoot of Laura Wingfield to the burning rose tattoo on Serafina's breast, to the anatomy lesson for Alma Winemiller, to the dung heap of the Reverend Shannon, to the burning of Lady Torrance's father, to the cannibal death of Sebastian Venable.

The death of Lady Torrance on stage takes on some of the qualities of Baroque Tragedy, but the whole last scene of *Orpheus Descending* is grotesque and seems to be designed as much for its terrifying force as for any sense of tragic significance. On the other hand, the play, *Suddenly Last Summer*, is precisely constructed to achieve the rhythm of melomantic imminence in the telling of the life of Sebastian Venable so as to achieve the greatest effect of Gothic horror. Mrs. Venable begins by describing to Dr. Cukrowicz her doting affection for her son. We are prepared early for the image of carnivorous animals by the Melville story of the Galapagos birds eating the newborn turtles. We next see Mrs. Holly and George sweep down upon Catherine to force her to change her story, but in the end the story of the death of Sebastian Venable as a victim of cannibalism is all told. Like many of the grotesqueries in Williams it is reported as having happened off stage and at some distance in time, but told by what may be an emotionally disturbed person, it contains sufficient horror in the telling. The melomantic feeling in the play, however, is demonstrated by the doctor's willingness to accept the story, to therefore leave Catherine free of her oppressive family, and to disappoint the vultures, Mrs. Holly and George, who would have the story otherwise. Within the limits of this short twentieth-century play we can still experience the rhythm of subjugation in the confinement of Catherine, the pursuit of the true but horrible story by the doctor, and the final safety for Catherine, whom the doctor protects from being hurt by Mrs. Venable. Because of Catherine's honesty and openness we become involved in her plight. Because we do not know her story, we wait with impatience for its telling. Because we are committed to her desire for freedom, we can sense some satisfaction only if we see that she is safe from Mrs. Venable. One cannot doubt the excitement of the grotesque and the horrible in this play, but one does doubt the level of human enrichment to be gained from the sequences of storytelling which are portrayed here. It would seem to be evident that sensational theatre created solely for sensation has always evoked this sense of futility, this disappointment at the waste of high human energy.

### The Byronic Hero

Throughout most of the nineteenth century, the characteristics of Gothic drama and literature became hallmarks of romantic drama in general. The remorseful and guilty hero which appeared in Byron's *Manfred* and *Sardanapalus* as well as in more popular plays such as *Bertram* and *Black-Eyed Susan* continued in almost all Western popular literature. They were later seen in *The Drunkard, Ten Nights in a Bar-Room,* and in the more lavish setting of *The Bells* as played by Henry Irving. The anti-drinking plays were obviously moralistic melodramas of a very common type, and *The Bells* also tried to teach a moral lesson concerning the value of listening to one's own conscience. In the latter case, however, it is the Gothic fear of the Burgomeister, Mathias, which enthralls the audience and creates the sense of imminence. This reliance on suspense and fearful anticipation continues through all the mystery melodramas, but the tortured Byronic hero appears in numerous guises in various kinds of plays to the present day.

Sometimes the guilty hero reforms and remains alive as with Elmer Rice's character, George Simon, in *Counselor-at-Law* (1931) and more recently in a melomantic epic for novel and screen, the Reverend Abner Hale in *Hawaii*. But there are still a few such agents who suffer and die, as in the case of James McLeod in *Detective Story* by Sidney Kingsley (1949); or the pathetic adultress, Rose Pemberton, in *The Living Room* by Graham Greene (1953); or the equally pathetic Lady Torrance in Williams' *Orpheus Descending.* The latter plays may on occasion be designated as tragedies just as *The London Merchant* was two hundred years ago. They do not, however, concern characters who have taken their destinies into their own hands by the moral choices which they have made. What happens to them is either fortuitous or it is a punishment dealt them by the dramatist rather than a consequence due to their own will. A final death scene is melomantic rather than tragic when it punishes a wayward, or immoral, or antisocial agent. The death of a leading character in the Byronic plays, therefore, will cause the audience to feel that a fortunate retribution has come to one who deserved it.

Perhaps in our time, the most extensive attempts to create the remorseful and guilty hero have been those of Eugene O'Neill. The latter has presented, with the utmost skill in characterization, some of the most tormented souls known to all of melomantic drama. Perhaps those more memorable than the others have been: Robert Mayo in *Beyond the Horizon,* Ephraim Cabot in *Desire Under the Elms,* Dion Anthony in *The Great God Brown,* Orin in *Mourning Becomes Electra,* Don Parritt in *The Iceman Cometh,* James Tyrone in *Long Day's Journey Into Night,* and Con Melody in *A Touch of the Poet.* Certainly in the drama of our century one could not find a body of writing of more intense emotionality, of characters with greater suffering or with any greater sense of their own guilt than in the plays of Eugene O'Neill. The one character who seems to struggle against his destiny in a tragic way is that of the coal stoker, Yank, in *The Hairy Ape.* He seems to be the one O'Neill character who sets out to do something about his ignorance, backwardness, and failure; but because of his place in society, he merely makes an attempt to reach out for a better way of life and is thrown back each time. His one last effort is thus to try to overpower the real ape and, in doing so, he dies from his mistake. In acting out his own volition and meeting his destiny he achieves some of the characteristics of the common man as a tragic hero, but one does not sense in Yank any moral strength other than his determination. One does not see the sacrifice of self for others, but Yank is nonetheless tragic in his confrontation, his interaction, and his destiny.

By and large, however, the major characters of O'Neill are

onlookers at the despair and misery of the stormy lives around them; they do not make the kind of choices which lead them to any certain fate. Hickey, the salesman, in *The Iceman Cometh* is more like a spirit of doom who has descended upon the inmates of Harry Hope's Saloon. He talks, argues, cajoles, and preaches about the need for giving up illusions when he has already struck back at society by murdering his wife before he enters the action of the play. In this case, the dramatic action is a representation of a purely verbal interaction of derelicts in an "out-of-the-way" place. Most of the agents in the play simply despair for their circumstance in life or promise themselves they will do better in the future, but the only thing that "happens" in the play is that after hearing Hickey's moralizing preachments, Don Parritt, after four acts, goes out the door and commits suicide. In *Long Day's Journey Into Night,* the Tyrone family simply sinks into helpless dissipation as the mother goes quietly insane and ultimately toward death with overdoses of morphine. Andrew and Ruth in *Beyond the Horizon* watch Robert die and stand helplessly awaiting their own dismal future to materialize. Eben and Abby in *Desire Under the Elms* go off to prison for infanticide, ignorantly content with the thought that they are still in love. Nina and Marsden in *Strange Interlude,* after her husband's death, say good-bye to Nina's son and to her former lover, as if a life of happiness lay before them without any of those familiar people whom they hope to forget. In *Mourning Becomes Electra,* Lavinia can look forward to a battle with her sense of guilt and to boredom, but nothing else seems to be in store. She contemplates suicide, and sees only the punishment of nothingness; her destiny is really unknown. Even the great Kublai Khan in *Marco Millions* looks sadly at the dead body of his granddaughter, Kukachin, without knowing any other conclusion to his vain hopes than that she would be remembered by the mercenary Marco Polo.

In each and every serious play, the dreams of O'Neill's heroes and heroines remain unrealized, and death is no answer to those who remain alive. There are no real villains except the wasted lives that all these people live for themselves to the utmost of futility. Over and over again, O'Neill dramatizes the struggle of intelligent and vital characters to find some meaning, some worth, some happiness in their impossible surroundings of despair, conflict, and ill fortune. There is no history in his stories of Lazarus or of Marco Polo; there is no tragedy in his imitations of ancient Greek drama; there is no melodrama in his contemporary stories because the evil in man is not punished nor is the good rewarded; but the pathos of both Gothic and Byronic drama is exemplified in the deep frustration, despair, and remorse evinced by O'Neill's characters.

We know that in melomantic plays, the goodhearted people attain some forgiveness or expiation for the mistakes they have made, and so it is with Robert Mayo, Eben Cabot, Anna Christie, Dion Anthony, and even Con Melody in *A Touch of the Poet.* What one may discover, therefore, is that the principal characters of O'Neill are introduced in sympathetic form, they are depicted in their subjugation to old Mayo, or to Ephraim Cabot, or to Chris Christopherson, or to James Tyrone, or to William Brown, or to Christine Mannon, or to the Kublai Khan himself. They are then pursued by the dreams and ideals that have inspired their interaction with these subjugators; they are caught in conflict, not with palpable villains, but with the drive to live. This pursuit is brought to a climax of desire and need, like Kukachin's desire for Marco Polo, like Robert's need for Ruth's love while he is pursued by the haunting call of a far distant horizon, like Dion Anthony's need for Margaret's love as he is pursued by the ideal of creative power, like Orin's need for Lavinia's love as his guilt pursues him to his suicide, like Mary Tyrone's need for morphine as her family disintegrates around her. Instead of the usual tender resolution which shows the expiation of sins, or, as in more pathetic melodramas, a moral victory in the death of the heroine, O'Neill drains all hope from the living characters so that their existence is destined to become a haunting shadow of their former lives. The resulting despair and futility in the audience does not destroy the earlier dramatic effectiveness, but it may diminish, for some, the sense of involvement, and of commitment, and of fulfillment in the end.

Melomantic Drama, which includes all of the tragicomedy, historical drama, pageant drama, melodrama, social drama, mystery, and horror plays that have been written, represents the largest body of dramatic writing in the Western world. The pathetic melodramas and the Byronic plays are perhaps the saddest plays of all, and large segments of the audience enjoy weeping for poor unfortunate characters, the victims of circumstance, the enemies of evil and also those who are enemies of themselves. The audience does not demand that the principal figures in these plays have any great tragic stature; most spectators would find it difficult to judge themselves by such standards. Instead, they appreciate the melomantic hero who is capable of some suffering and who, like themselves, is helpless against the world.

There has been no slackening in the production of such plays from *The London Merchant* in 1731 to *The Great White Hope* in 1969. There always seems to be another pathetic victim of misfortune or aggression to appeal to the compassion of an audience. Most of them have sufficient will to find their misfortune, but it is usually only by coincidence that they are able to achieve any equilibrium in the end—at their own death or that of the villain. George Barnwell is free of the greed and lust which have overcome him only when he has been executed, and Jay Follet in *All the Way Home* is free of the terrors of alcoholism only in his fatal accident. In the latter play, the characters are just as beautiful and as interesting as people can be; and drunkenness, waywardness, and death are awesome and fearsome figures in the background which augment our involvement and our commitment to the beautiful heroine, Mary, and her little boy, Rufus. But, instead of any tragic sense of destiny, theirs is a new awareness and acceptance of life, and all is well with the whole world at the end.

For the melomantic hero there is victory through conquering evil and there is victory through death. The victory through death is in apotheosis; either his death is a punishment which will serve as an example to wrongdoers or it is a pathetic memory of a soul which is free at last. His is not a tragic death; his life has been sacrificed to coincidence and circumstance but not at his choice in the cause of truth or justice. Nor, as in ironic plays, is he impaled on the horns of a dilemma whose solution would be possible only if he could move the society in which he has lived. The character Ill in *The Visit* sees that his life would be saved if the community was not selfish. Bérenger in *Rhinoceros* also suffers and is defeated, but it is ironic that he sees a way out of the dilemma, that he sees the uselessness of his society's distintegration before it comes. In this different type of play, we are confronted with a disjunction in man's ideals; we are faced with man's divorcement from the status quo; and we are sent through scenes of ambiguity and dilemma in search of disillusionment. In such instances, we experience a different form of dramatic art: that of Ironic Drama.

# VI.

## Ironic Drama: Its Quality and Its Meaning

". . . whether Ibsen the habitual ironist did not intend some irony. . . ."
                                                             —John Gassner, 1965

There seem to be more possibilities in the aesthetic experience of drama than those recognized by tradition. Besides the romantic archetype of Melomantic Drama, there seems to be another area of experience which is neither tragedy nor comedy but which tends to mix pity and anxiety with laughter. As suggested earlier, there is a kind of drama, with both light and somber values, which exploits the artistic quality of "the irony of fate" but is not tragicomic in nature.

The power of good over evil may be explicitly demonstrated in melodrama or it may be implied in the plays of social reform, but it is only in Ironic Drama that one finds the forces of change in an ambiguous juxtaposition in which the audience is faced with the dilemma of choosing not one but both commitments, one on each side of a conflict. We find analogous ironic situations when two or more political parties, two football teams, or two armies at war, pray to the "same" God for victory. In Melomantic Drama we know the good characters to pray for; in Ironic Drama we usually must choose between the lesser of two evils, or accept both.

The dramatic action symbolizing an ironic juxtaposition in human engagement carries through a disjunction of disparate ideals or opposing values in terms of a rebellion against the status quo, and in terms of the ambiguity of an unresolved dilemma. We are presented with two views of life, disjoined but not necessarily in active conflict (*See* Chart XIII). In *The Wild Duck*, Gregers Werle and Hjalmar Ekdal are intimate and long-time acquaintances who find themselves at opposite poles in their thinking. Gregers Werle represents "the claim of the ideal" as Ibsen puts it; and Hjalmar, the claims of commonplace prudence and security. Their disjunction is not enacted as a struggle but is shown ironically in their interaction when Gregers tries to help Hjalmar but instead brings about the suicide of Hedwig. It is he, who denies and denounces the aims of his father in putting up a deceptive front, and who then attacks the complacency of the Ekdal family. After the death of Hedwig, we are struck with the fact that this idealist, who wanted only the best for his friend, is really the guilty one and yet is the one who goes free of pain; and we are left with the dilemma of feeling that the truth remains ideally best but that human beings may not be able to accept it, or may feel forced to destroy themselves because of it. Such an unresolved dilemma is often created in Ironic Drama from the results of the interaction of disparate ideals. We are often made to feel the ambiguity in the consequence of the engagement which *is* and *is not* rationally acceptable. The dramatic analogue of ironic human action, therefore, includes a confrontation in which is presented one person's disjunction from another by reason of their opposite goals. It includes the interaction of agents who reveal their divorcement and rebellion from the status quo. It includes the consequence of this interaction in terms of the cessation of hostilities, leaving the opposing sides in ambiguity or in dilemma.

A unity of action is maintained in Ironic Drama by the persistent opposition of the two equal forces at hand. The contrast may be between the forces of idealism and expediency as in *The Wild Duck;* or the epitome of a conservative status quo in the character of George Tesman may be opposed to the radical claim of the ideal in his wife, Hedda; or, in a sardonic vein, as in *The Physi-*

## CHART XIII
## THE ANALOGUE OF IRONIC DRAMA

### The Symbolic Rhythm of Ironic Engagements

| Confrontation | Interaction | Consequence |
|---|---|---|
| Man's Disjunction from Man by His Disparate Ideals | His Divorcement and Rebellion from the Status Quo | The Cessation of Hostilities in Ambiguity or Dilemma |

### The Source of Its Dramatic Qualities

| The Sense of Involvement | The Sense of Revelation | The Sense of Commitment | The Sense of Fulfillment |
|---|---|---|---|
| Being Captivated by the Struggle Between the Ambiguous Ends and Means. | Discovery of the Disparity between Ideals, Motives, and Acts. | The Ambivalent Choice of Ambiguity and Disparity. | The Acceptance of Dilemma and Disjunction in Man's Ideals and Motives. |

| The Sense of Imminence |
|---|
| Anticipation from the Disparate Motives of Idealism and Expediency or of Conformity and License. |

*cists* by Dürrenmatt, the knowledge of science for social power and control may be contrasted with the knowledge of science for personal fame and prestige. In no case is it a simple conflict between good and evil. Ironic Drama is skeptical of the virtue of both sides, and instead of a resolution of conflicts, the struggle simply ceases because of the dilemma in which the characters are left. Its intelligent skepticism is often disillusioning and even satisfying while it remains on the humane side of nihilism; when it is immersed in morbidity and cruelty, some audiences may avoid it to maintain their self-confidence. But Ironic Drama is not weak tragedy or confused tragicomedy; it is the dramatic creation of disjunction, dilemma, and disillusion which purges the acid from our souls. This kind of play has been with us since the beginning of our drama.

## Euripides

From the very beginnings of Western Drama, in the ironic works of Euripides, we find the balance of two disparate views of life thrust against each other in mockery and disdain. One of the earliest examples is the play, *Alcestis,* written about 438 B.C. Although Phoebus-Apollo tells us of the death of Alcestis at the opening, we are made to wonder curiously about its necessity when he and Death argue like fishwives about which one of them has the right to kill her or spare her life. We seem to anticipate trouble, but we do not fear this captious sardonic Death. Ordinarily one expects the subject of death to be treated seriously in poetry and in the theatre, but there are few plays in which it is employed so adroitly as to show the ironic contrast between the cowardliness of a king and the courage of his queen.

In the *Alcestis,* the heroine's death is something about which all the characters argue, but about which only Heracles can really do anything. Heracles himself is an amusing drunken strong man who blunders into the house of Admetus at a particularly inopportune moment. The whole situation is incongruous at times and is pitiful at other times. Each of the two people for whom we have sympathy is portrayed as suffering from the loss of the other. While there does exist an element of opposition to their well-being; it seems to come from two very different directions.

In the confrontation, there is the figure of Death or Prince of Hades who insists that the life of Alcestis must be taken if Admetus does not die. There is Pheres, the father of Admetus, who refuses to die for his son in any case because he claims to love his life as much as his son does his own. There is the faithful and all-loving wife speaking more wisdom than the wise king; there is the strong king showing more fear of death and Hades than the woman shows. Not the loving husband, or traditional hero figure, is the one to conquer death; it is, instead, in the interaction of the opposing forces, that a bodacious and sometimes tipsy God-hero, Heracles, is able to foil Hades and bring Alcestis back alive for Admetus.

On the other hand, the happy ending in no way points to comedy. The altercation between Apollo and Death is not treated as a joke so much as it is a rehearsal of an eternal duel between the force which fosters the development of life and that which determines its decay. It is for the sake of dramatic irony that Apollo foretells, just after Death's exit, how Alcestis will be rescued from death. It is ironic that after the Gods have debated and challenged each other regarding the time and reason of the deaths of both Admetus and Alcestis, these two are destined to live and die naturally in the end. It is also ironic that there is more faithfulness, more honesty and wisdom in a "mere" woman (*Poetics*, 1454a 20) than in a great King—who should have been all these things to his people. But the chief irony of the whole engagement is in its consequence which shows the supposedly devoted husband taking a strange woman into his house just prior to welcoming his most loving and self-sacrificing wife.

The *Alcestis* is obviously not a melodrama in which the good people are rewarded and the evil punished. Here, there is no emphasis on the rewards of virtue as there would be in a tragi-comedy. It is true that the play is resolved by the seeming coincidence of Heracles' visit to Admetus, but it is also a fact that Apollo prophesied this event. Under careful scrutiny, the play can hardly be presented as a Melomantic Drama because its ironic portrayal of mistaken trust and false alliances are too obvious.

In the *Ion*, the *Orestes*, and the *Bacchae* which came at the end of Euripides' career, one discovers the culmination of the development of Ironic Form in Greek dramaturgy. The *Ion* is especially notable because the whole human engagement is dependent upon the structural device of "dramatic irony." Euripides not only tells the audience, in the first speech of Hermes, the myth upon which the action is based but continues throughout to make us aware that the agents do not recognize those to whom they are speaking. Neither Creusa nor Ion know each other as mother and son, as we do in the audience. Ion does not know that Xuthus is to be his father by order of Apollo. The audience is aware that Creusa is actually plotting, with the aid of the old man, the murder of her own son, but she does not know it. It is, therefore, doubly ironic that these two should be pitted against each other in a kind of life and death struggle at the moment when the Priestess reveals the cradle which proves them to be mother and son. All then ends in dilemma since these two must live in the falsehood that Ion is the son of Xuthus and not of Creusa. The audience is torn between their sense of truth and their sympathy for mother and son. Ion and Xuthus represent the traditional faith in the Greek pantheon. Creusa is the rebel partially because of her experience with Apollo and partially because Xuthus' son would be a threat to her dominance as a queen. In the audience, we cannot resolve this dilemma because Euripides has shown the incompatibility of Greek pantheism with rational human justice. If the gods are followed religiously as in the final declarations of Athene, Xuthus is given a son and Creusa must deny her claim to him. If truth were followed, Xuthus would have to give up his belief that Ion was his son and Creusa would be able to acknowledge him. It is on the horns of this dilemma that Euripides impaled his audience and made them feel the disjunction between these characters and their beliefs. It is ambiguous as to whether happiness can be known by any of them. Few dramatic plots have been more thoroughly symbolic of the ironic course of human existence than this one; since, here, the truth itself is doubted as a possible solution.

The *Orestes* is perhaps an even more demanding and difficult play to enjoy if for no other reason than that it is one of bitter and caustic irony. Unlike the tragic trilogy of Aeschylus, the *Orestes* shows with a bitter humor how it would have been for

Helen to return with Menelaus to Argos and face all the Greeks who had lost someone in the Trojan War. In this play, Euripides mocks the dignity of the house of Atreus. He makes of Menelaus a mercenery warrior who has no friends with which to help Orestes. Helen and her daughter are the ungrateful house guests of Electra and her brother and are making uncomfortable demands instead of finding safety there. When the elders of Argos plan to kill Orestes and Electra in order to avenge the death of Clytemnestra, Menelaus will not help them. Orestes and Pylades then plan to murder Helen and hold her daughter hostage. At that point, Euripides presents the most ironic *deus ex machina* of all his plays by having Apollo save Helen from death although she deserved it most; by having him give all of Sparta to Menelaus who is shown as the most incompetent and greedy of all leaders; then give his daughter to Orestes who is just about to kill her, and give Pylades to Electra because they are both such careful planners of murder. No modern parody of the ancient story could have made the action of the play a more sardonic contradiction of the myth as it was known to the original audience. The ancient heroes in the play, ironically, are motivated only by self-interest and greed. Menelaus, Helen, and their daughter are shown disjoined from their unwilling hosts, Electra and Orestes. They clash in the crisis of Orestes' death sentence when suddenly, in desperation, he seeks his freedom by threatening Hermione. The audience is left in ironic dilemma after Apollo instructs the other characters to accept a destiny which is a contradiction of their present circumstances. It is then no longer possible to choose as heroes either the agents of tribal justice, Orestes and Electra, or those destined by the gods to destroy Troy with a waste of Grecian lives. Any choice made by the audience is a bitter choice.

In the *Bacchae*, which was probably the last play of Euripides, there is an even more scathing use of ironic rhythm. The disjunction of disparate ideals is seen in the confrontation of the temporal power of Pentheus against the godly power of Dionysus. Without any indication of religious faith, King Pentheus throws the intruder, Dionysus, into chains and hopes to evict him from the land. The irony is evident from the very beginning when we are aware that Dionysus is at once the most terrible and the mildest of the gods, an effeminate but also a cruel god, and that he speaks not as himself but as a follower of the god. He soon forces on Pentheus a decision which seems like a spell. Pentheus becomes one who longs to see the maenads dance and is willing to dress as one of them in order to observe them closely. Thus, Pentheus must act ironically against his very nature and against all that he had claimed at first. The interaction portrays the willingness of Pentheus to go into the hills to see the maenads dance in their Dionysiac rites. It is then reported that Agave, the mother of Pentheus, leads the bacchantes in tearing the king limb from limb and bringing his head back to the palace. The consequence is that the mother, being released from her bacchic frenzy, must recognize what she has done to her own son and must suffer henceforth from her bitter discovery. The ultimate meaning of the play would seem to be that the religious ecstasy which is demanded by the gods, *the fervor of man's faith,* is, ironically, that which often leads to his own irrational destruction.

With even closer scrutiny, it may be observed that Euripides' mocking criticism of religion, logic, and tragedy may have led him to create a distinct dramatic analogue referred to here as Ironic Drama. In the history of dramatic literature, one discovers that the aesthetic experience of numerous dramas since the Greek period correspond closely to the Ironic plays of Euripides. Using a number of examples from a variety of periods, it is possible to show the persistence of the form as well as its essential nature.

It is not merely the quality of irony in what is said or the device of irony in the structure of the play that marks the unity of ironic drama; it is, more particularly, the constant juxtaposition of two valid sources of psychic strength which, when pitted against each other in strenuous interaction are incapable of reaching equilibrium. In the more sombre versions of Ironic Drama a life may be destroyed as in the *Bacchae,* or in *Hedda Gabler,* or in *The Visit of the Old Lady,* but the ambiguity of the opposing forces still remains. Happiness is unknown to either side. Euripides was able to dramatize the human engagement in terms of tragedy, but it was in the Ironic Drama that he presented the first clear examples of this form. Whether in the more sombre vein of the *Orestes* or in the easier and more pleasant vein of the

*Alcestis,* we have examples of this form of drama again in our century written by a variety of authors from a variety of points of view. The physical structure of the ironic sequence of action has changed considerably since the day of Euripides just as it has in the case of Tragedy, but the aesthetic feeling quality engendered by the whole image together with its import gives all such plays their formal consistency.

One may well ask whether Ironic Drama is a believable imitation of human life, or whether this is of any concern here. The answer lies in the nature of dramatic art itself. As an analogue of an ironic human engagement consisting of a confrontation, an interaction with culmination, and a consequence, an ironic play, like any dramatic production, calls to our minds immediately the movements and sounds of human beings. Even when the theatrical image is a brief fragment, and the dramatic experience is only partial in its evocation, there is the possibility of ironic quality if not complete ironic form. Two bounding ping-pong balls can be made to represent some aspect of a human engagement as in the play *Balls* by Paul Foster. Here, there is only so much of life as can be imagined from what is said or intimated by the sounds, and only so much of that which applies to the smallest segment of human engagament which is the conversation. This does not take it out of the realm of drama; it simply confines drama to a fragment, and its experience to a short segment of time. Some recent ironic plays such as *The American Dream* by Edward Albee, *The New Tenant* by Eugene Ionesco, and *Motel* by van Itallie are short plays which are effective for a brief period of time but which do not contain the same force of imminence, revelation, and fulfillment that one may find at a performance of a longer work such as *The Sea Gull.*

## Chekhov

Chekhov and a number of other dramatists since the beginning of the century have been recognized as writers of a realistic drama of the commonplace.[1] Some of their plays will be found to be modern tragedies, some sentimental or pathetic comedies, some melodramas, and some Ironic Dramas. Those which follow the form of Chekhov will be easily recognized as ironic. Beginning with *The Sea Gull* there is the light humor of the characters who surround Nina and Trepleff. Even the sad Masha is amusing in her disgruntled nagging of Medvedenko, and nearly all are capable of laughing at themselves even as we all laugh at the bad play performed by Nina. There is a feeling that the disjunction of both Nina and Trepleff from the world at large is something which separates them from each other. Nina longs for the world outside—the urban world of excitement. Trepleff longs for the achievement of art, and they are both met with rebuffs from a "country gentleman" society which includes the doctor, his mother, his Uncle Sorin, and Trigorin, the ideal "man of the world." As in each of the plays of Chekhov, those who represent the status quo are disjoined from those who are rebels in their hearts; the old culture is juxtaposed to the new. Some of the ironic disjunction occurs because those in one group are seldom in love with one another but with someone on the other side; Trepleff loves Nina, Nina loves Trigorin, and Masha loves Trepleff. It is sardonic to see Trepleff followed and annoyed by the others, but it is pathetic to see Masha cry for Trepleff. It is ironic that he who needs love the most is the one who is unable to accept it from his mother or from Masha, and he is in anguish because he has lost Nina. After waiting for months for her return, Trepleff talks to her only to learn that she can love no one but Trigorin; but his reaction is like that in certain old romantic plays in which the hero blames his failure in love for his failure in creativity. Trepleff destroys all of his writings and then commits suicide. And, as in *Hedda Gabler*, there is no tragedy because it is the disjunction of two ideals which has brought them to their ambiguous ends: Hedda and Trepleff, failures in both creativity and love, are worth little alive and worth nothing dead. The consequence is suicide and the audience must be satisfied with what will always remain a dilemma. How can one capture the world and also realize one's self? Such ironic problems are often ambiguous because they are neither happy nor sad. Their value, of course, lies in the freedom of thought which they foster. It is not so much that they leave us feeling ambivalent and uncertain as that they stretch our consciousness to believe in the infinite variety of forms which human happiness might take. The irony of *The Sea Gull* makes us appeal to reason and to ask: Why could not Nina see the beauty of sharing a creative life with Trepleff? Why could not Trepleff see Nina's need for the scope of the great hustling world and go with her, however briefly, into that world to share in her expressiveness? One of the ironies of human engagement is that these alternatives are so easy to suggest and so difficult to accomplish.

Chekhov did achieve a realistic mode of dramatic writing. The language is simple, natural speech; the setting is the environment, as he saw it, in which people lived, and the conditions of the society he depicted were exactly what he found and what his contemporaries would also find in the life about them.[2] In such plays of naturalistic origin among the works of Ibsen, Hauptmann, and Chekhov, irony can be no less obviously the essential import of the dramatic engagement. The more recent ironic dramas of Ionesco and Dürrenmatt are certainly more caustic, more cutting, and show somewhat more brilliant contrasts perhaps, but they are no more definitely ironic than *The Cherry Orchard.*

From first to last in *The Cherry Orchard* there are some characters like the student, Trofimov, and Lyubov's daughters, Anya and Varya, who are secure in the traditional life but who see possibilities for the future. Others, like Lyubov and her brother, are tied to the past and will probably not relinquish it. These, then, are the opposite of the merchant, Lopakhin, who comes to buy and subdivide the cherry orchard. He is the only one to see the commercial advantages at hand, the value of selling part of the old estate and of developing the rest. But he is not a greedy miser from out of comedy; he is a friend of the most lovable person of all, Madame Ranevsky. He wants to help her, but he is the son of a former slave who sees the practical road to prosperity. In comedy, such a point of view would be found on the side of procreation and aimed at the enjoyment of the Good Life. Here, it is set against the cultural idealists who already have a good life and would rot in it if those like Lopakhin would let them. The irony persists and even increases in this play as we discover that what is best for the traditionalists is what will destroy their whole way of life; what is best for Lyubov is that her estate be sold, and it is that which nearly breaks her spirit. Whereas marriage would be good for Varya, she cannot attract either Ephidov, whom she comes to despise, or Lopakhin who does not notice her and does not respond. What Anya looks forward to are quiet reading sessions with her mother, but she will probably have none of that after her schooling is finished. The final irony is that Firs, who by long practice should serve Madame Ranevsky wherever she goes, is left behind to die in the old mansion in which he has always served her family. The new cannot shed all vestiges of the old, and the old can do nothing without the life of the new. Thus, the irony of *The Cherry Orchard* is the irony of life itself.

There are not only comic, and tragic, and melomantic circumstances in the course of ordinary human existence; there are also ironic ones which fill us with wonder. They are contrary to what is expected at the moment, but they seem to be the most plausible and just in the end. Just as Aristotle found the death of Mitys' killer filled with awe, so do we today find the sale of the cherry orchard most remarkable as it goes to a former slave. After showing how certain scenes in *The Cherry Orchard* are contrary to what one would ordinarily expect, J. L. Styan writes: "We have the authority of the cumulative ironies to doubt what we see and hear."[3] It is not so much the dramatic causes that we doubt but the results. For example, we do not doubt the fact of Anya's longing for a return to childhood, but for ironic purposes, we are made to doubt that she could ever live again at home. To the extent that we recognize the futile aspirations of Chekhov's characters, to that extent do we recognize the natural qualities which are inherent in his dramatic engagements. His are "realistic" dramas and are imitations of life to the extent that they are artistic symbols of the life he knew. It would be difficult to discover improbabilities in the portrayal of engagements so close to the life of the dramatist. At the same time, it is not out of place to question the universal recognition and appeal which such a portrayal may have. The plays of Chekhov would probably be more often rejected for their lack of activity or violence than for their portrayal of everyday life. They do not appear to have been designed to surprise and ridicule as comedy does; nor were they designed to frighten us with death as tragedy does. They seem, instead, to shock and stimulate us with the ironic incongruities of ordinary human existence.

### Ionesco and Livings

A similar quality seems to be evident in the work of Eugene Ionesco. The disparity between aspiration and achievement as shown in *The Chairs* is understandable and appreciable in a wide variety of cultural contexts. The disparity between shared beliefs and mechanical, complete conformity as shown in his *Rhinoceros* is also easily understood the world around. In *The New Tenant* the disparity and incongruity between the neat orderly acquisition of furniture and the unbridled desire to acquire every piece of it that can be stored in the cubic space of an apartment should be universally recognized for its irony.

Following Albert Camus with his notion that the human condition is "absurd," a number of critics have linked the plays of Ionesco, Beckett, Sartre, Genet, Pinter, and Dürrenmatt with the philosophy of existentialism and with a "Theatre of the Absurd."[4] Because of their obvious serious quality, it is probably the case that these plays come closer to being "existential" than they do to being as foolish and silly as indicated by the word, "absurd." However others may use these terms, it should be noted here that existential drama abounds in sardonic disparities, hopeless dilemmas, and severely grotesque ironies. Certainly these elements in Genet, Pinter, Ionesco, and Livings bear out the view that the old customs and manners of society are threadbare and that the "red tape" and busy work of our bureaucracies and institutions are a stupid waste of human energy. Such disparities and grotesqueries are seen in our attempts at communication. In *The Bald Soprano* especially, one is impressed by the incongruousness of both the Smiths and the Martins, of the Maid, of The Fire Chief, and of nearly everything they say. In one sense, it is ironic that the guests come just when the Smiths are going to bed. It is ironic that the Smiths excuse themselves to change their clothes just as their guests come. It is ironic that Mr. and Mrs. Martin speak as if they had just met. But it is essentially a dramatic distinction that must be made. It is dramatically ludicrous for these things to proceed as they do, but since no volition is involved in the action —no character wills the events that transpire—no comedy evolves out of what is said and done. What one sees in the theatre is based upon distortion and disjunction in every sound and gesture. Some of the irony arises from the implications of the lines and some from what transpires as when The Fire Chief appears at the door after the fourth ring and not before. But not this event or any similar one in the play is a result of rational motivation. Each moment is amusing and ridiculous because it is all so surprising and unexpected, and we are no longer captivated by the traditional devices of comic incidents in a story as we are by the ironic satire of conventional manners.

A similar kind of experience is evoked by the play, *Eh?* by Henry Livings, but it is not, in this case, devoid of the aesthetic qualities which excite and draw the spectator into the concerns and involvements of the character portrayed. *Eh?* is probably more than the "inspired silliness," or "simple farce," that some reviewers of its first performance would have it. Instead, the play evokes an ironic vision of the contemporary world of commerce as seen through the eyes of a poet. We see the disjunction between the rigid senseless conformity of the commercial enterprise and the free individual, Brose, who has come to ask for a job as a boiler tender in the dye factory. Getting the job done, however stupid and unnecessary it may be, is the aim of Manager Price; he has all the necessary equipment to do it; the situation is technologically stable. Into the factory comes Brose, who is questioned as to his being a satisfactory worker. His reply is:

> I'm satisfactory all right. Always been satisfactory. All my school reports: satisfactory satisfactory satisfactory. I went to the Grammar School, you know. . . . I did Latin. *Satis* meaning enough, *factory* meaning works: Satisfactory. Had enough of work.[5]

Here we find a character similar to Chaplin in *Modern Times* rebelling against the machine, not simply as the poor speechless victim but, this time, as a voluble and vehement rebel who attacks conformity, rigid schedules, mechanical duties, and slavery to the factory and who avoids any adherence to such traditional duties as to church, family, boss, or work. This is modern man not doing what the sociologists predict at all, but a man growing hallucinogenic mushrooms in a boiler room which to him is a fascinating toy. His bride whom he brings into this room to live is no ordinary prize won in the struggle for life and love as in a comedy. She is simply another of the fixtures with which he must contend in the button-pushing existence of the modern mass man. He wins his arguments with the manager by being more witty and by reducing the latter's stipulations to absurdity. He wins the argument with the preacher by drawing him into nonsequiturs of logic which nearly derange the prelate's mind. He comes out superior to the personnel secretary by reducing her to certain Freudian repressions which she has been trying to find in him. Nor is there any love duet ending in a dramatic symbol of marriage or of sexual union. Brose's wife finds it just as difficult as anyone to understand this man. Her ironic remark is: "The trouble with getting inside your head is that once I'm there I'm on my own." She has no provocative ability to draw him into the vegetative female world of blossoming, germinating, and bearing fruit. Brose seems to be a master of growing psychedelic mushrooms, but his power can only lead to the destruction of the dye works. We in the audience are left again on the horns of an ironic dilemma; freedom from all duty seems perfectly idyllic, but, to achieve that state, how can we sacrifice the world of productivity which is so helpful to our drive for freedom?

To be sure, the play, *Eh?*, is as funny as any comedy to appear in recent times. To achieve its full value as drama, however, is to emphasize its disjunctions, the disparity between what is said and what is usually the case in the world, to capture the import of the symbolic rebel who stands against the status quo, and to capture the ambiguity in which we all stand whether committed to freedom or to the world of commerce. It has the rhythmic structure of the wittiest and most amusing ironic drama; it does have the intellectual bite of satire, but it lacks the bitter hopelessness of the drama of cruelty; it offers none of the easy solutions to worn-out problems of good and evil which are offered by melomantic plays. It does stand between Tragedy and Comedy, since it is a ludicrous study of the common man with serious overtones, and this helps to assure us of its place in Ironic Drama.

## Durrenmatt

To find Ironic Drama in its simplest most direct generic type, one can turn to the Swiss play of Friedrich Dürrenmatt, *The Visit of the Old Lady (Der Besuch der alten Dame)*. Here again we have a play described by its author as "this comedy with a tragic end," not like what one discovers among the tragicomedies of an earlier period, but a kind of play with a different sort of experience to offer. The expectation of the arrival of a wealthy heiress into a community of bankrupt people can evoke nothing less than the strongest sense of imminence as we hear more and more of the confrontation between Ill and Claire. We do get some intimations of death with the coffin, with the return of capital punishment, and with the saying of last rights; but this is not the suspense of melodrama because Ill and all his neighbors speak to Claire in happy anticipation until the bribe is announced and the revenge is proclaimed. By that time we are involved with the characters of Ill and Claire so that we want to know the whole interaction between them in the past. We are shocked by the tale told of Ill's bribing the witnesses at the former trial, and we are even more shocked when Claire asks the town of Gullen for his life. This is not the romance of *Romeo and Juliet* in which love conquers death; nor is it the satire of *Man and Superman* in which the female is proved to be superior; it is Ironic Drama in which a rigorous single standard of sexual morality is juxtaposed to the lenient complacency of the double standard. We discover the faults in each symbolic character as when the mistakes of weakness and softness in Ill are compared with the faults of revenge and hate in Claire. Yet, however much we might be committed to the cause of Ill who is reminded of his error by both the Mayor and the Priest, we also tend to sympathize with the need of the community and of his family to be repaid for the wrong done to them by Claire when she bought out each industry and locked its doors. More than anything else, we see the ironic circumstance of this man who must buy his last moments of prosperity for himself and his family with his own life. We see how, ironically, the world is led to think that he died for joy at learning that Madame Zachanassian had given this little town a million pounds in endowment in memory of her friendship with Alfred Ill in their childhood. As in many Ironic Dramas, we are not finally committed to a single course of action by any one agent in the play. We are, instead, committed to the ambivalence found in the moral dilemma which divides two disparate ideals in their interaction. In Ill's character we find traditionalism followed in the easiest most expedient way as he lives out the consequences of the double standard; in Claire Zachanassian we find the rebel challenging that standard of morality with the strongest means possible, that of complete economic power and authority which has to be applied with ruthlessness to bring about her desired revenge and to convince the obdurate reactionaries of its justice. Her cruel victory is one not often seen in real life, but the ambiguity of ironic drama leaves open the possibility that she may have been right.

In another of his plays, *Romulus the Great,* Dürrenmatt has captured some of the simplicity of Euripides' ironic dramas. Against the tried and true traditions of standing off the enemy at all costs as recommended by Mares, his Minister of War; of sacrificing one's life for one's country as in the case of his daughter Rea; of fleeing to a new land to take up the war again as in the case of his wife Julia; of sacrificing his love for Rome as does Emilian; Romulus ironically does all of the opposite things to help undermine the power of his empire and to help bring it to an end. Romulus sells or gives away the leaves from his laurel crown, the jewels from his sword, the busts and statuary from his palace so that he can be free to feed his chickens. We are amused, at first, at the satire of a powerful Roman Emperor, but as he comes in conflict with his soldiers, with his daughter, and with his wife, we see the ironic seriousness with which he expects to carry out his own, and Rome's, capitulation. Instead of making a tragic choice for the integrity of the Empire and its continuation, Romulus chooses its destruction in the belief that this will serve mankind better in the end. One then suspects him of hoping to become a martyr in this deed until, ironically, in the end, his Teutonic captor persuades him that if he will not continue as Emperor, he must at least reside in exile after giving up the throne; he becomes the only one who is saved after trying so hard to die with the empire. Speaking of his characterization, Dürrenmatt has written:

> Look closely at what kind of a human I have sketched here: surely a witty man, a man at ease and humane, but in the last analysis, a human being who proceeds with the utmost firmness and lack of consideration for others, a man who does not shrink from demanding the same absoluteness of purpose from others. He is indeed a dangerous fellow, a man determined to die. That is the terror lying within this imperial chicken-fancier, this judge of the world disguised as a fool. His tragedy lies in the comedy of his end; instead of a sacrificial death he has earned for himself retirement. But then—and this alone is what makes him great— he has the wisdom and the insight to accept his fate.[6]

The author probably does not mean great in the tragic sense, since he has admitted that the tragedy of the character "lies in the comedy of his end"; in other words, his dignity and power have been reduced, ironically, to nothing by the meanness and vacuity of his ultimate fortune. His rebellion against the status quo has been worked out in his interaction with each of the characters associated with him. He has denied the validity of the old conventional modes of honor, duty, and patriotism, and we see in his denial of aggression, the very strength of his humanity in opposing his enemy. He permits his family to attempt to save their own lives by going to Sicily, but they accidentally die at sea. Every direction of the dramatic action turns on the irony of its opposite as in the *Ion* and the *Alcestis* of Euripides.

An examination of the other works of Dürrenmatt shows his continuous interest in the portrayal of the ironic disparity between man's ideals and loyalties. Some of his other plays which show this interest are *The Physicists, The Blind Man, An Angel Comes to Babylon,* and *The Marriage of Mr. Mississippi.* The last is a long altercation between Anastasia and Mr. Mississippi, showing the complications, intrigues, and conflicts which might possibly arise in the complex turmoil of a marriage and a political career based upon blackmail and hate. Unfortunately, our sense of imminence is practically destroyed by the loquacity of the characters and our sense of involvement is destroyed by our lack of sympathy for these humorless and insidious characters. Any sense of commitment is impossible simply because too many different characters in their asides appeal to the audience for sympathy and understanding without any of them being more convincing than the other. Our sense of fulfillment is cheated, not only because of uncertainty and ambiguity, but because there is no indication of any possible alternatives other than nihilism. Our dramatist has shown at verbose lengths the destructive nature of political, religious, and social tyranny unrestrained; and, as a consequence, the rhythmic structure which he has projected for the theatre may lack the aesthetic power to hold the interest of the audience. But this is not to deny that some of the speeches are bitterly ironic and are of interest because of that.

Most of the plays of Dürrenmatt, however, have been effective in the theatre and have caused considerable discussion concerning their dramatic significance. Many of the critical commentaries have pointed to the ironic substance of his work. Writing of *Der Blinde*, Dürrenmatt himself has said: "I wanted to juxtapose the word against the dramatic place, to turn the word against the scene. The blind duke believes he is living in his well-preserved castle whereas he is living in a ruin; he thinks he is humbling himself before Wallenstein, but sinks to his knees before a slave."[7] The essence of irony is in every incident of this play and it informs the entire rhythm of its engagement. *The Physicists* is another such ironic drama with perhaps more immediate relevance to the dilemma of scientific discovery versus man's responsibility for his own preservation. In the play, the scientists have tried to escape public censure and greed by living in an insane asylum. They each commit murder in order to preserve their solitude, but by that time they discover they are the absolute prisoners of a true egomaniac who operates the asylum. The dramatist seems to leave his audience in the ambiguous state of not knowing whether man can pursue knowledge, administer its use, and still retain either his sanity or his humanity.

Dürrenmatt, of course, is not the first dramatist to weave so much ideational material into a play as to make it obscure. Such plays have been shelved in the libraries of the Western world for several hundred years. In the English-speaking world alone, there have been Elizabethan plays such as *Gorbuduc; or Ferrex and Porrex* by Thomas Sackville and Thomas Norton, romantic poetic effusions such as Byron's *Manfred,* and in our own century *The Dynasts* by Thomas Hardy. One can be almost certain that there is no place for these plays in the theatre, but it is not alone weighty thought and verbosity which lead to obscurity. Sometimes it is the unspoken which makes a play most vague. For example, one might observe that it is often difficult to determine the source of dramatic power in the work of Luigi Pirandello.

## Pirandello

There is an abundance of irony in the plays of Pirandello. Some of them come closer to achieving ironic form in their essence than do others. His first play, *Lumis di Sicilia* (*Sicilian Limes,* 1910), is naturalistic in its mode and tells rather directly the story of a Sicilian peasant who is insulted and degraded by wealthier and better-educated townspeople. The dramatist did not resolve the peasant's problems, but let the incidents speak for themselves. Such a technique did not produce the effective fulfillment that he was to create in later plays. He begins in the play, *Tutto per bene* (*All for the Best,* 1920), to bring the juxtaposition of disparate goals to their ironic end. When the man discovers that his dead wife had not been faithful, he would like revenge, but his only recourse is to continue after twenty years to pretend that he mourns for a good and faithful wife. Trust and loyalty must in the end be given theatrical pretense when the relationship upon which they were built becomes a lie. The lie, as in most of Pirandello's plays, becomes the opposition to the normal, traditional way of living, and forces the characters into a world of make-believe in order to live out their lives with any sanity. This becomes most obvious in the theatrical tour de force entitled *Sei personaggi in cerca d'autore* (*Six Characters in Search of an Author,* 1921). The actors know no other life than acting roles in the theatre, and the characters know no other life than being the creatures imagined by an author. In this case it is the characters who work out the incidents of the story, and the players who fail in imitating what the characters intend. Pirandello presents the people of the theatre as faced with this ironic contrast, and he compounds the irony by making the sordid story of the characters one of mistaken identity which ends not in make-believe but in the actual death of the little boy. An unexpected ending, of course, does not ensure the essential experience of ironic form, but in this play, the contrast between illusion and reality is vividly portrayed in terms of theatrical environment. The claim of illusion is so strong among the actors and their manager, the claim of reality is so strong among the invented characters, that one's feeling for dramatic quality is well sustained throughout, and one's interest and attention are held. From a structural point of view, it appears to be unfortunate that nearly the whole interest is attached to the story of the characters and that only a passing glance is given to the lives of the actors who remain in the scene throughout the entire play except in the second act when they attempt, ironically, to perform the roles of the characters. There would be a greater sense of imminence and discovery if there was less philosophizing on the part of the Father. There would be a greater sense of involvement, if there was one of the agents, either actor or character, whose destiny really mattered to the audience.

Such a character is Signora Frola in *Così è, se vi pare* (*Right You Are! If You Think You Are*, 1918). Signora Frola is a gentle person who would like to keep her family affairs to herself, and as a victim of a disastrous earthquake, she has not felt any impulse to get out socially and pay visits to the neighbors. She has suffered a great deal from the earthquake; she may even have suffered the loss of her daughter. The problem of truth and appearance is made the dominant subject of the play; it is portrayed by showing that each person involved in the disaster has a different conception of it and of the relationships that exist in the Ponza family. The ironic form is developed by means of showing in confrontation the disjunction between what the community *believes* to be the truth and what the victims say *is* the truth. As Signor Ponza tells it, Signora Frola has gone insane from grief at losing her daughter. As a result, we in the audience feel the force of irony when we hear first one and then the other tell about the girl who has become Ponza's wife; she may or may not be the daughter of Signora Frola. The end is the ambiguous consequence of finding the dilemma unresolved by the girl herself, who claims she is not what they say she is. Again, this is entirely possible as a truthful and sincere human engagement provided we understand that some, or all three, of the principal characters are acting roles, or pretending to know something, or hiding the truth. Both Frola and her son-in-law are disturbing elements in the complacent community of public opinion represented or symbolized by the gossiping neighbors, but the one rebel against the status quo in this play is Lamberto Laudisi, who tries to tell the neighbors that they cannot come closer to truth than what they are able to observe from the testimony of the participants. The community cannot accept this, and, ironically, they continue to dispute with Laudisi on the very point which the ending of the play would tend to verify. Pirandello persisted in making the claim dramatically and ironically that the truth, in any case, is only that which it seems to be and nothing more.

He reiterates this theme in ironic form in at least three other interesting plays, *Enrico IV*, 1922, *Come Tu Mi Vuoi* (*As You Desire Me*, 1930), and *Ciascuno A Suo Modo* (*Each in His Own Way*, 1924). Perhaps more than in any other of his works, his *Enrico* possesses the clearest exposition of man's uncertainty concerning the identification of insanity. That it should be nursed and compassionately accepted seems not to be questioned in the play, but how it should be treated by near relatives presents an imminent concern, particularly when one of them is a former mistress. Dramatic irony is employed as a device from the very beginning by letting the audience know that the play takes place in the contemporary world, and that Enrico expects everyone in the household to act as if it were eight hundred years prior, and that every detail of living must conform to the eleventh century. In the last scene, not even the audience knows the degree of madness to which this man has succumbed. After revealing his pretense and after denouncing both the Marchioness and Belcredi, Enrico drives a sword into the latter for having ruined his entire life. It is ironic that in trying to demonstrate the utmost sanity, this man shows the greatest degree of insane jealousy by murdering the object of his hate. In the end, he must continue the role of being insane or accept his punishment as a murderer. His dilemma is ours in the sense that we are forced to ask ourselves whether our only defense in the modern world against the cruelty of avaricious people is to seek the seclusion of a madhouse.

More is required of Ironic Drama as a form than merely a strange sort of discovery or reversal at the curtain line of a play. In Pirandello, the ideational content, the import of his plays reveals the great disparity between accepting the world on faith, or remaining always skeptical of it. To the extent that Pirandello urges doubt and protests our faith, he is following the polemic way of the thesis playwright. Seen in the light of the polemicist, his plays may lack, for some, the sharp delineation of dilemmas that we find in Euripides or in Dürrenmatt, while at the same time, the ambiguity of his endings is as ironic as any in all of dramatic literature.

There is also a certain piquant irony in the endings of the plays of Ferenc Molnár, but his *Liliom* is tragicomedy, and *The Guardsman* is a drawing-room comedy of a very high order. The rest seem to be comedies of intrigue which make delightful entertainment but which do not follow the sardonic, disjunctive rhythms of Ironic Drama. In *Liliom*, our involvement becomes very great in the love affair of the leading characters. We love Julie for her unspoiled innocence. We know Liliom is a ne'er-do-well, but we admire his strength and bravado and his obvious love of Julie. We wait expectantly for the robbery to be successful, but we are not surprised that it failed and that Liliom died. More than anything else we feel the pathos of Liliom's return to earth and his attempt to show a kindness which he was unable to show in life. It may be somewhat ironic that he slapped his little daughter without her feeling it just as he had slapped her mother, but this does not make an Ironic Drama out of a very sentimental, melomantic one.

## Shakespeare and the Jacobeans

Shakespeare perhaps went further than any dramatist in attempting to give a tragicomic ending to his essentially ironic plays. This seems to have occurred in *Measure for Measure, All's*

*Well That Ends Well,* and *Troilus and Cressida.* The ironic disbalance or disjunction in *All's Well That Ends Well* appears in the marked disparity between the honesty and forthrightness of Helena (aided by The Countess, and Diana) and the greedy chicanery which motivates Parolles to lead Bertram astray. In the tragedies of Shakespeare, that which weighs in the balance of his human encounters are truth and justice; here, they are very doubtful eventualities. Bertram, in his desire to please his king, cares not for the injustice of his abandonment of Helena. In his desire to have Diana later on, he cares not for the truth about his purchase of her virginity. In the comedies of Shakespeare, the superior force of womankind's procreative and vegetative rationale grows superior to man's animalistic propensity to devour the world so that it can be remade to his own specifications. But in this ironic play, it is *deception* which brings out the truth from Parolles and brings a just response from Bertram as Helena's husband. Only by pretending death, only by submitting to lechery and adultery, does it seem possible for the women to demonstrate the value of honesty and justice in the course of social interaction. That the same is true in politics is shown by the political exchange between Lafeu, Bertram, and Parolles. Only a false and impossible task brings forth the true nature of Parolles and his schemes for power and influence. Only by allowing a trap to be set could Bertram learn what a perfidious liar and cheat his follower, Parolles, really was. It is a pleasure to see him caught and punished. It is pleasant to marvel at the wit of the clown. It is pleasant to see Helena win her husband in the end. But these pleasantries only heighten the ironic quality of the whole plot, which portrays the conflict between a materialistic expediency represented by the will of Bertram and the idealism of love and marriage held by Helena. This is brought to its culmination by Helena's scheme to use in a ruse the very words of Bertram so that he would, in the end, marry her. It does, nonetheless, leave us with the dilemma as to whether such a marriage has any hope of succeeding and if, perhaps, it would have been better had Helena not insisted on having Bertram in the first place. It is irony rather than comedy that makes us doubt the power of the "Life Force" in the face of persistent faithlessness.

If, in the realm of Ironic Drama, *All's Well That Ends Well* is a dark play among the more sardonic works of Shakespeare, then *Measure for Measure* is somewhat more so. It is a much more carefully written play and seldom wavers from the realistic style of the dramatist's domestic scenes. It puts in the ironic balance the heavy-handed and hypocritical moral duplicity of Angelo against the honest idealism of Isabella. Angelo, by his insistence upon law and order and moral restraint, becomes in his break with his own principles the most hypocritical lecher of all drama. Isabella cannot preserve her ideals except by deceiving Angelo with a substitute for herself in his bed. In a simpler version of ironic drama or in a tragicomedy, this device might complete the conflict between Isabella and Angelo, but in this play the irony is compounded further. Angelo does not save Claudio's life as he bargained. Instead, another ruse must be perpetrated by the Duke in order that Claudio be saved. He has the head of Ragozine sent to Angelo in place of Claudio's. Again it is ironically uncertain as to whether it requires more lying and deception to correct injustice in the powerful than one man can rightfully afford. In these two plays of Shakespeare, the ideals of truth and justice are made most needful and impressive by their very absence. He demonstrates most forcefully in *Measure for Measure* how ironic it is that both truth and justice can often be made manifest only by false and injurious intrigues. In comedy, the falsity and injury are also ever present, but the audience never has any doubt in a comedy but what they can be vanquished by the forces of common sense and by the joy of living; it has been so demonstrated in theatrical performance year after year since the dawn of human history. In Ironic Drama, however, we begin to have grave doubts about the viability of common sense and the possibility of a good productive life. Perhaps all is not well that only seems to end well, and perhaps truth and justice cannot really be secure where one must resort to lying and deception in order to remain alive.

Not all ironic plays, however, end with the principal characters still alive. The harsher examples of this genre include not only the *Bacchae, Hedda Gabler,* and *The Visit,* but also Shakespeare's *Troilus and Cressida.* With Patroclus' death, Achilles'

faith is lost, and in Hector's death, all of Troy's is lost. Yet, ironically, that which is valued most and lost to Troilus is the love of
Cressida which was secured through Pandarus with no little ex-
penditure of effort. In the disparity between love and war, the
ironies are compounded by those who wage them both. It is
ironic that a young man of such high position and stature as
Troilus should depend upon Pandarus to woo the fair Cressida
even though her father was a Trojan who was partial to the
Greeks. It is evident that Troilus has more leisure to think about
his love for Cressida than he does about how to fight in the war.
In the course of war, it is shown that Achilles would have been
the better match for Hector, but Ulysses invents a craftier way of
setting Ajax against the Trojan hero. It is not a little ironic that
it requires as much cunning and persuasion to get Achilles to
meet with Agamemnon as it does to get Cressida to speak with
Troilus. In both cases, the dialogue becomes a banter of ironic
disparities. In the case of the Greek generals, one ironic comparison is found in that all the faults which Ajax finds in Achilles
are precisely the faults of Ajax:

*Ajax.*   If I go to him, with my arm'd fist I'll pash him
         Over the face.
*Agam.*   O, no you shall not go.
*Ajax.*   An a'be proud with me, I'll pheeze his pride:
         Let me go to him.
*Ulyss.*  Not for the worth that hangs upon our quarrel.
*Ajax.*   A paltry, insolent fellow!
*Nest.*   How he describes himself! [Aside.
*Ajax.*   Can he not be sociable?
*Ulyss.*  The raven chides blackness. [Aside.
*Ajax.*   I'll let his humours blood.
*Agam.*   He will be the physician that should be the patient.
         [Aside.
*Ajax.*   An all men were o' my mind!
*Ulyss.*  Wit would be out of fashion. [Aside.
*Ajax.*   A' Should not bear it so, a' should eat swords first:
         Shall pride carry it?
*Nest.*   An't would, you'd carry half. [Aside.
*Ulyss.*  He would have ten shares. [Aside.
*Ajax.*   I will knead him, I'll make him supple.
*Nest.*   He's not yet through warm: force him with praises:
         Pour in, pour in; his ambition is dry. [Aside.

*Ulyss.* My lord, you feed too much on this dislike.

(Act II, Sc. iii)

Ajax is a victim of ridicule, and such might be the dialogue of comedy except that the generals are leading Ajax to his death because they believe him *not* to be as great a warrior as Achilles or Hector whose challenge he is set to meet. In the case of love, Troilus and Cressida meet with banter on their lips, but it is not the playful sarcasm of Beatrice and Benedick, it is the challenge of a warrior against the skepticism of a sophisticated lady:

*Tro.*  O Cressida, how often have I wish'd me thus?
*Cres.* Wish'd, my lord?—The gods grant?—O my lord!
*Tro.*  What should they grant? What makes this pretty abruption?
        What too curious dreg espies my sweet lady in the fountain of our love?
*Cres.* More dregs than water, if my fears have eyes.
*Tro.*  Fears make devils of cherubins; they never see truly.
*Cres.* Blind fear, that seeing reason leads, finds safer footing than blind reason stumbling without fear:
        To fear the worst oft cures the worse.
*Tro.*  O, let my lady apprehend no fear: in all Cupid's pageant there is presented no monster.
*Cres.* Nor nothing monstrous neither?
*Tro.*  Nothing, but our undertakings; when we vow to weep seas, live in fire, eat rockes, tame tigers; thinking it harder for our mistress to devise imposition enough, than for us to undergo any difficulty imposed. This is the monstrosity in love, lady—that the will is infinite, and the execution confined; that the desire is boundless, and the act a slave to limit.
*Cres.* They say, all lovers swear more performance than they are able, and yet reserve an ability that they never perform; vowing more than the perfection of ten, and discharging less than the tenth part of one. They that have the voice of lions, and the act of hares, are they not monsters?

(Act III, Sc. ii)

And, instead of this antithetical description of lover's claims leading to love and marriage as in Comedy, it leads to desire, then to deception, and finally to default. Instead of deception leading to infidelity and death as in neo-classic tragedy, it leads to disillusionment for Troilus and a lost challenge. This, with the loss of Hector, meant the loss of Troy and virtually the end of everything worthwhile for Troilus. Before the fatal day, the Trojan Hector says: "Goodnight, sweet lord Menelaus," and the master ironist, Thersites, comments: "Sweet draught: Sweet, quoth'a! sweet sink, sweet sewer." No one individual agent in this play is responsible for turning the tables on tradition and conformity, but several do. Achilles does not seek out an opportunity to fight with Hector but shuns it until the very end. Troilus does not seek out Cressida but has Pandarus do it for him. Cressida swears eternal love to Troilus, but she disavows it at the first opportunity. Love and War are thus balanced on the ironic lever of tradition versus freedom. All members of Hector's family plead with him not to go to war on the fatal day, but he listens to none of them. It is no friend of Troilus who shows him Cressida being unfaithful with Diomed; it is the Greek enemy Ulysses who does so. All the traditional expectations that one might have of faithfulness in love and courage in war are severely questioned in this bitter but brilliant Ironic Drama. The audience is left with the dilemma as to whether honesty and faith can be counted on realistically in the conduct of human affairs or whether we must rely on their opposites.

Following the Elizabethan plays of Shakespeare, there appear a number of bitter and sardonic comedies such as Ben Jonson's *Volpone* and some of his later plays which seem to possess the traditional rhythmic patterns of comedy, but which are so filled with ironic contrasts and disjunctions as to warrant a reconsideration of their qualities.[8] It is also apparent that our disappointment with certain so-called "tragedies" of the Jacobean and Caroline stage such as John Webster's *The White Devil*, Middleton and Rowley's *The Changeling*, and John Ford's *The Broken Heart* have to do with the ironic qualities and devices which tend to color these works in unique ways and show them not to be in the realm of traditional dramatic structures.

The play, *Volpone*, which is often listed as a comedy, has very little to do with the joy of living or the celebration of love. It is a bitter satire and a brilliant revelation of corruption, but the deviations are not meliorated. The distorted moral characters of both the gulls and the gullers remain as grotesque and deformed as are the strange creatures known as Nano the dwarf, Castrone the eunuch, and Androgyno the hermaphrodite. Volpone and his parasite, Mosca, show the wealth they have acquired and the deception through which it is obtained. In each meeting with every greedy heir looking for Volpone's acquisitions, the audience is fully aware that the expectant heir is being cheated of all he may have to give, but that the victim remains ignorant of it until the very end. As in the older classics of Plautus, the scenes of disguise all depend upon the technique of dramatic irony so that the audience is fully aware of the gull and how he is being gulled. In comedy, the gull is usually fooled into believing that unless he acts in a certain way, he will lose his property. In the ironic form, those who are fooled may *actually* be cheated of their wealth, their wives, their good names, or even life itself. Corvino, through his avarice, actually relinquishes all claim to his wife in taking her to Volpone; Corbaccio actually disinherits his son in his will. In the end, Mosca is actually ordered to be a galley slave and Volpone is actually thrown into prison to starve and die. There is very little comedy in these events, but since the interaction of the play as a whole is a struggle between avarice of one kind and another, the ironic disjunction appears when the miserliness of Volpone and Mosca is realized through deception and the avarice of the vultures is actualized in hypocrisy. At the end, the audience is left to wonder whether the deceptions of the former are any worse than the crafty greed of those they deceived. It is true that the schemers are brought to justice, but there is apparently no end to the mischief which may be wrought by those guilty of avarice. It is surely ironic that Volpone, who thought himself a master of deception should be the most deceived by Mosca in the end.

In the "tragedies" of the period, a similar disjunction occurs between those who would preserve honor, truth, or chastity and those who would neglect or destroy them. The chief figures seem incapable of making moral choices in the face of those of evil intent. Not only does virtue fail in its own behalf, but dishonesty seems to succeed in the cause of deception without interruption.

It is ironic in Webster that the vengeful relatives have so much more perseverance, more fortune on their side, and apparently more intelligence than his beautiful heroines, Vittoria Corombona and the Duchess of Malfi. In *The Changeling*, it is De Flores, the servant, who possesses the craft and malevolent intelligence to destroy all possibility of Beatrice's happiness and then to seduce her. It is not tragic that they should be imprisoned and commit suicide; it is ironic that only the will to destroy is unassailable in such a misbegotten alliance. The question then arises as to what hope there may be for a decadent society. Ironically, it is difficult to see how man can destroy his own destructiveness.

## Bitter Irony

Those performances in the modern theatre which match the bitterness and cruelty of Jacobean drama are the allegorical masques by Peter Weiss and Jean Genet, particularly the *Marat/Sade* and *The Balcony*. These masques do not achieve ironic form in drama simply because they do not portray the engagement of human life in terms of acts of will, nor of their interaction, nor of their consequences. Such portrayals are allegorically represented in masques and not in any way structured in the rhythmic patterns of dramatic form. Similar ideas in Shakespeare, Ibsen, Pirandello, or Shaw, may appear as brilliant expositions of the critical and skeptical point of view indigenous to either ironic drama or to satiric comedy. In Weiss and Genet, they are more like allegorical pageants; they are more like fanciful dialogues than they are drama. *A Man's a Man* by Bertolt Brecht and others of his so-called "Epic Theatre" plays are also of the style and mode of the masque rather than of episodic drama. One of the chief reasons for this is that the agents who speak in these productions do not have character in any dramatic sense, are not motivated by choice, and can cause no human engagement. When there is no confrontation of the will, then there is little possibility for the experience of imminence, involvement, or commitment. Like the dialogues of Plato and the masques of Ben Jonson, the modern masque tends to be chiefly a matter of revelation and discursive statement with some witty and scurrilous speeches thrown in to keep verbally alive the sequence of spectacles. The masque has always been highly theatrical, but it has always been produced for didactic purposes for a coterie audience and only occasionally to delight the general audience.

Some of the cruelty found in these contemporary masques of darkness appears in certain plays such as those of a more recent ironist, Harold Pinter. In *The Homecoming,* the confrontation appears at once between the harsh domination of a thoroughly masculine and ruthless family of men and a young feminine newcomer, Ruth, who is brought home by her husband, Teddy. None of the men at home hesitate one moment to attempt to seduce Ruth as a kind of declaration of their faith in a traditional male prerogative. Ruth instantly senses their approach to her and begs her husband to take her away. Teddy is blind to the problem and insists that she stay even though reluctantly. His brothers Joey and Lenny proceed in their separate ways to seduce Ruth even before the very eyes of her husband. Joey demonstrates that he is a very capable boxer and will permit no interference from Teddy, the husband. Max, the father, who has lost his wife from an unhappy marriage, finds it promising to have this young woman in the house, since she seems perfectly willing to go to bed with Joey even when the latter appears impotent. The intellectual Teddy, who is a professor of philosophy in an American university, is forced to stand by calmly while his father and brothers persuade Ruth to stay with them as a prostitute whom they will furnish with a nice apartment if she will give them a percentage. As a rebel of superior intelligence, she agrees to stay provided they will take her on her own terms and follow her instructions. She completely reverses the position of traditional male authority and domination, and the audience is left to consider the ironic possibility that all co-operative activity between the sexes would cease to exist at such time that their only palpable activity was sexual. Pinter demonstrates by this play that a total involvement with sex would be the end of man's interest in it. It shows ironically that human lives bartered on the slave block of sex would be worth nothing at all, since all the limits set would be purely commercial ones and the family as such would become simply another business. It would apparently be a business in which all the females were prostitutes in executive control of all property and of all available funds. The men, like the characters in this play, would simply be males at stud for the purposes of procreation. The modern ironist shows that man has perhaps always wanted to have all the cake and to eat it too, but the ironic wonder of it appears in the fact that to have all the cake is to have nothing else at all.

Other contemporary playwrights in a bitter mood have treated the dilemma of love and sex in modern society, but perhaps the most serious one is Jean Anouilh. The latter had good reason for classing his plays in at least four types; calling the dark, sombre ones "Pièces Noires" and the harsh bitter ones "Pièces Grinçantes," as opposed to "Pièces Roses" and "Pièces Brillantes" both of which were lighter and more amusing.[9] Although Anouilh is much more gentle than Brecht, Dürrenmatt, Genet, or Ghelderode, he is nonetheless, in both the dark plays and the harsh plays, essentially an ironist. In the dark play *La Sauvage* (translated with a characteristically American euphemism as *Restless Heart*), we find the idealistic rebel, Thérèse, being prepared by her parents to marry the rich opportunist, Florent France. There is the immediate triangle of love to create an immediate suspense, but it is not long before we hear of difficulties from the objective and intelligent Hartmann, who realizes that it will be difficult to match the brilliant rich musician, Florent, with the sensitive, fragile, but poor Thérèse. Our anticipation comes not only from wanting to know the outcome of the triangle but from feeling the irony of the imminent failure of such a love affair and marriage. Florent's beautiful hope, always shown beside Thérèse's nagging and painful doubt, fills all of the preparations for the wedding with ironic imminence. Irony also permeates the struggle between the two lovers because of the sardonic truth with which Anouilh shows the rich man's expediency and the poor girl's idealism again and again at odds. Conflict alone, however, is not the essence of irony in this case or in any other. It is, as much as anything, the ironic revelation of the common, brutal, vulgar Gosta and Tarde who have been brought into the world of Florent France by Thérèse and who create the vivid sense of disjunction, misplacement, and hurt which we experience throughout this play. We fear the temper of Gosta, and it makes us wonder how Thérèse could ever be attached to two such opposite kinds of people.

*La Sauvage* is thus especially ironic in its sense of revelation. Some of the important discoveries made are those of Thérèse concerning the incongruous situation in which she finds herself. She discovers that her parents are crude "money grubbers" beside Florent, and that beside him, Gosta is coarse and greedy, a "simple, violent man." In Ironic Drama there are very often two major plot discoveries related to the disjoined and paradoxical concepts which are in strong contrast to each other. We find Thérèse discovering that Florent has moments when he needs her and is not entirely self-sufficient. Upon that discovery, there is no doubt in her mind but what her father represents the worst in human life and that Florent will be the most wonderful husband in the world and that she will be very happy. Her last major discovery, however, is quite the opposite. She has again seen her father, who has come some distance to warn her that Gosta is coming to murder her fiancé. Gosta himself appears in all his anger and is scolded by Thérèse who, in turn, shows him what a shameful slovenly person he is; but in his very weakness, in the very failure that he admits, and in the confession of his desire for revenge, Thérèse discovers that she does in fact belong to the world of the striving, poor, embittered people that she has left behind chiefly because she believes that they are alive and that the happy idle rich are essentially dead.

As we become involved more and more with Thérèse and her fiancé, Florent France, we develop certain expectations for their happiness; we discover, as they do, that their particular ways of life are worlds apart. We are torn, as in all Ironic Drama, between being committed to one kind of happiness which they might achieve together and another kind with which they could be content—apart from each other. As in other Ironic Dramas we are forced into a stoic acceptance of ambivalence toward the destiny of the chief characters and, finding the situation ambiguous, we will often be uncertain as to our own commitments. It is this uncertainty plus the dismay that we feel at the inadequacy of mankind which gives to Ironic Drama its strong piquant taste.

Thérése does not have the moral choice which is forced upon Antigone, but they are both faced with dilemmas that might be considered insuperable by most human beings. Antigone, whether conceived by Anouilh or Sophocles, must choose between a "living death" and a dead sort of living. Thérèse choses the degraded poverty-stricken life, but we do not know what her destiny will *ultimately* be. We are struck by the irony of her having a world of beauty and love laid at her feet and of her rejecting it for reasons which seem at first to be strange and unhappy ones but which, on second thought, may be the only ones which could satisfy her. The fulfillment that we sense from this play is a disjunctive consequence. It grows from the incongruity of our last view of Thérèse whose happiness seems not to lie in the good life as it would in comedy but in the harsh, cruel world of failure and crudity to which, ironically, she had been born. We doubt the end, but we are forced to accept it; it has a bitter tang, but we admire it for its truth. In *Ardélé*, by Anouilh, the problems of married love in a variety of situations are treated sardonically and bitterly not only with regard to a married couple but from the point of view of mistress and lover as well. We see how the General suffers from having a wife whom he has driven insane with jealousy, but we also see how indifferent Ada, his housekeeper and mistress, is. We see how bitter the Count and the Countess are toward each other, but we also see how Villardieu tries desperately to have the Countess all to himself and cannot. The young couple, Nicholas and his brother's wife Nathalie, might have had a happy marriage once, but the latter insists on being true to her husband who is away on business in China. The only normally monogamous relationship that exists in the play is that between the hunchbacked Aunt Ardélé and her unknown boy friend, who is also a hunchback. All the other characters despise this relationship because of the physical deformity of the couple, but they do not see how deformed is their own love by comparison. The irony of love in deformity as opposed to deformity in love is the central disjunction which each couple demonstrates in their relationship. Perhaps the most sardonic contrast is that in which Villardieu finds his situation full of grief because the Count and Countess show such a normal marital concern for each other. Another amusingly sardonic touch includes the Peacock which calls "Leon! Leon!" throughout the play just as the unhappy Emily does from her room. There are also the gruesome children, Toto and his cousin, Marie Christine, who dress up in their elders' clothes and carry on married "scenes" in which they tear at each other in pretended marriage quarrels. The children's view of marriage seems to be that of Jean Anouilh who shows that it is a kind of hell on earth. Whether a better system of non-French and non-Catholic divorce laws and customs would solve these problems is not considered here. This play, however, is another example of Anouilh's mastery of ironic form by means of which he persistently shows in play after play the impossibility of both romance and expediency prevailing in the same marriage. His plays seem to demonstrate that a marriage for convenience cannot be transformed into a marriage for love in any case, but the characters left alive are seldom granted any hope.

The aesthetic qualities of this play are strongly ironic in nature. The sense of imminence is awakened carefully in *Ardélé* by the persistent secrecy in which each person must carry on his illicit affair. The mordant situations breed our anticipation of a catastrophe to occur at any moment. We become involved with each of the affairs because the participants are engaging, charming, affectionate, and misguided persons. They love each other and they are in conflict with each other; it is not strange that they are confused. The Count is the most rational as well as the most agreeable individual of them all, but no one listens to his suggestions to let Ardélé have her own normal love affair. Our anticipations are all revealed in good time. We learn the nature of the General's marriage, the difficulties of the Countess, the early love of Nicholas and Nathalie, the sad deformed condition in which Ardélé must live, and we are even shown the General's life, Emily, in all of her anger and hate. In each case, the revelation is of the disparity between our normal expectations of happy love and the actual sad circumstance. Yet, in no case is one point of view so obviously right that we can become committed to it. We are never convinced that Emily's fate is her own fault; we are not even certain about any of the others. As in all ironic drama, we are committed to the ambiguity of good and bad in every act of will and in every interaction which grows out of the ironic disjunction which is depicted in human engagement. We excuse all of the characters in *Ardélé* for their moral deviations, but the Count and Nicholas and the children intimate that perhaps there could be a better way to achieve a greater happiness in marriage. Our only sense of fulfillment here is that Ardélé and her lover are finally free of anguish in their suicide and that the children, because they have seen so much and heard so much, may strive to avoid the pitfalls of their elders. The ironic dilemma remains, however, as to whether it might be better to be deformed than to suffer the deformities of love.

Although there are equally pathetic and frightening deformities in Ionesco's plays *Amédée* and *Rhinoceros,* the forms of these two plays are noticeably different. In *Amédée, or How to Get Rid of It,* the purposive behavior of disposing of a dead body is shared by man and wife who bicker in the age-old tradition of domestic farce. As in older farce, they are attempting to hide or dispose of that which cannot be hidden. It is like trying to hide Bottom with the Ass's Head, or hiding Falstaff in the laundry basket. The physical struggle to move the gradually growing body is a ridiculous process which they try to keep secret from the neighbors. Although their living dream of the past brings up some very serious questions about the difference between illusion and reality, between what is human and what is inhuman, the desire of Amédée is always for life and love. He is frustrated by the fact of the grotesque body; he is frustrated by a mercenary and callous wife; he is frustrated by the uncomprehending people in the world outside; but he continues to pursue his own vision until his miraculous ascent into the air with the body wound around him. Then he is free of the frustrations; then he has some hope of happiness. He had dreamt of Madeleine, his wife, as his loved one, but she turned away from him in their struggle with the frustrations of the world. He is then freed in this fanciful comedy to achieve his dream elsewhere and we are satisfied that the celebration of the good life will occur in another place and time for him or in another world. The play ends with comic hopefulness rather than with ironic doubt.

On the other hand, the monsters in *Rhinoceros* are not simply creatures to fear and to hate for their ugliness, they are the images of natural innocence, of commonality, and of strong tradition, of which the whole community longs to become a part. At first, one laughs at the pseudo-rationality of the logician and the Old Gentleman as well as the commonplaceness of those who weep for their hurt cats and their broken saucers. One sympathizes with Bérenger, who seems to be trying to make some sense of the whole situation, but who has a certain compassion for his employer and fellow workers. We became more certainly involved with him in his attempt to patch up his friendship with Jean. We see at once the contrast between Bèrenger and the stiff, traditional, dogmatic stereotypes of conformity, Papillon and Botard.

In the first act we are not aware that Daisy and Dudard are anything other than possessed of the same common sense as Bèrenger. One of the ironic effects in the play is the revelation of each succeeding character who becomes a rhinoceros, and the chief factor of imminence is our anticipation of which one will be next among those with whom we have become acquainted. But the ironic disjunction between the humane concern for people as epitomized by Bèrenger and the mercenary, dogmatic egotism of the traditionalists such as Jean is the core about which the rhythmic structure is built.

In the third act, the rebel, Bèrenger, declares himself irrevocably against those who are willing to submit to the appeal of the rhinoceroses, and he remains skeptical of that appeal to the end. It is only at the end that one of the audience's kin, Daisy, is drawn into the web of sympathy and attachment to the cause of the rhinoceros. Daisy is steadfast in her affection for Bèrenger and in her common-sense attitude until Bèrenger suggests that they can save the human race by having children. Then she is no longer sure that such a course would be desirable. She is no longer sure that their way is the better way. It may be, as she says while pointing to the shadows of rhinoceroses on the walls:

Those are the real people. They look happy. They're content to be what they are. They were right to do what they did.[10]

This attitude is the source of the ironic ambiguity in which the audience is left at the end of the play when Bèrenger becomes the only living human being who has resisted the appeal of the strong, energetic, happy animals which are everywhere. As in all the great ironic dramas, the chief satisfaction is seeing clearly the age-old dilemma of man that rises between his desire to be a contented, unquestioning, law-abiding creature of conformity and his equally strong desire to be the skeptical striving, searching, changing creator and destroyer of his own environment. It may be that the play, *Rhinoceros,* is so fully occupied with symbolizing the contrast between the contented animal and the doubtful man, that it does not clearly show the process of creative thought as opposed to the state of difference and habit which characterize the lives of the characters who turn into animals. But the form of Ironic Drama does not allow for happy constructive solutions. It is only complete and fulfilling in its form when it achieves a full sense of ambivalence in the audience.

Ambivalence, felt in the audience as a result of dramatic ambiguity, is dependent upon contradictions in meaning to the extent that dramatic irony provides such contradictions. In concluding an ironic play, a dramatist does not signify by overt action or words a positive proposition concerning the human engagement which has been symbolized in the play, but instead, creates a question which depends upon the spectator to answer in terms of the disjunction of ideologies which have been dramatized. Thus, in *Rhinoceros,* one might suppose that the author is asking for sympathy with those who, like Bèrenger, can successfully oppose the temptation to become rhinoceroses like everybody else; but the ambiguity appears when one realizes that this character is left more desolate, more uncertain, more lonely, and more in despair than those who have been transformed. In one sense, his way of acting has been the least satisfactory of all the ways shown in the play. There is, therefore, the possibility of finding both interpretations evident: that the rhinoceroses represent the defeat of humanity, or that they represent the only adequate solution to the problem of human life. With this ambiguous effect, the ending can only evoke ambivalence toward the situation in which Bèrenger finds himself, and this ambivalence is the desired result of ironic ambiguity and dilemma, and, therefore, the chief source of the audience's satisfaction.

In all other forms of drama, fulfillment consists of the positive feelings of resolution, of unraveling, of conclusion, of answers to questions, and therefore of denouement. In the ironic play, however, there are too many unanswered questions for it to be considered or unraveled. This is the case simply because dilemmas cannot be resolved, ambiguities cannot be clarified, and what has been disjoined cannot be made whole. Dilemmas are the only possible consequences for the rebellion of the social critic and for the disjunction of disparate ideals. Hegelian reconciliation is impossible without new definitions, new laws, new knowledge, and the reconstitution of society. It may be that some of our laws and customs, which were controlling factors in the *Ion* of Euripides or in *Measure for Measure* by Shakespeare, may have since been sufficiently altered so as to modify our concerns for the dilemmas which are presented therein, but the fundamental problems of fidelity and family integrity in a monogamous society, such as these plays present, are still with us today. Likewise, some of the intrigue associated with the ironic plays of Anouilh, especially *La Sauvage* and *Ardéle*, may be due to the marriage customs of France, but again, it is the institution of marriage itself which is responsible for the dilemmas in which these characters are caught in these plays.

When considering the great ironic dramatists from Euripides to Anouilh, it is clear that neither the social critic nor the social rebel has chosen any particular church or institution as the source of man's difficulties. They have been more concerned to show the unreasonable way in which men adhere to worn-out customs and mores at the same time that they neglect reliable ones. As indicated earlier, perhaps no one has demonstrated more clearly than George Bernard Shaw how Ironic Drama may hold both unquestioning faith and reliance on will power in utter disdain. However spiritually justified the young Joan of Arc may seem to be, her blind faith is amusingly childish and naïve. However rational was the Catholic Church in denouncing her claims, it was foolish to think it could nullify the power of her faith by burning her at the stake. Shaw obviously did well not to make his play a Comedy or a Tragedy or a pathetic melodrama with the Church as the villain. The ironic juxtaposition of these two great forces of faith and will in the story of St. Joan is made by Shaw into a most serious example of the Ironic Form. He demonstrated this with great clarity in the Epilogue of the play. He shows the serious and melodic litany of praise which each character renders to Joan after her canonization. In ironic contrast, each character then gives his answer to Joan's question: "Shall I come back to you a living woman?" They all plead with her not to return but to let them die in peace and not to make them suffer any further the anguish of her struggle to save France. We in the audience have been made to feel the pathos of her death, and we are now suddenly forced to smile wryly at the fact that we would not know what to do if she were to return to life. Our ironic dilemma remains to the effect that how ever we may admire or worship any genius or saint and feel pity at their death, we could not really accept their return to earth and their continuation in the martyrdom which made them famous. Certain plays of Shaw like *St. Joan,* while exemplifying witty and critical types of drama, are nonetheless in Ironic Form and include *Mrs. Warren's Profession, The Doctor's Dilemma,* and *Heartbreak House.* The style, the structure, and the techniques in the latter plays may in some ways be similar, but the experience is not that of comedy in which we arrive at that moment when the joy of living has been vindicated by a victory over those of neurotic and deviant bents.

In *The Doctor's Dilemma,* it is not possible to determine at the end whether it would be better for Doctor Ridgeon to save the good but ordinary Blenkinsop or the brilliant artist, Louis Dubedat. This is also an ironic play on the subject of men and women because it portrays Ridgeon as being willing to sacrifice a man for love of his wife and then, ironically, to lose her because he is too old-fashioned and tradition-bound to understand her faith in love and her admiration for her unconventional painter-husband. The doctor's will to cure the sick and his great skill in doing so are of no avail in his struggle for domination over Jennifer Dubedat. His conceit turns every success to naught; Jennifer's failure becomes her greatest triumph. Shaw's irony seems to be that death without new life is as unthinkable as life without death. In *Heartbreak House,* a similar struggle between the sexes is continued ad nauseum. Each and every character is contrasted with another, and it is ironically demonstrated that although monogamy is the only available marriage custom, it is the one deterrent to freedom among those drawn to Heartbreak House. Indeed, all the characters who meet in this house are deeply in need of love and happiness, but Shaw shows them ironically incapable of either one, although they seem to be kept interested in life by burglaries and bombings. The dilemma seems to be that whereas it is well nigh impossible to sacrifice practical reason for one's faith in love and compassion, it is equally impossible to live with complete callousness and abandon. As in the plays of Chekhov, Shaw has symbolized a whole generation which, because of its uselessness, failed utterly no matter which way it turned. Such avant-garde ideas in Edwardian England may have been uniquely interesting then. Perhaps to later generations *Heartbreak House* will seem to be overloaded with circumlocution in spite of its telling irony and its wealth of Shavian wit.

It may be that more recent playwrights have written plays in this form which are more pertinent to contemporary social problems, but there can be little doubt that Ibsen, Chekhov, and Shaw contributed some of the most artistic examples of Ironic Drama to be seen in the theatre of the world. The question as to why this form seems to have appeared again in modern times is one that we need to pursue, but it is evident that Ironic Drama, like other forms, cannot easily be divorced from the cultural context in which it is conceived. Like Melomantic Drama it contains elements of ethical conflict which may be as strong as in any melodrama or social thesis play, but there is no tragicomic image of poetic justice nor of good and evil in conflict. The horrors of Gothic drama are transformed in it by mordant wit and sardonic satire. It may be as serious as tragedy and as ridiculous as farce, and like them, it will suffer from any overdose of sentimentality. We can be as amused at Ephidov as we are at the fool in *King Lear,* but we could never be as romantically involved in *Rhinoceros* as we are in Schiller's *Maria Stuart* or Maxwell Anderson's *Mary of Scotland.* We only become sentimental over Hedda Gabler when the actress makes the mistake of interpreting her as a romantic misguided heroine instead of as the ambiguously sexless enchantress which she must appear to be.

At the same time, as a "symbol of articulated feeling," Ironic Drama may be distinguished from other forms in its view of human engagement. Unlike Tragedy which celebrates man's will to impregnate the earth with his ideals, and unlike Comedy which celebrates man's faith in the perpetual nourishment of the Life Force, Ironic Drama celebrates the pessimistic view that man may not have either the faith or the will to achieve his ideals, but that he may have the expedient ability to preserve his species at least until he can discover a better way of life. Bitter and cruel examples of Ironic Drama do not hold out any hope for man, but those who continue to create and to enjoy such drama are living proof of the ever-present faith that aesthetic experience in the theatre, however cruel, is still a desirable and engrossing pursuit of man.

# VII.

# A Contemporary Dilemma

"I defend the plays I have written, and I know that, though they might have been better in another manner, they would not have had the vogue which they have had; for sometimes that which is contrary to what is just, for that very reason, pleases the taste."
—Lope de Vega Carpio, 1609

The more dynamic the society, and the more change that is being undergone, the more expressive are its artists, and the more varied are the viable forms that one finds in its theatre. In the

Golden Ages of dramatic invention including fifth-century Greece, third-century Rome, the Ages of Elizabeth in England, of Lope de Vega in Spain, of Louis the XIV in France, and of Romanticism in Europe, England and America, audiences were responsive to several kinds of plays. Now, in the last third of the twentieth century, one finds not only an eclectic audience but also a divided audience which must choose between the spectacle of the musical, the sentimental or violent movie, the ironic avant-garde play or film, the dinner-theatre comedy, and the melomantic soap opera. This divided audience has developed from both a larger population eager to attend various media of theatre and an increased variety of tastes that have pleaded for satisfaction. The subsequent changes have grown right out of the history of modern drama.

The coming of Ibsen, Hauptmann, Zola, Brieux, Chekhov, and Shaw at the end of the nineteenth century meant that thoughtful and inquiring minds were at last assuming their rightful place in the vanguard of the theatre. The abundant but trivial works of commercial playwrights were being challenged by sincere and dedicated artists with new dramatic ideas. Apparently with a greater emphasis being given to science, its philosophy and its method, there was more and more attention paid by the leading dramatists to the problems of society and of psychopathology and how these problems actually arose among various classes of people. The new playwrights felt they could be a part of the movement to examine human society under a microscope and to depict both the individual deviations as well as the class problems in the most scientific and objective way. Most of the plays were didactic if not polemic and they were dedicated to the style known as naturalism. Their form, however, is somewhat more elusive. For every genuine comedy such as *The Inspector General* by Gogol and *The Bear Rug* by Hauptmann, or for every tragedy such as Hebbel's *Maria Magdalena* or Ibsen's *Ghosts* there were hundreds of plays which were obviously something else. Those which were most polemic, such as Brieux's *The Red Robe* or Becque's *The Vultures*, maintained the style of naturalism in the theatre, but they argued with all the force of melodrama that the good are oppressed and that evil must be destroyed if human society is to be preserved. In another vein, we experience in the serious plays of Hauptmann, such as *Rose Berndt* and *The Rats,* those human engagements which seem to be fated to end in failure. The rhythm of these plays is similar to that of the "fate-tragedies" of German Romanticism, but there is an overwhelming sense of irony in these serious works of Hauptmann, and we sense the acid in the cynically portrayed fate of his characters.

With the coming of the scientific age, philosophic determinism tends to replace the reliance on either "fate" or "destiny" as the lot of human beings. Environmental determinism is relied upon to a great extent in the dramatic writing in the last quarter of the nineteenth century. This did not decrease the unbelievable motivations, the loud and long exhortations to morality, or the violent suicides and stabbings as seen in romantic tragedy at the beginning of that century. What one discovers, then, in a period often refered to as an "age of naturalism" in drama, are the spectacular devices of death and destruction formerly seen in either melodrama or romantic tragedy, both of which become "naturalistic" in such pathetic works as Sudermann's *Die Heimat* (*Magda,* 1893) and Tolstoy's *The Power of Darkness* (1887).

With scientific investigation, experimentation, and thinking came also the doubt and the skepticism which drove all of our arts into new and varied paths. The lyric poets became "symbolists" and "imagists"; the painters became "impressionists" and "cubists"; the musicians became "romanticists" and then "impressionists"; and the playwrights became "realists" and then "expressionists." It was obviously not that science of itself inspired such movements in the arts, but that skepticism among intellectuals tended to direct our artistry away from traditional modes and forms to new means of expression, new manners of approach, and finally to new treatments of the old forms. (*See* Chart VII).

In the work of some significant playwrights at the turn of the century can be seen the conceptual visions which led in yet another direction. Ibsen, Strindberg, Chekhov, and Shaw who began with the old types of well-made, Melomantic Drama became, with the new scepticism, more ironic. The old simple struggle against evil human ways in their respective plays—*A Doll's House, The Countess Julie, Ivanov,* and *Widowers' Houses*

—soon was replaced in their development as dramatists and think-
ers by the disturbing disjunctions in their ironic plays: *The Wild
Duck, The Dance of Death, Uncle Vanya,* and *Mrs. Warren's
Profession.* As has been pointed out earlier, these are very different plays from the customary social dramas of the old school.
They no longer take for granted the improvability of human
society as did the older melomantic works. They are Ironic
Drama in all their biting, sardonic skepticism, and they all leave
the audience in the ultimate dilemma of feeling that man cannot
improve his situation without destroying much of what he has
already established. It might be argued that Chekhov's political
successors did this very thing in the Russian revolution, that a
doubt had been raised by Chekhov; that his people were aware
of their oppression and that many believed revolution to be the
way to make a better world. But one cannot really hold Chekhov
responsible for the changes that were wrought in the succeeding
years. The world of historical fact is different from the imaginative world in the plays, and the conceptual vision of human engagement changes whenever we move from life to art.

Nevertheless, in dramatic art, the ironic plays of Euripides
brought with them a new skeptical view of the world after the
tragedies of Sophocles. The ironic plays of Webster, Marston,
and Ford brought with them a cynical and cruel view after the
tragedies of Shakespeare. The ironic plays of Alfred de Musset
brought with them a sardonic and piquant quality after the
romantic tragedies of Dumas *père* and Victor Hugo. The twentieth
century presents a different problem simply because the Ironic
Drama of our day from Pirandello, Brecht, and Dürrenmatt to
Ionesco, Genet, and Pinter follows upon a tradition of melomantic
plays rather than coming after tragedies in the realm of serious
drama. The modern revolution in drama has not only been fostered by increased doubt and skepticism but also a freedom in
expression, freedom in morality, and freedom in thought which
could never have been achieved under the Victorian restraints
of the nineteenth century. It has taken nearly a hundred years
for the moral restrictions on language to be lifted from playwrights so that they can put in the mouths of their characters

he words which they really would say under the stress of vio-
ence in which they are portrayed.

A change is also evident in the customs and manners of the
characters depicted. It would be difficult to accept the language
and manners of the characters in *Little Women* as appropriate
for the characters in Brecht's *Mother Courage*. What has happened in this regard is that the idea of naturalism, which pur-
ported to treat all that was natural in both art and literature, has
been superseded by the grotesque in either morbid satires after
Alfred Jarry or the theatre of cruelty as conceived by Antonin
Artaud. In the days of Emile Zola, that which was most natural
became pathological in the theatre simply because scientific
thought, as exemplified by medical science, was faced with an
enormous number of diseased conditions in the human being
which could be observed clinically but for which there were few
explanations and no remedies. The dramatist found the same
thing true of society at large and began to depict all that was
ugly, sick, oppressed, or exploited in human engagement regardless of the lack of cures. It was thus that the "problem play"
became prominent in many quarters, yet there seemed to be no
actual achievement of a new form. The form of most problem
plays takes us through the same melomantic sequence that we
discover in the previous era: that of the subjection of good
people, followed by the pursuit of virtue to the point of terror,
to an ultimate condition of safety through a negative quiescence
or a death and apotheosis.

Such a use of the "naturalistic" play as a problem-solving
device has had a number of repercussions in twentieth-century
dramatic theatre. Those with a particular bent for revolt against
tradition and moral restraint began to take the reins of the avant-
garde. Decade after decade they drew the interest of certain
coterie groups in our society away from that large body of the
middle class who supported the financially successful commercial
theatre. As Professor Shattuck has suggested in *The Banquet
Years*, it may have been that the revolt began with Alfred Jarry
and his play, *Ubu Roi*, at the Théâtre de l'Oeuvre on December
10, 1896. Jarry's scathing parody of tragedy caused much discus-

sion then among the literati and can still create differences of opinon because of its scatalogical language, its satirical condemnation of Shakespearean tragedy, and its morbid view of humanity.

Although a similar rebellion against the traditional theatre was carried on by Cocteau, Vitrac, and Artaud, there were others whose rebellion was expressed in other ways. André Antoine produced plays in a large room on a second floor in Paris, and J. T. Grein produced Ibsen in London on Sunday afternoon to avoid censorship. In America, the most enterprising rebellion during the first quarter of this century was to be seen among the non-commercial groups who started what were called "little theatres." Their avowed intention was to produce original works that no longer borrowed the worn-out styles which had become habitual in the commercial theatre, but most of these theatres eventually succumbed to the necessities of competitive commerce. They could produce only what sponsoring socialites would buy.

Today, the flame of revolt is again burning vigorously. The first overt act in the United States was the move in the nineteen fifties to "off" Broadway, which made it possible to perform both new plays and classics without the burden of high costs found "on" Broadway. Some of the original works were interesting, but the rebellion became more intense, and the avant-garde, in order to express itself freely, began to move to the cafés, churches, factory rooms, and garages which now constitute what is called "off-off" Broadway. In this manner, they have tried to escape all association with conformist theatre and conformist art of every kind. The present avant-garde wants no restraints whatever on its invention and wants to have theatrical presentation so free of order and direction that it simply "happens" on the stage or in the audience, or both.[1] In doing so, they often go beyond the bounds of dramatic art and return to primitive dancing and expression without any concern for drama or dramatic form. Those of the vanguard still interested in drama, such as Arthur Kopit, Adamov, Edward Albee, David Rabe, Ferlinghetti, van Itallie, and Jack Gelber, seem to write what might be called stage pieces without traditional form. It is interesting to note that *Tiny Alice*, however much irony it contains, is very much like an old melodrama with the subjection of Julian and then his destruction by a cruel faction after he is made out to be corruptible. Jack Gelber's *The Connection,* however shocking, or disgusting, or unique it may seem, may be simply another naturalistic problem play without any resolution or consequence. But the latter play in 1959 did not come as close to the clinical problem of drug addiction as did the documentary treatment of it in *The Concept* as written and performed in 1968 by patients who were on their way to being cured. The improvisational aspects of some performances in musical productions such as *Hair, Jesus Christ Superstar,* and *Godspell* do not seem as yet to hold any promise of a new form in dramatic art. But this is not to say that these new and different spectacles have not contributed to our understanding and appreciation of theatre in the twentieth century.

The area of drama which seems to have been expanded most in the modern theatre is that of Irony. In recent years, since the advent of what have been called absurdist plays, the playwright's tendency has been toward Ironic Drama. The mode of irony was adapted very early from European plays such as Ionesco's *The Bald Soprano* by Edward Albee in *The American Dream* and *The Zoo Story.* In the first, with all its non-sense dialogue, there is persistent satire showing the decay of all the things taken for granted by middle-class Americans. Even the names of the characters are "Mommy" and "Daddy" and "Grandma," but they are anything but traditional in their responses. They do show how silly many of the platitudes regarding family relationships can be, but this play is not so comprehensive or caustic as the later play of Albee's, *A Delicate Balance.* In this case, the irony stems from the disparities between parents and daughter, between the witty woman who controls her family and the lovelorn sister who lives by her passions, and between the will to act and the will to maintain serenity in Tobias. He fails to be a source of strength because he indulges himself in contemplative thought, and he hesitates to make any decisions. He is ironically the source of disjunction between himself and his friends and between himself and his wife. In the end, Tobias opens the way to danger and terror in his family by wanting merely to protect them from such things. As one commentator would say, it achieves "the irony that belongs to the best modern theatre."[2]

Irony, on some occasions, can be digested easily as in *You Know I Can't Hear You When the Water's Running,* but it can be more difficult to evoke smiles in such a play as *The Effect of Gamma Rays on Man-in-the-Moon Marigolds.* Beatrice, the mother in this play, is bitterly despondent. One can only laugh nervously at her outbursts which seem to have no logic behind them but which seem to symbolize the anguish of our whole modern society in its loneliness, its disjunction from the main stream of affluence, and its ill treatment of its fellow members. It is probably true that Tillie seeks the same quality of success in her dreams and in her actual school projects as the most sentimental heroine of a former period, but her victory is empty and lonely without any recognition from either her mother or her sister who are lost in their own worlds. It is ironic that her interest in science and knowledge could grow in an atmosphere of hostility and neurosis which is depicted in this play. Perhaps the author means to imply that it is ironic for our society to take such an interest in space exploration when the disintegration of family, and the common man's anti-intellectualism, and his moral degeneration are so pervasive in that same society.

A similar thematic emphasis appears in the play of David Rabe called *Sticks and Bones* in which the degenerative process is epitomized by man's disregard and misunderstanding of the Vietnam War and especially the indiscriminate sexual promiscuity of the soldier in that war. Here an irrational bigotry is illustrated by Ozzie, the father, in the values he places on games, and hunting, and sexual dominance beyond anything remotely related to education. The decay of the family is shown by the complete failure of communication in the family unit and by the disjunction that comes from the fear that the son will marry a Vietnamese girl instead of a white, Anglo-Saxon Protestant. In his previous play, *The Basic Training of Pavlo Hummel,* Rabe had concerned himself chiefly with the disillusionment of the American soldier in Vietnam and his rebellion against the military industrial complex which seemed to be responsible for America's involvement in that war. Rabe infused both these plays with such excess energy, such strong language, and such violent reactions among the characters as to shock many audiences and to please all those with similar sympathies and similar views of society.

Our political and social life has been also demonstrably criticized by Jules Feiffer in *Little Murders* and *The White House Murder Case*—the first more socially concerned with society's acceptance of violence in general and the second with the political acceptance of brutality for political ends alone. In the second play, the historical incident of the murder of the President's wife is invented for the sake of theatrical excitement, but for all his stretching of audience credibility, Feiffer continues to evoke interest for grotesque, bitter, and ironic incidents.

There continues to be an ever-wider interest in such plays, especially among the most literate audiences, for a variety of reasons. For the coterie audience the list of bold plays accredited with appropriate intellectual relevance continues to grow. In 1968, there was *America Hurrah* by Jean-Claude van Itallie which excoriated the vapidity of hypocritical patriots and the stupidity of those who "see America first" by going from one motel to another. His play is neither comic nor tragic, but it is certainly ironic and full of bitter laughter. Van Itallie's next play, *The Serpent,* was more of a "structured ceremony," which would require the invention of directors and actors to create the full scale of details in the production. There is a scene in a hospital, then a scene depicting the Kennedy and King assassinations, and the rest of the ceremony is the creation of Adam and Eve and the begetting of the earliest names in Genesis. It is necessary for the entire cast of characters to represent the rhythmic copulation of all the Begats in the Bible. The author excuses the disorder in his play in the following way:

> The trip for the audience must be as carefully structured as any ancient mystery or initiation. But the form must reflect contemporary thought processes. And we don't think much in a linear fashion. Ideas overlap, themes recur, archetypal figures and events transform from shape to shape as they dominate our minds.[3]

What seems to be meant by "linear" for recent critics and authors is the chronological order of the storyteller who relates events in the sequence of their happening. The storyteller has not in the past attempted to make "ideas overlap," "themes recur," and "events transform from shape to shape" as in "contemporary thought processes" because he has wanted to give order to what he said. One of the chief aesthetic beauties of dramatic art has always been the rational order which has been given to human events so as to make them intelligible to a wide audience. This is not to deny that *The Serpent* could be intriguing or at least puzzling to a contemporary intellectual coterie, but it seems to lack the careful structure that the author hoped for it and it becomes then a ceremony for those already initiated in the new ways but not for any general group of spectators. The latter will not connect the begetting of the ancient prophets with the assassination of modern leaders.

One of the aesthetic problems of our time, therefore, is whether audiences will be habituated to non-linear and non-illusionistic images in their theatrical spaces. Theatre as ceremonial involvement is far removed from theatre as illusion or as the imitation of human action. One is not enthralled by magic when performing his own tricks. The change in aesthetic milieus is radical and revolutionary, and it may or may not have any permanence. But just as the Romans insisted upon communication as well as imitation, just as the Romantics insisted upon expression as well as illusion, so the contemporary avant-garde may add to our experience of theatre some of the aesthetic quality of the ceremony. The difficulty with the artistic validity of such a production as van Itallie's *The Serpent* is that it is more fleeting, more transitory, than any previous theatrical style. It seems to be possible to re-create the pleasures afforded by *Hamlet* and *Romeo and Juliet* again and again in different ages and in different ways, but the ceremonies of the theatre of involvement have not yet achieved their enduring form.

More effective in recent times have been those whose bitterness and cynicism leads them to the ironic revelation of society's disintegration. Sam Shepard's *Operation Sidewinder* is a spectacular example of this kind of production. The electronic snake, with its brilliant red eyes, that catches Honey in its coils and nearly strangles her on the desert is a unique image of death and destruction. The play is again episodic and is accompanied by country rock music, but there is enough continuity to keep the audience attentive from one image of death to another. It is, in its totality, the story of an obsessed Young Man who kills Dukie, then tries to seize the Air Force by putting dope in its reservoir. But he is thwarted by three black militants; by a carhop; by Mickey Free, the Indian; by Spider Lady, the shaman of the Hopis; by Captain Bovine; and the CIA; but, in the end, it is Honey's and the Young Man's relation to the Indians which give them some confidence. Finally a soldier destroys the snake and his victory is the destruction of the world. By contrast with the structured ceremony by van Itallie, this work fills out the form of Ironic Drama in its confrontation, interaction, and consequence. It leaves us in considerable doubt as to the value of either technological destruction or the acceptance of the Indian's spirituality. The end is apparently total disintegration. Such is the tenor of contemporary irony in the theatre.[4]

What influence these plays will have on society in general cannot yet be determined, but it is evident that in the not-too-distant past the response of the audience had been immediate and sometimes violent. When a dramatization of *The Idiot* by Dostoievski was performed in Warsaw, Poland, the audience literally rioted at the end before permitting the actors to leave the stage. They were apparently violently opposed to the play's thesis that a genuine attempt to live by Christian principles would end in disaster. A similar response was occasioned by the performance of John M. Synge's play, *The Playboy of the Western World,* when it was given in the Abbey Theatre, Dublin, in 1907. The audience seemed not able to accept the character of Christy Mahon as representative of his father. They rose up and shouted the play down. Not only the Irish of Dublin but also the Irish of New York, in 1911, felt much the same way, although this fact has in no way dimmed the aesthetic judgment that the play is Synge's best work.[5] Then, in 1926, when Sean O'Casey's play of the Easter Rebellion, *The Plough and the Stars,* was performed in Dublin, the audience was so riotous that the play had to be stopped before they would be quiet and allow it to continue. It is recorded that W. B. Yeats sprang upon the stage and shouted to the excited crowd:

> You have disgraced yourselves again. Is this to be an ever-recurring celebration of the arrival of Irish genius? Once more you have rocked the cradle of genius. The fame of O'Casey is born tonight. This is apotheosis.[6]

Nor were these the only examples of direct effects which some plays have had on society in the last one hundred years. The appeals made in the plays of Ibsen and Shaw for the education and emancipation of women were in several ways reflected in the campaigns of the suffragettes and the feminists for political and legal equality with men. The women, of course, were the active bargainers for justice, but the theatrical presentations of *A Doll's House, Hedda Gabler, Ghosts, Candida, Widowers' Houses, Mrs. Warren's Profession,* and *Man and Superman* surely were pertinent and helpful to their cause. Even dramatists in the United States saw the need to write plays which showed women in a subjugated position; and, among others, there appeared *Salvation Nell* by Edward Sheldon and *The Easiest Way* by Eugene Walters, the first of which showed the power of a woman to "redeem the goodness in a man" and the second of which showed how badly women could be treated by men even when the latter had professed great love for them. Some of these plays, of course, were more positive in their demand for women's rights and some were less thoughtful than Shaw's and Ibsen's. Nevertheless, it was after this period of playwriting that women began to seek a more secure position in society. At first, they were given the right to vote, the right to sue for divorce, to make a living wage, to sign contracts, and to be enlisted in the Marine Corps in World War I. Their struggle for equality is not yet won, but the better dramatists have done more to help their cause than all of the demonstrators in the world.

The clamor for reform and censorship in the theatre has usually sprung from sources outside the theatre. On such occasions, it is not the form of the experience or the form of dramatic art presented, but some fragment of thought, of language, or of spectacle which causes certain segments of society to react. The criticism of violence and sex in the media of cinema and television seems to be of that kind. So long as war and sex are sought after as sources of theatrical excitement, there will be those who will pander to such taste by displaying any kind of grossness in and for itself. On the other hand, the plays of Shakespeare are filled with scenes of war, violence, and sex which are present because of the importance of those human engagements which grow out of such problems. The need in modern drama is not to abolish all evidence of these factors in playwriting but to depict the moments of human decision and choice which develop beyond the level of sensationalism and in spite of it. These great moments can be portrayed in any of the essential forms of dramatic art.

As the century has gone along, the wars depicted on the stage have become less frequent (although they have continued full force on the screen), and the riots in the audience have subsided in lieu of "audience-participation shows" in which either some or all of the spectators enter into the "happenings" initiated by the performers. The latter type of event may have been less violent, but perhaps the former riots in the audience were more positive indications of the aesthetic power of the performance. In the present period, the frequency of actual wars in the political world and the frequency of actual riots in many troubled areas may or may not have reduced the desire for the experience of such conflicts either in the audience or on the stage. Violence in cinema and television is thought by many to be a menace to manners and morals, while at the same time there seems to be no reduction in the sexually exciting or physically violent as presented on the screen. The apparent tendency is for a large portion of the middle-class audience to continue to thrive on such scenes on the screen, while two smaller groups have become sharply divided between those who are opposed to all displays of violence in art, literature, and drama and those who persistently appeal to the audience to take part in the frenetic dancing and stripping down to nakedness which seems to be essential in certain hypertensive coterie groups.[7] Such a disjunction among thoughtful and intelligent people tends to divide our cultural milieu into two fairly strong schisms, identified on the one side as a polemic and cynical avant-gardism and on the other as a reactionary and complacent traditionalism. In intellectual circles we have those who would preserve the appreciation of art for a select group in a very few well-defined coteries by emphasizing the strange, unique, distorted, and limited forms which are quite outside the understanding and appreciation of the majority of people. Joseph Wood Krutch has described this select group as the "Establishment":

> The thesis propounded by some members of the Establishment seems to be that the emergence of a large public was an unmixed calamity and that since the time when it appeared, High Culture has been squeezed out by Mass Culture on the one hand and Middlebrow Culture on the other; also that of the two latter, both of which now flourish exuberantly, the Middlebrow is the worse, because it competes directly with the High and is likely to be mistaken for it by that larger public that believes it to be cultured when it is only vulgar.[8]

It would appear from Krutch's estimate of the situation that a conflict exists between High Culture and Middlebrow Culture, either of which may be mistaken for the other. There is also the possibility, however, that Middlebrow Culture may contain the traditionalists on the one hand and the avant-gardists on the other, with High Culture nearly "squeezed out" as he says, but with the major struggle going on between the two factions of the middle area and the larger mass of people. It is difficult for the traditional establishment to instruct the masses in their heritage at the same time that the iconoclastic vanguard is trying to destroy their idols. As a consequence, the "responsive audience" in the theatre is again being broken up into elite coteries such as those of the aristocrats and learned men of the Renaissance, who, in the sixteenth century, fostered two separate developments of lavish spectacle on the one hand, and of elegant neoclassicism on the other.

Today we have people in the business world, our "industrial socialites," who seem to be intent upon exploiting the commercial uses of all the arts, displaying their most obvious surface features and capitalizing upon their most sensational effects. They give support to dramatic art only when it is gaudy, superficial and salacious; they have discovered that musical comedy and certain topical farces will often give a good return on their investment and will satisfy their own obvious tastes. These people form one side of the Middlebrow Culture and are often referred to as the Establishment. They are associated with business and industry, but they are encouraged by certain theatrical celebrities who see them as the chief source of their own fame. They differ markedly from that much smaller group of highly educated people who, because of their specialized backgrounds, have much more advanced ideas concerning art, literature, and philosophy. The latter group, which Krutch refers to as our "Highbrow Culture," is dwindling because it is no longer as innovative as the new avant-garde and because it does not control the purse strings of the socialites.

The Middlebrow extremists seem to insist on the abolition of all form in art. They apparently support those competitions in painting in which a chimpanzee is likely to win first prize, as one did in Tokyo in 1969. They apparently support those experiments in music in which no musical instruments are used and in which sounds are made that only a few human ears can endure. They seem to be so bored with the traditional forms which have been developed in the theatre that they want the audience to participate with them in frenetic gyrations and nudist-colony antics. They reject most of the ideals of Highbrow, and Lowbrow Cultures; they also extend beyond the labels of "beatnik," "yippie" and "camp" as fast as they are invented. They remain always in the vanguard of those who rebel against old styles and old forms of human expression. We get from them mixtures of all styles, mixtures of all forms, and mixtures of all kinds of art. Some apparently hope to establish the "intermedia arts" as if somehow painting, poetry, music, drama, sculpture, and dance had never been brought together in a context of "total theatre." They are mistaken in this because of the Renaissance festivals of the Italian Doges, the masques of Jonson and Jones in seventeenth-century England, the brilliant garden theatre fetes of French queens, the "stupendous extravaganzas" of the nineteenth century, and the spectacles of Max Reinhardt and Norman Bel Geddes in the twentieth.

But the desire to create "total theatre" must not therefore be denied to anyone. None of these ideas for the transformation and reconstitution of the theatre should be discounted or rejected. They may be the very ideas which will shape the ways of expression in all of the arts of the future. Some innovations in the contemporary theatre, however, would seem to bear out the old adage that "complete freedom from restraint leads to anarchy and chaos." It would seem that freedom of expression in the arts may have gone as far as it can go. In looking at past experience for some assistance in dealing with the "artistic explosion," we find that freedom and license in the Restoration theatre of England were finally curbed by religious and ethical restraints in the early eighteenth century. In the late Roman Empire we find that freedom and license in the theatre were finally curbed by the establishment of Christian emperors. We must also note that neither of these restraining forces destroyed the theatre in any permanent sense. Neither will our theatre be destroyed by internal restraints or by political cataclysm.

Theatrical experience in the past would seem to give evidence that the most effective alterations and additions were not total revolutions but were artistic innovations of great merit. The first construction of a dramatic entity in the early Greek theatre by Thespis was such an innovation. The dramatic use of iambic pentameter was such an innovation. The theatrical use of perspective in Renaissance Italy was such an innovation. The invention of the panoramic plot in the Elizabethan theatre was such an innovation. Ibsen's succinct fusion of thought and structure was such an innovation. Since no one can determine the longevity of a flash of insight, it should be reasonable for the responsive audience to hope for and to expect innovation, variety, and novelty from any theatre which purports to be devoted to artistic work. Once the audience has learned to enjoy new experiences, the styles of production will change, the stages will become more flexible, the actors will become better able to project new ideas, and it may be that even the form of drama will develop new configurations by which to convey thought and feeling.

Thus far in the history of human culture there have developed only a limited number of formal types by which dramatic construction has been meaningful to an audience (*See* Chart VII). Traditionally, they have been grouped around those congeries of feeling which we recognize as Comedy and Tragedy. Now, it is evident that those types of drama which are neither comedy nor tragedy should be distinguished according to the poetic justice central to Melomantic Drama on the one hand and the imminence of human failure found in Ironic Drama on the other. It now seems apparent that aesthetic choices may depend, on the one hand, upon strong predispositions toward definite kinds of aesthetic experience, and upon educated responses to archetypal patterns of behavior on the other.

The great majority of audiences across the world will continue to seek out and be satisfied with the bland and easy experiences of light comedy and simple melomantic plays. There will be others who prefer the more emotional and pathetic types of Melodrama and romantic Tragedy. Whereas pathos and farce have almost equal appeal in the dramatic theatre, it may be possible for popular taste to be moved to include both classical Comedy and classical Tragedy. It will be for smaller groups of sophisticates and intellectuals to bring to the theatre those skeptical and sometimes bitter works which achieve Ironic Form on some occasions and which may have no form whatever at other times. Yet, in all these well-established types, the basic desires and drives of people continue to be their greatest concern, and imaginative solutions to their problems continue to be the most sought-after ingredient in dramatic art. The theatre will probably continue to make drama as spectacular as it can, but the satisfaction of audiences may be the theatre's most essential need.

It is to be expected that nearly every new type of play will show its similarity to those types which are already substantial representatives of the forms that have appealed to aesthetic tastes throughout the world. The commercial establishment will probably continue to foster the writing of Melomantic Drama because it knows that the sentimental reassurance of goodness in man is essential to the support of a prosperous and growing economy of satisfied customers. The artistic innovators in the vanguard, on the other hand, will continue in the immediate future to create Ironic Drama, hoping to emulate the artistic excellence of Pirandello, Dürrenmatt, and Ionesco in that form. It would seem that the temper of this twentieth *fin-de-siècle* will become increasingly interested in the moral and spiritual doubt which is evident in Ironic plays. Modern man will probably never entirely reject the salubrious and inspiriting message of hope that springs from light comedy and pleasant melomantic plays; but, on the other hand, it cannot step back from disillusionment and skepticism and ignore any longer the crucial and incisive criticism of human society that is always evident in satiric Comedy, in ethical Tragedy, and is the very essence of meaning and feeling in Ironic Drama.

# Notes

### Chapter I

1. John E. Boodin, "The Discovery of Form," *Journal of the History of Ideas,* IV (1943) 177.

2. Plato, *The Symposium,* 211e-212a., trans. J. L. Davies and D. J. Vaughan (London: Loeb Library, 1888). Cf. Paul Friedlander, *Plato—An Introduction* (New York, Pentheon, 1958), pp. 16-31.

3. Plato, *The Republic,* 534b., trans. J. L. Davies and D. J. Vaughan (London: Loeb Library, 1888).

4. Aristotle, *The Poetics,* 1450⁶-1451ᵇ., trans. Ingram Bywater in *The Rhetoric and Poetics of Aristotle,* ed Friedrich Solmsen, (New York: Modern Library, 1954), pp. 233-235.

5. Horace, *Letter to the Pisos* (Ars Poetica), IL. 289-294., trans. Sir Theodore Martin, *The Works of Horace* (London: Loeb Library, 1888), II, 386.

6. Giraldi Cinthio, "On the Composition of Comedies and Tragedies," trans. Alban H. Gilbert, *Literary Criticism, Plato to Dryden* (New York: American Book Co., 1940), pp. 260-261.

7. G. W. F. Hegel, *Hegel on Tragedy,* eds. A. and H. Paolucci (New York: Anchor Books, 1962, p. 45.

8. Hegel, pp. 73-75.

9. William Archer, *Playmaking, A Manual of Craftsmanship* (Boston: Small Maynard, 1912), p. 137.

10. Gustav Freytag, *Technik des Dramas* (Leipzig: Hirzel, 1901), pp. 102-122.

11. Archer, chaps. VI, VII, XII, XIII, XVIII, XXI.

12. Francis Fergusson, *The Idea of a Theatre* (Princeton: Princeton University Press, 1949), p. 31.

13. John Howard Lawson, *The Theory and Technique of Playwriting and Screenwriting* (New York: Putnam, 1949), Book one, Part 4, Sections II, III, IV, V.

14. The treatments of Form in works from the sixteenth, nineteenth, and twentieth centuries are not identical, but the similarities in structural analysis by those named are obvious.

15. G. B. Shaw, *Dramatic Opinions and Essays* (New York: Brentano's, 1928), I, 116-124.

16. Archie J. Bahm, "Aesthetic Experience and Moral Experience," *Journal of Philosophy*, LV (September, 1958), 842.

17. Susanne K. Langer, *Feeling and Form, A Theory of Art* (New York: Scribner's, 1953), pp. 72, 259, 306-325.

18. Stephen C. Pepper, *Aesthetic Quality* (New York: Scribner's, 1937), pp. 43-44.

19. C. G. Jung, *Psychological Reflections*, ed. Jolande Jocobi (New York: Harper & Row, 1961), p. 36.

20. Jung, p. 181. See also C. G. Jung, *Complete Works*, "The Archetypes and the Collective Unconscious," IX, trans. R. F. C. Hill (New York: Bollingen Foundation, 1961).

21. Stephen C. Pepper, *Principles of Art Appreciation* (New York: Harcourt, 1949), pp. 27-38.

22. George Steiner, *The Death of Tragedy* (New York: Knopf, 1961), pp. 303-350.

23. Joseph Golden, *The Death of Tinkerbell* (Syracuse: Syracuse University Press, 1967), pp. 108-138.

## Chapter II

1. Arthur Koestler, *The Act of Creation* (New York: Macmillan, 1964), p. 96.

2. Ivor B. Hart, *The World of Leonardo Da Vinci* (New York: Viking, 1961), pp. 307-339.

3. William Shakespeare, *Romeo and Juliet*, A New Variorum edition by Horace A. Furness, Revised (New York: Dover, 1963), p. 361, 415-424. Accepting the considered judgment of scholars that the quarto versions may possibly have been hastily copied plays made for ready sale at the time of the early performances, one can only hope with some authorities that there was opportunity for Shakespeare to make further revisions himself before he completed the version that we find in the Folio of 1623.

4. Theodor Lipps, "Empathy, Inner Imitation, and Sense-Feelings" in *A Modern Book of Aesthetics*, ed. Melvin Rader (New York: Holt, Rinehart and Winston, 1960), pp. 374-382.

5. Karl Groos, *The Play of Man,* trans. Elizabeth Baldwin (New York: Appleton, 1912), pp. 173-186, 232-237, 300-313.

6. Herbert S. Langfeld, *The Aesthetic Attitude* (New York: Harcourt, Brace, 1920), p. 137.

7. Samuel Selden, *First Steps in Acting* (New York: Appleton-Century Crofts, 1947), p. 5.

8. Bertolt Brecht, "Kleines Organon fur das Theater," trans. John Willett, *Brecht on Theatre* and also Beatrice Gottlieb, "A Little Organum for the Theatre," *Accent* XI, 1 (Winter, 1951), p. 13.

9. Susanne K. Langer, *Problems of Art* (New York: Scribner's 1957), pp. 5-6.

10. Richard McKeon, "Literary Criticism and the Concept of Imitation in Antiquity," *Critics and Criticism* ed. R. S. Crane (Chicago: The University of Chicago Press, 1952), pp. 147-175. Cf. Auerbach, *Mimesis.*

11. William Shakespeare, *Hamlet,* Act I, Scene I.

12. Brander Matthews, *A Study of the Drama* (Boston: Houghton Mifflin Company, 1910), p. 224.

## Chapter III

1. Irwin C. Lieb, *The Four Faces of Man* (Philadelphia: University of Pennsylvania Press, 1971), pp. 1-24.

2. George Steiner, *The Death of Tragedy* (New York: Alfred A. Knopf, Inc., 1961), pp. 3-10

3. Compare the New York theatre critics reviews of these plays.

4. Hegel, *Hegel on Tragedy,* pp. 71-76.

5. Renè Rapin, "Reflections on the Poetics of Aristotle," trans. Thomas Rhymer in *Dramatic Essays of the Neoclassic Age,* ed. Henry Adams and Baxter Hathaway (New York: Columbia University Press, 1950), p. 128.

6. J. L. Styan, *Dark Comedy: The Development of Modern Comic Tragedy* (Cambridge: Cambridge University Press, 1963), p. 119.

## Chapter IV

1. Stark Young, "New Ibsen," *The New Republic,* LXXV (January 1, 1936), p. 230.

2. Susanne K. Langer, *Feeling and Form,* pp. 333-351.

3. Samuel T. Coleridge, "Greek Drama," a lecture, *Literary Remains* Vol. II (London, 1836).

4. George Meredith, *An Essay on Comedy and the Uses of the Comic Spirit* (New York: Scribner's, 1897). If there seems to be a dearth of such plays in the second half of the twentieth century, it is not that we do not pursue pleasure; it is that we no longer believe in the satisfaction of contentment. Although Jerry and Gittel in *Two for the Seesaw* are somewhat appealing personalities, their ironic love affair does not lead to the joy of life but to the pathetic dilemma of a futile relationship and to

ultimate rejection. Later, in *Barefoot in the Park* by Neil Simon, we again meet lovers who work their way through folly and discord to a happy married life.

5. Henri Bergson, *Laughter, An Essay on the Meaning of the Comic* (London: Macmillan, 1911), pp. 31-34.

## Chapter V

1. Karl S. Guthke, *Modern Tragicomedy* (New York: Random House, 1966), pp. 3-44.

2. Cf. Ernest Bernbaum, *The Drama of Sensibility* (Cambridge, Mass.: Harvard University Press, 1915) and Karl S. Guthke, *Modern Tragicomedy* (New York: Random House, 1966).

3. Denis Diderot, "On Dramatic Poetry," in John Gassner and Ralph Allen, *Theatre and Drama in the Making* (Boston: Houghton Mifflin, 1964), pp. 466-67.

4. *Ibid.*, p. 468.

5. In the nineteenth century there were at least 264 performances of this play in New York City alone. *See* G. C. D. Odell, *Annals of the New York Stage* (New York: Columbia University Press, 1927-1939), Vols. III-XI.

6. A. E. Morgan, *English Plays, 1660-1820* (New York: Harper, 1935), p. 639.

7. *Ibid.*, p. 644.

8. *Ibid.*, p. 650.

9. *The London Stage, 1660-1800*, Parts II, III, and IV, ed. by Emmett L. Avery, Arthur Scouten, and G. W. Stone, Jr. (Carbondale, Ill.: Southern Illinois University Press, 1960-1965).

10. Jordan Miller, *American Dramatic Literature* (New York: McGraw-Hill, 1961), p. 77.

## Chapter VI

1. Harold R. Walley, *The Book of the Play, An Introduction to Drama* (New York: Scribner's, 1950), p. 407.

2. *The Plays of Anton Chekov*, trans. Constance Garnett (New York: Modern Library, 1929), p. 185.

3. J. L. Styan, *Dark Comedy*, p. 105.

4. Cf. Martin Esslin, *The Theatre of the Absurd* (Garden City, New York: Doubleday, 1961) and George E. Wellwarth, *The Theatre of Protest and Paradox* (New York: New York University Press, 1964).

5. Henry Livings, *Eh?* (New York: Hill & Wang, 1965), p. 20.

6. Friedrich Dürrenmatt, *Four Plays* (New York: Grove Press, 1965), p. 119.

7. *Ibid.*, p. 18.

8. Larry S. Champion, *Ben Jonson's 'Dotages,' A Reconsideration of the Late Plays* (Lexington: The University Press of Kentucky, 1967).

9. Philippe Jolivet, *Le Theatre de Jean Anouilh* (Paris: Michel Brient et Cie, 1963), pp. 5-17.

10. Eugene Ionesco, *Rhinoceros, and Other Plays* (New York: Grove Press, 1960).

### Chapter VII

1. Julian Beck, *The Life of the Theatre* (San Francisco: City Lights Books, 1972), Units 6-9.

2. Tom F. Driver, *Romantic Quest and Modern Query, A History of Modern Theatre* (New York: Dell Publishing Co., Inc., 1970), pp. 283-323.

3. Jean-Claude van Itallie, *The Serpent* (New York: Atheneum, 1969), p. 3.

4. John Lahr, *Astonish Me, Adventures in Contemporary Theatre* (New York: The Viking Press, 1973), pp. 15, 16, 102-119.

5. Ellis-Fermor, Una M., *The Irish Dramatic Movement* (London: Methuen, 1945).

6. Charles H. Whitman, *Representative Modern Dramas* (New York: Macmillan, 1936), p. 787.

7. Jean-Jacques Lebel, "On the Necessity of Violation," *The Drama Review*, XIII, T41 (Fall, 1968), pp. 89-105.

8. Joseph Wood Krutch, "If You Don't Mind My Saying So," *The American Scholar* (Winter, 1967), p. 14.

# Selected Readings in Dramatic Theory

## Collections of Essays

Adams, Allan H., and Baxter Hathaway (eds.), *Dramatic Essays of the Neoclassic Age.* New York: Columbia University Press, 1950.

Allen, Gay W., and Henry H. Clark (eds.), *Literary Criticism, Pope to Croce.* New York: American Book Company, 1941.

Bogard, Travis, and William Oliver (eds.), *Modern Drama: Essays in Criticism.* London: Oxford University Press, Inc., 1965.

Calderwood, J. L., and H. E. Toliver (eds.), *Perspectives on Drama.* New York: Oxford University Press, Inc., 1968.

Corrigan, Robert, and James L. Rosenberg (eds.), *The Context and Craft of Drama.* San Francisco: Chandler Publishing Company, 1964.

Crane, Richard S. (ed.), *Critics and Criticism.* Chicago: The University of Chicago Press, 1952.

Gilbert, Allan H., *Literary Criticism—Plato to Dryden*. New York: American Book Company, 1940.

Hyman, Stanley E., *The Critical Performance, An Anthology of American and British Literary Criticism*. New York: Vintage Books, 1965.

Schorer, Mark, Josephine Miles, and Gordon McKenzie. *Criticism: The Foundations of Modern Literary Judgment*. New York: Harcourt, Brace, 1948.


## General Sources

Abel, Lionel, *Metatheatre*. New York: Hill & Wang, 1963.

Archer, William, *Playmaking*. Boston: Small, Maynard, 1912.

Aristole, *Poetics,* trans. by Ingram Bywater in *The Works of Aristotle,* edited by Richard McKeon. New York: Random House, 1941.

―――――, *The Rhetoric and Poetics of Aristotle*. New York: Modern Library, Inc., 1942.

Atkinson, Brooks, *Broadway Scrapbook*. New York: Theatre Arts, 1947

Auerbach, Erich, *Mimesis*. Berne: A. Francke, 1946.

Barrault, Jean-Louis, *The Theatre* (trans. John Ciardi). New York: Hill & Wang, 1961.

Bentley, Eric, *The Life of the Drama*. New York: Atheneum Publishers, 1967.

Bernbaum, Ernest, *The Drama of Sensibility*. Cambridge, Massachusetts: Harvard University Press, 1915.

Brecht, Bertolt, "A Little Organum of the Theatre" *Accent,* XI (Winter, 1951), 13.

Brown, John Mason, *Two on the Aisle*. New York: W. W. Norton & Company, Inc., 1938.

Brunetière, Ferdinand, *The Law of the Drama* (trans. Phillip M. Hayden). "Papers on Playmaking" First Series, Vol. III. New York: Dramatic Museum, Columbia University, 1914.

Burke, Kenneth, *The Philosophy of Literary Form—Studies in Symbolic Action*. Baton Rouge: Louisiana State University Press, 1941.

Coleridge, Samuel Taylor, Biographia Literaria (1817; especially chapters I-IV, XIV to XXII). New York: Everyman's Library, 1908.

Daiches, David, *Literature and Society*. Chicago: University of Chicago Press, 1953.

Dewey, John, *Art as Experience*. New York: Capricorn, 1934.

Doran, Madeleine, *Endeavors of Art, A Study of Form in Elizabethan Drama*. Madison: University of Wisconsin Press, 1954.

Egri, Lajos, *The Art of Dramatic Writing*. New York: Simon & Schuster, Inc., 1946.

Eliot, T. S., *Poetry and Drama*. Cambridge: Harvard University Press, 1951.

Esslin, Martin, *The Theatre of the Absurd*. Garden City, New York: Doubleday & Company, Inc., 1961.

Fergusson, Francis, *The Idea of a Theatre*. Princeton: Princeton University Press, 1949.

Freytag, Gustav, *The Technique of the Drama* (trans. by Elias J. MacEwan). Chicago: Griggs, 1895.

Frye, Northrop, *Anatomy of Criticism*. Princeton: Princeton University Press, 1957.

Garland, Hamlin, *Crumbling Idols*. Chicago: Stone and Kimball, 1894.

Gorelick, Mordecai, *New Theatres for Old*. New York: Samuel French, Inc., 1940.

Greene, Theodore M., *The Arts and the Art of Criticism*. Princeton, Princeton University Press, 1940.

Guthke, Karl S., *Modern Tragicomedy*. New York: Random House, Inc., 1966.

Harap, Louis, *Social Roots of the Arts*. New York: International, 1949.

Hegel, George W. F., *The Philosophy of Fine Art* (trans. by F. P. B. Osmaston). London: G. Bell and Sons, Ltd., 1920.

Hoffman, Frederick J., *Freudianism and the Literary Mind*. Baton Rouge: Louisiana State University Press, 1945.

Horace, *Ars Poetica,* in Fairclough, H. Rushton. *Horace: Satires, Epistles, and Ars Poetica*. New York: Loeb Classical Library, Harvard University Press, 1926.

Hugo, Victor, *Preface de Cromwell et Hernani* (ed. by Effinger). Chicago: University of Chicago Press, 1900.

Huneker, James G., *Iconoclasts, A Book of Dramatists*. New York: Charles Scribner's, 1907.

Hunt, Leigh, *Leigh Hunt's Dramatic Criticism, 1808-1831* (ed. Houtchens). New York: Columbia University Press, 1949.

Lamb, Charles, *Dramatic Essays* (ed. by Brander Matthews). New York: Dodd, Mead & Company, 1891.

Langer, Susanne K., *Philosophy in a New Key*. Cambridge: Harvard University Press, 1942.

_____, *Feeling and Form: A Theory of Art*. New York: Charles Scribner's Sons, 1953.

Lawson, John Howard, *Theory and Technique of Playwriting*. New York: G. P. Putnam's Sons, 1936.

Little, A. M. G., *Myth and Society in Attic Drama*. New York: Columbia University Press, 1942.

Miller, Jordan, *American Dramatic Literature*. New York: McGraw-Hill Book Company, 1961.

Mukerjee, Radhakamal, *The Social Function of Art*. New York: Philosophical Library, 1954.

Nathan, George Jean, *The World of George Jean Nathan*. New York: Alfred A. Knopf, Inc., 1953.

Nicoll, R. A., *The Theatre and Dramatic Theory*. London: George G. Harrap & Company, Ltd., 1962.

Nietzsche, Friedrich, *The Birth of Tragedy* (1877) (trans. W. A. Haussman), London: G. Allen & Unwin, 1923.

Peacock, Ronald, *The Art of Drama*. London: Routledge and Kegan Paul, Ltd., 1957.

Pepper, Stephen, *The Basis of Criticism in the Arts*. Cambridge: Harvard University Press, 1945.

————, *Aesthetic Quality*. New York: Charles Scribner's 1938.

Plato, "The Ion" in *Dialogues* (ed. and trans. Benjamin Jowett). Oxford: Oxford University Press, Inc., 1892.

————, *The Republic*, Books II, III, X (Jowett). Oxford: Oxford University Press, Inc., 1892.

Read, Herbert, *Art and Society*. London: Faber and Faber, Ltd., 1950.

Rolland, Romain, *The People's Theatre* (trans. B. H. Clark). New York: Holt, 1918.

Saint-Denis, Michel, *Theatre: The Rediscovery of Style*. New York: Theatre Arts, 1960.

Sainte-Beuve, C. A., *Portraits of the Seventeenth Century Historic and Literary* (trans. Katherine P. Wormeley). New York: G. P. Putnam, 1909.

Sarcey, Francisque, *Quarante Ans de Theatre* (8 Vols.). Paris: Biblioteque Des Annales, Politique et Litteraires, 1900-1902.

Sartre, Jean-Paul, *The Psychology of Imagination*. New York: Philosophical Library, 1948.

Schlegel, August Wilhelm, *Lectures on Dramatic Art and Literature* (trans. John Black). London: Bell and Daldy, 1871.

Schopenhauer, Arthur, *The World as Will and Idea*. London: K. Paul, Trench, Trubner, 1909.

Sedgewick, G. G., *Of Irony, Especially in Drama*. Ontario: University of Toronto Press, 1934.

Selden, Samuel, *Man in His Theatre*. Chapel Hill: University of North Carolina Press, 1957.

Shaw, G. B., *The Quintessence of Ibsenism*. New York: Brentano's, 1909.

Spencer, Herbert, "The Philosophy of Style," in *Theories of Style* (ed. Lane Cooper). New York: Macmillan, 1912.

Stanislavsky, Constantin, *My Life in Art* (trans. J. J. Robbins). Boston: Little, Brown and Company, 1938.

States, Bert O., *Irony and Drama, A Poetics*. Ithaca: Cornell University Press, 1971.

Taine, Hippolyte, *History of English Literature* (trans. J. Scott Clark). New York: Colonial Press, 1900.

Thompson, Alan R., *The Anatomy of Drama*. Berkeley: University of California Press, 1946.

————, *The Dry Mock, A Study of Irony in Drama*. Berkeley: University of California Press, 1948.

Thomson, George, *Aeschylus and Athens*. London: Chatto & Windus Ltd., 1957.

Wellwarth, George E., *The Theatre of Protest and Paradox*. New York: New York University Press, 1964.

Young, Stark, *The Flower in Drama*. New York: Charles Scribner's, 1923.

## Theory of Tragedy

Anderson, Maxwell, *The Essence of Tragedy*. Washington: Anderson House, 1939.

Brooks, Cleanth (ed.), *Tragic Themes in Western Literature*. New Haven: Yale University Press, 1955.

Cooper, Lane, *The Meaning and Influence of Aristotle's Poetics*. Boston: Marshall Jones, 1923.

Else, Gerald F., *Aristotle's Poetics: The Argument*. Cambridge: Harvard University Press, 1957.

Hathorn, R. Y., *Tragedy, Myth, and Mystery*. Bloomington: Indiana University Press, 1962.

Jones, J. H. F., *On Aristotle and Greek Tragedy*. New York: Oxford University Press, 1962.

Mandel, Oscar, *A Definition of Tragedy*. New York: New York University Press, 1961.

Muller, H. J., *The Spirit of Tragedy* New York: Alfred A. Knopf, Inc., 1956.

O'Connor, W. V., *Climates of Tragedy*. Baton Rouge: Louisiana State University, 1943.

Olson, Elder, *Tragedy and the Theory of Drama*. Detroit: Wayne State University Press, 1961.

Prior, Moody, *The Language of Tragedy*. New York: Columbia University Press, 1947.

Sewall, R. B., *The Vision of Tragedy*. New Haven: Yale University Press, 1959.

Steiner, George, *The Death of Tragedy*. New York: Alfred A. Knopf, Inc., 1961.

## Theory of Comedy

Bergson, Henri, *Laughter: An Essay on the Meaning of the Comic*. New York: Macmillan, 1921.

Cornford, Francis M., *The Origin of Attic Comedy*. Cambridge: Harvard University Press, 1934.

Feibleman, James, *In Praise of Comedy*. New York: Russell and Russell Publishers, 1962.

Freud, Sigmund, *Wit and Its Relation to the Unconscious*. London: Moffat Yard, 1916.

Lewis, D. B. W., *Molière: The Comic Mask*. New York: Coward McCann, 1959.

Meredith, George, *An Essay on Comedy and the Uses of Comic Spirit*. Ithaca: Cornell University Press, (1946).

Potts, L. J., *Comedy*. London: Hutchinson's University Library, 1948.

Smith, Willard, *The Nature of Comedy*. Boston: Gorham Press, 1930.

Styan, J. L., *Dark Comedy: The Development of Modern Comic Tragedy*. London: Cambridge University Press, 1963.

## Contemporary Ideas

Beck, Julian, *The Life of the Theatre*. San Francisco, City Lights Books, Inc., 1972.

Corrigan, Robert, *The Theatre in Search of a Fix*. New York: The Delacorte Press, 1973.

Grotowski, Jerzy, *Towards a Poor Theatre*. New York: Simon & Schuster, Inc., 1968.

Kirby, E. T. (ed), *Total Theatre, A Critical Anthology*. New York: E. P. Dutton & Co., Inc., 1969.

Lahr, John, *Astonish Me, Adventures in Contemporary Theatre*. New York: The Viking Press, Inc., 1973.

Poland, Albert, and Bruce Mailman, *The Off-Off Broadway Book*. New York: The Bobbs-Merrill Co., Inc., 1972.

Schechner, Richard, *Environmental Theatre*. New York: Hawthorn Books, Inc., 1973.

# Index

## Authors, Critics, Playwrights

## Play Titles